PRAISE FOR *DON'T HURRY ME DOWN TO HADES*

"Susannah J. Ural's *Don't Hurry Me Down to Hades* masterfully recounts the Civil War, relying on the voices of the people who experienced it. Her narrative captures its vastness and violence, moving North to South, battlefield to homefront, but also includes poignant moments of intimacy and loss… The result is a fresh and engaging account of the conflict."

Lesley J. Gordon, Editor, *Civil War History*

"Compelling voices that will reward anyone seeking nuance rather than a simple narrative."

Gary W. Gallagher, author of *The Union War* and *The Confederate War*

"Susannah J. Ural reminds us that the Civil War was fought by real people with families and deep emotional connections… This is the Civil War as lived experience, vibrantly and movingly written."

Professor Anne Sarah Rubin, author of *A Shattered Nation*

"Gracefully written and powerfully argued, *Don't Hurry Me Down to Hades* offers an eye-opening new perspective on the Civil War's social and cultural history."

Professor Amy Murrell Taylor, author of *The Divided Family in Civil War America*

"Taking her sources as her co-authors, Susannah Ural ferries us deep inside the maelstrom of the Civil War to its very heart, where we realize anew that war is not a sequence of battles but a vast mosaic of heart-rending family crises. Beautifully written, exhaustively researched, and highly recommended."

Professor Steve Berry, author of *House of Abraham*

"In this dramatic, expertly conceived and executed work...[Ural] deftly weaves the words and lives of the participants into a narrative of rare depth and insight. What she achieves is to go beyond the simple daily routings of the historical actors, as the powerful letters and journals she includes give readers a sense of the internal struggles that flowed through every facet of the war and society itself... For Civil War enthusiasts and historians of the era, this is a must read."

T. Maxwell-Long, California State University, San Bernardino, *Choice: Current Review for Academic Libraries*, June 2014

"Ural's fine combination of military history and personal saga uses original documents to excellent effect."

Publisher's Weekly

"The author highlights the social and cultural history of the American Civil War by linking new, rare accounts of families and ordinary citizens who witnessed the war with a compelling contextual analysis of the period."

Military History Quarterly

DON'T HURRY ME DOWN TO HADES

OSPREY
PUBLISHING

DON'T HURRY ME DOWN TO HADES

SOLDIERS AND FAMILIES IN AMERICA'S CIVIL WAR

SUSANNAH J. URAL

For my family:
The Urals, the Rasberrys,
and the best of us all,
Robby Bruce

First published in Great Britain in 2013 by Osprey Publishing,
PO Box 883, Oxford, OX1 9PL, UK
PO Box 3985, New York, NY 10185-3985, USA
E-mail: info@ospreypublishing.com

OSPREY PUBLISHING, PART OF BLOOMSBURY PUBLISHING PLC

A CIP catalogue record for this book is available from the British Library

ISBN: 978 1 4728 0910 0
e-book ISBN: 978 1 4728 0672 7
PDF ISBN: 978 1 4728 0671 0

Index by Alison Worthington
Typeset in Sabon LT Std
Printed in China through Worldprint Ltd

15 16 17 18 19 10 9 8 7 6 5 4 3 2 1

Front cover: Union officers with a cannon at Fair Oaks, Virginia. Photographed by James F. Gibson, June 1862. (The Granger Collection/Topfoto)

Osprey Publishing supports the Woodland Trust, the UK's leading woodland conservation charity. Between 2014 and 2018 our donations will be spent on their Centenary Woods project in the UK.

www.ospreypublishing.com

❧ CONTENTS ❧

LIST OF ILLUSTRATIONS

Plate Section 1

15th Street Presbyterian Church, Washington, D.C., ca. 1890s. This photo shows the church as it would have appeared around the time Francis Grimké served as its minister. *Library of Congress Prints and Photographs Division Washington, D.C.*

Charlotte Forten, ca. 1870s. *Photography Collection, Miriam and Ira D. Wallach Division of Art, Prints and Photographs, The New York Public Library, Astor, Lenox and Tilden Foundations.*

Abraham and Tad Lincoln, 1865. *Library of Congress Prints and Photographs Division Washington, D.C.*

Willie and Tad Lincoln with their cousin Lockwood Todd in 1861. *Library of Congress Prints and Photographs Division Washington, D.C.*

Willie Lincoln, ca. 1861. *Library of Congress Prints and Photographs Division Washington, D.C.*

Mary Todd Lincoln in 1861. *Library of Congress Prints and Photographs Division Washington, D.C.*

Lieutenant General Ulysses S. Grant, ca. 1864. *National Archives at College Park, Maryland, USA*

Ulysses S. Grant photographed with his family after war. © *Oscar White/CORBIS*

Jefferson Davis and Varina Howell Davis the year they married, 1845. *Photography Collection, Miriam and Ira D. Wallach Division of Art, Prints and Photographs, The New York Public Library, Astor, Lenox and Tilden Foundations*

Winnie Davis, the daughter of Jefferson and Varina Davis, born during the height of the Civil War. Beloved by Confederate veterans, she was dubbed the "Daughter of the Confederacy." She died from an illness, possibly malaria, at the age of 34. © *CORBIS*

LIST OF ILLUSTRATIONS

Jefferson Davis's inauguration as Confederate president on February 18, 1861, in Montgomery, Alabama. *Library of Congress Prints and Photographs Division Washington, D.C.*

Leaders of both the Union and the Confederacy drew on conventional images of women at the heart of the family. Loyalty to kin and community, it was hoped, would ensure that most women endured losses with patient martyrdom. *Courtesy of New York Historical Society*

Family in camp with the 31st Pennsylvania Infantry Regiment, ca 1861–65. Two poses. Civil War families often hoped to visit their soldiers, while others would come to stay with their men during the long winter encampments. It is not clear from this photo whether the soldier's family is just visiting or staying, but hints of domestic home life abound, right down to the little boy's puppy. *Library of Congress Prints and Photographs Division Washington, D.C.*

Dead in front of Dunker Church, the Battle of Antietam, Sharpsburg, Maryland, September 1862. *Library of Congress Prints and Photographs Division Washington, D.C.*

Confederate dead behind the Stone Wall at the Battle of Fredericksburg, Virginia, December, 1862. *Library of Congress Prints and Photographs Division Washington, D.C.*

Unidentified Union girl in mourning dress. Man in photo is identified as her father, a Union cavalryman. *Library of Congress Prints and Photographs Division Washington, D.C.*

The reverse of "The Children of the Battlefield" image shown below. *Library of Congress Prints and Photographs Division Washington, D.C.*

The Children of the Battlefield. Frank, Alice, and Freddie Humiston, ca. 1860s. This was one of the reprinted images of the Humiston children that was sold to raise funds for the Orphanage at Gettysburg. *Library of Congress Prints and Photographs Division Washington, D.C.*

James Madison Bowler and Elizabeth Bowler, 1862. *Minnesota Historical Society*

James Rodgers Loughridge, ca. 1861–65. *James Rodgers Loughridge Papers, Pre 1838–1972, Pearce Civil War Collection, Navarro College, Corsicana, Texas*

Mary Felicia Martin Loughridge, ca. 1880s–1890s(?). *James Rodgers Loughridge Papers, Pre 1838–1972, Pearce Civil War Collection, Navarro College, Corsicana, Texas*

Andrew Nelson Erskine in 1853. *Photo courtesy of and reproduced with permission by Erskine descents Melissa Laird Lingwall and Melinda Laird Kilian.*

Sarah Katherine "Kate" Stone Hudson, date unknown. *John Q. Anderson Papers, Louisiana and Lower Mississippi Valley Collections, Louisiana State University Libraries, Baton Rouge, Louisiana*

William T. Shepherd, ca. 1860. *Kenosha County Historical Society, Kenosha, Wisconsin*

James Rodgers Loughridge, ca. 1861–65. This wartime photo of Loughridge shows him without the polish of a studio photo and uniform, and more realistically captures how he and other Confederate officers looked during the war. *Photo courtesy of David L. Loughridge, Plano, Texas*

Taylor Battery Monument, Rosehill Cemetery, Chicago, Illinois. The inscription at the base reads, "I die for liberty, boys: go back and man the gun," the famous dying words of Taylor Battery member Oscar E. Beckers at the battle for Fort Donelson, February 1862. *Photo courtesy of Kurt H. Hackemer, Vermillion, South Dakota*

Example of the "kiss" symbols J.R. Loughridge always drew in his wartime letters home to his wife, Felicia, and daughters, Mary and Ella. Taken from July 25, 1863 letter. *James Rodgers Loughridge Papers, Pre 1838–1972, Pearce Civil War Collection, Navarro College, Corsicana, Texas*

Mary and Ella Loughridge, ca. 1860s–1870s. *James Rodgers Loughridge Papers, Pre 1838–1972, Pearce Civil War Collection, Navarro College, Corsicana, Texas*

Wilbur Fisk, ca. 1861–65. *Courtesy John Gibson*

Wilbur Fisk, ca. 1890s. *Photo reproduced from a Congregational Yearbook courtesy of Peter Fisk*

U.S. Senator and Colonel Edward D. Baker, killed at the Battle of Ball's Bluff, October 16, 1861. *Library of Congress Prints and Photographs Division Washington, D.C.*

Plate Section 2

Lieutenant General Ulysses S. Grant, ca. 1864–65. *National Archives at College Park, Maryland, USA*

Confederate General Robert E. Lee (center) and Major General George Washington Curtis Lee (left), his eldest son, and Lieutenant Colonel Walter H. Taylor (right). © *Bettman/CORBIS*

On April 9, 1865, General Robert E. Lee surrendered the Confederate Army of Northern Virginia to Lieutenant General Ulysses S. Grant at the home of Wilmer

LIST OF ILLUSTRATIONS

and Virginia McLean in the rural town of Appomattox Court House, Virginia. © *National Geographic Society/CORBIS*

President Abraham Lincoln with General George McClellan in a tent at the Antietam battlefield in October 1862. © *Bettman/CORBIS*

Three young African-American boys huddle against a pillar amidst the ruins of Charleston, South Carolina, ca. 1861–1865. © *CORBIS*

Commodore Franklin Buchanan, Confederate States Navy, ca. 1861–65. *Library of Congress Prints and Photographs Division Washington, D.C.*

Unknown African American soldier, wife, and two daughters, ca. 1863–65. *Library of Congress Prints and Photographs Division Washington, D.C.*

Jefferson Davis's plantation home, Brierfield, after it was occupied by Union troops and Freedman's Bureau workers. They had a celebration there on July 4th in 1864, one year after Vicksburg surrendered, with a banner marking "The House that Jeff built." *Unidentified source*

Confederate dead lying behind the stone wall on Marye's Heights, Fredericksburg, Virginia, ca. 1861–1865. *Library of Congress Prints and Photographs Division Washington, D.C.*

Union defenses on Little Round Top at the Battle of Gettysburg, ca. 1863. *Library of Congress Prints and Photographs Division Washington, D.C.*

The gate house cemetery at Gettysburg. *Library of Congress Prints and Photographs Division Washington, D.C.*

General William Tecumseh Sherman photographed in 1865. Note the black armband he wears in honor of the late President Abraham Lincoln. © *Hulton-Deutsch Collection/CORBIS*

General Ulysses S. Grant's forces at Young's Point north of Vicksburg, March 1863. © *CORBIS*

William Seward and his daughter, Fanny, ca. 1861–1865. *Courtesy Mississippi Department of Archives and History*

Frederick W. Seward, ca. 1860–65. *Library of Congress Prints and Photographs Division Washington, D.C.*

William H. Seward, ca. 1865. *National Archives at College Park, Maryland, USA*

Nellie Nugent Somerville, ca. 1920s. *Courtesy Mississippi Department of Archives and History*

Weapons captured from Lincoln's assassins and an original poster offering a reward for any information. © *Hulton-Deutsch Collection/CORBIS*

An artist's impression of the moment John Wilkes Booth leaned forward to shoot President Abraham Lincoln as he watched a play at Ford's Theater in Washington, D.C., in 1865. © *Bettman/CORBIS*

Annie Surratt, ca. 1860–65. *National Archives at College Park, Maryland, USA*

Lewis Powell aka Lewis Payne during his trial, ca. 1865. *Library of Congress Prints and Photographs Division Washington, D.C.*

Lewis Powell aka Lewis Payne during his trial, ca. 1865. *Library of Congress Prints and Photographs Division Washington, D.C.*

Clara Harris, ca. 1860–65. *National Archives at College Park, Maryland, USA*

Major Henry Rathbone, c. 1860–65. *National Archives at College Park, Maryland, USA*

Mary Surratt, ca. 1865. *National Archives at College Park, Maryland, USA*

A group of freed slaves who worked as laborers and servants for the 13th Massachusetts Infantry Regiment during the Civil War. © *CORBIS*

An idealized depiction of life for slaves both before and after emancipation. The reality was much starker. © *Bettman/CORBIS*

⮞ ACKNOWLEDGMENTS ⮜

This project began in the late spring of 2010 in Lexington, Virginia, at my favorite academic conference of the year, the Society for Military History's annual meeting. My colleague and good friend, Andy Wiest, was discussing the possibility of publishing his history of a U.S. Army company's experience in Vietnam with Osprey Publishing (it's since been released and it's brilliant: *The Boys of '67*), and he mentioned that they were looking for a Civil War historian to write a book for them that was about how soldiers *and* civilians experienced the war. That's when I first met Kelli Christiansen, John Tintera, and Kate Moore. All of them, as well Marcus Cowper later on in the process, have been incredibly supportive of my crazy work schedule and the happy distractions of the mom of an eight-year-old boy, and I cannot thank them enough for the opportunity to write this book, and their patience and support along the way. Kelli, though, deserves special thanks. This book would not be nearly as strong as it is without her editorial expertise and advice, not to mention her pep talks and friendship. Thank you, Kelli.

My colleagues in the history department at the University of Southern Mississippi deserve thanks, too, for their tremendous support throughout this process. Special thanks in particular go to Kyle Zelner, Andy Wiest, Phyllis Jestice, and Heather Stur for reading sections of the manuscript and offering invaluable advice, and to Cindy Hodge for helping me find the peace and quiet to write. Thanks, too, to fellow historian and friend Kurt Hackemer, Professor of History and Associate Vice President of

Academic Affairs at the University of South Dakota. Kurt first made me aware of William Shepherd's letters, which Kurt published in a beautifully edited collection entitled *To Rescue My Native Land*. He also deserves tremendous thanks—the drinks are on me in perpetuity—for reading the entire manuscript with a critical eye.

Archivists and librarians have been of great help along the way. I want to thank Jennifer Brannock of Southern Mississippi's McCain Archives, Holly Beasley Wait and Jennifer Coleman of the Pearce Library and Museum at Navarro College in Corsicana, Texas, Tara Laver and Judy Bolton of the Louisiana State University Libraries Special Collections, Eileen Fay and Lori Birrell of the Department of Rare Books & Special Collections at the University of Rochester, Eric Mortenson of the Minnesota Historical Society, Thomas Lisanti of the New York Public Library, the staff of the Kenosha County (Minnesota) Historical Society, Frank A. O'Reilly of the Fredericksburg and Spotsylvania (Virginia) National Military Park, and Elbert Hilliard, Anne Webster, and Betty Uzman of the Mississippi Department of Archives and History. I'm also grateful to the archives, institutions, and organizations who have made so much valuable material and scholarly analysis available online over the last decade or so. There's a wealth of information out there, but I continue to be impressed and thankful for those who make the time to ensure that the information they're providing is accurate and accompanied by the historical analysis that places it in its proper context. I have carefully listed these sites, with Osprey Publishing's support, in the endnotes so readers may enjoy many of the original sources that are tied to this story.

I want to thank the descendants who provided letters, images, and detailed genealogical information that helped me to humanize the experiences of American families at war. Key portions of this book would not have been possible without the generosity of Melissa Laird Lingwall and Melinda Laird Kilian, Andrew and Ann Erskine's great-great-granddaughters; David L. Loughridge, the great-grandson of James Rodgers and Felicia Loughridge; Martha Hartzog, the great-granddaughter of William "Howdy" Martin; Peter Fisk, the great-grandnephew of Wilbur and Angelina Fisk; and Gay Bennett Yerger, the great-grandniece of Helen Johnstone.

ACKNOWLEDGMENTS

Thanks are also due to my students. I shared stories from this book with my especially bright undergraduate U.S. Civil War era class in the fall of 2012, and they helped me realize what worked, what had to go, and asked the kinds of questions that inspired me to dig deeper into some of my best accounts. Special thanks go to Anna Todd, Tina McLendon, Shawna Guidry, James Freeman, J. C. Diaz, Warren Hennessy, Rebecca McLaughlin, Andrew Dinkins, Joseph Ezell, and David Howard. Thanks, too, to my graduate students in HI563: The U.S. Civil War era, and for the students with whom I had lengthy discussions about their Civil War theses and dissertations. You have inspired my work just as much as I have influenced yours. Special thanks for that go to: Allan Branstiter, Ruth White, Stephanie Seal, Angela Riotto, Rebecca Zimmer, Dennis Conklin, Samantha Taylor, Aaron Foster, Lynn Wartberg, John Mangipano, Tyler Rotter, Jonathan Snyder, Joseph Wise, Joel Bius, and Ryan Keating. And an extra thank you to Stephanie Seal, who worked wonders with the images for this book.

In the end, though, my greatest thanks go to my family. Without them, none of this matters. My love of history began with my parents, William F. and Sue C. Ural, who have read portions of this book as my test audience. They've been my strongest critics *and* supporters, a rare and beautiful combination, through every step of my life. They'll always, thankfully, be my parents, but they're also two of my dearest friends. Thanks also go to my family by marriage and friendship in Canton, Mississippi, who include Myra Mizell Sandidge, who shares my fascination with the Civil War and who provided sources on Mississippi in particular. Thanks, too, to Norman Gainey, whose questions about this project and thoughts on Mississippians at war inspired portions of this work. My biggest thanks to my Canton family, however, goes to Sandra Rasberry, my mother-in-law, who tracked down books, local historians, and even families who appear in this book and in a future project. We share a love of history and politics that remind me daily that I really lucked out in the mother-in-law category.

I want to thank, too, the two women who have carried me through the bad times, cheered me on in good times, and laughed with me every step of the way. My "therapists" and best friends, Peggy Douglas Waterman and Fran Rogers Garcia Phillips of Southport, North Carolina, are friendship personified. I adore you.

But the best for last.... My son, Robby, would go off on adventures with "Ras" (his stepdad and best friend) to give me quiet writing time, encouraged me when I was tired of clicking away at the computer, and believed in me with the pure faith that only an eight-year-old knows. As any parent can tell you, a child's love and laughter can get you through some pretty rough days. For every single second we've had, thank you, Roo-bear. I love you.

And finally, my husband, John Rasberry. For once in my life, words don't suffice. What can I say? He hung the moon. Probably more than anyone else, John deserves credit for this book's completion. I've lost count of the number of nights we've sat on the porch discussing this project. It's not that he's particularly interested in the Civil War or even in history. It's that he believed in me and my ability to tell this story, and for that I owe him everything.

It's a rare thing to look up one day and realize you have it all.

Is it possible to have another "last" or "final" acknowledgment? I hope you, reader, will grant me this. My father died between the time I wrote the acknowledgments above, which my parents read, and the time they appeared in the final proofs. I've thought of changing some things, but won't. "Don't get greedy," he'd say. "You still have it all." And I do. But I miss you, Daddy.

☙ FOREWORD ❧

The Civil War directly affected a far higher percentage of the American population than any other conflict. More than three million men enrolled in national armies, thousands of others participated in brutal guerrilla operations, people caught in the path of contending forces suffered vast disruptions in their lives, and civilians behind the lines in both the United States and the Confederacy dealt with unsettling change regarding political, economic, and familial circumstances. Military operations intersected in myriad ways with life on the home front, and the shifting tides of martial fortune brought fluctuations in morale that left the final verdict in doubt until deep into the war's last year.

The wartime generation created a rich lode of testimony that illuminates what Walt Whitman called "the fervid atmosphere and typical events" of the conflict. Their words, recorded in letters and diaries during the war and in memoirs retrospectively, afford an unmatched opportunity to appreciate the kaleidoscopic range of human experiences. Exploring this evidence in chronological order restores a sense of contingent uncertainty—an uncertainty often lost when beginning with knowledge of Appomattox and working backward to find explanations for what seem, across a century and a half, to have been preordained outcomes. Union triumph and slavery's end were not inevitable, as evidence from the time makes very clear. Either side could have won the war; indeed, Confederate prospects in 1861 were much better than those of the thirteen colonies against mighty Great Britain in

1776. And as late as the summer of 1864, freedom for millions of enslaved African Americans remained far from guaranteed, dependent upon Republican success in the ensuing autumn elections that, in turn, relied on good news from battlefields in Georgia and Virginia during September and October.

The compelling voices in *Don't Hurry Me Down to Hades* carry readers back into the mid-nineteenth century, offering a splendid array of descriptive and analytical lenses. Woven into a chronological framework and reflecting spacious geographical reach, these firsthand accounts reward anyone seeking nuance rather than a simple narrative. Attitudes toward emancipation and slavery afford an excellent example of this phenomenon. Modern Americans often conflate attitudes toward the institution of slavery and toward enslaved black people. In fact, most white people, even in the non-slaveholding states, harbored intensely racist attitudes by twenty-first-century standards. Yet most of the loyal white citizenry eventually supported adding emancipation to their larger goal of preserving the Union. They did so primarily because killing slavery would help end the Confederate rebellion, restore a democratic republic that offered a large percentage of its citizenry a voice in self-government and the opportunity to rise economically, and protect against future internal threats to the nation's viability.

Two witnesses from *Don't Hurry Me Down to Hades* help explain how ideas about slavery and emancipation figured in the loyal citizenry's thinking. David Hopkins, a U.S. sailor, demanded no "compromise with traitors" who menaced the Union. Acknowledging wrongs "done to the Negro race," he nonetheless insisted that the "men who have struck this blow at our government are on to playing for a bigger strike than the right to hold ... or extend slavery. It is intended to be a death blow to our form of Government." For Hopkins, Union predominated, something the small number of white abolitionists knew held true for most of their fellow citizens. In July 1861, New Yorker John Jay got to the heart of how emancipation could be added to the goal of preserving the Union. Rather than present a case for the morality of ending slavery (abolitionists had taken that approach for decades with relatively little effect), Jay suggested it be cast as a means to the end of preserving the Union:

FOREWORD

"Every battle fought will teach our soldiers & the nation at large that slavery is the great cause of the war, ... that slavery must be abolished as our army advances as a military necessity – & that slavery must be either abolished or utterly paralyzed to enable us to conclude a peaceful settlement of this rebellion, in such a manner that the industry & prosperity of the North shall never more be imperiled by it ...." When Abraham Lincoln issued his Emancipation Proclamation in January 1863, he echoed Jay's reliance on military necessity rather than morality as the basis for action.

Such interpretive gems abound in the pages that follow. They convey a gripping immediacy from battlefields large and small, from households mourning the loss of soldiers, from politicians and military officers reaching decisions that touched millions, and from individuals struggling to define the limits of national sacrifice. All who seek to understand the Civil War should look first to those who lived it, who understood better than any others what Union soldier Willie Shepherd called "the sad reality of our War."

Gary Gallagher
John L. Nau III Professor of History, University of Virginia
June 2013

➣ INTRODUCTION ⇐

They stood together, the wife leaning close to her husband. She grasped his rough hand in hers and begged him not to go. She reminded him that she had lost her father, her mother, her brothers. He, her husband, was all she had in this world. All but their boy. Stay home, she pleaded, "[b]efore you orphan your son and make your wife a widow." There was no point in continuing to fight in a war that would only lead to death, she argued. Looking at their infant child, she asked, "Have you no pity for *him*, our helpless son? Or me, and the destiny that weighs me down, your widow, now so soon?"

Looking at the tears streaming down her face, her husband smiled gently. He had to fight, he explained. He would "die of shame" if he failed to defend their home. Besides, it really wasn't up to him. He had been raised on tales of honor and sacrifice to the point where fighting "in the front ranks" to win his "father great glory, glory for myself," was all he knew how to do. Some day, he explained, his father would die, their land might perish, and he himself might be killed. But how could he turn away now? How could he lay down his weapons and watch his wife and son enslaved under the foot of a tyrant and know he had failed to do everything in his power to prevent that?

Holding their infant son in his arms, the husband kissed him, and laughing, he tossed him in the air, again and again, escaping for a moment the war and the death that surrounded them. And then the man prayed, his wife still close against him, that of their son his countrymen would one day say, "He is a better man than his father" and "a joy to his mother's heart."

Still crying softly, the wife took the baby in her arms, smiling through her heartache, and the husband softened, asking, "Why so much grief?" as he stroked her arm. "No man will hurry me down to Hades, against my fate. And fate? No one alive has ever escaped it, neither brave man nor coward, I tell you—it's born with us the day that we are born."[1]

This wartime family was neither Union nor Confederate, though it could have been either. They were Homer's Hector and Andromache in the midst of the Trojan War. Hector's faith that defeat would ensure the loss of all they held dear was a fear that echoed throughout homes on both sides of Mason's and Dixon's line during the American Civil War. Andromache's belief that the war mattered little if it meant the loss of her beloved Hector wove through those homes as well.

Don't Hurry Me Down to Hades is the story of how American families endured their nation's bloodiest conflict. For many of them, it was just as much a struggle for survival as the Trojan War was for Hector and Andromache. That was certainly the case for the slaves who escaped to engage in a desperate fight for freedom in the Union Army. It was also how white Americans understood the need for secession or the fight to save the Union, both sides struggling to preserve the legacy America's founding generation had left them. Seeing it as a fight for freedom was what made victory so essential, it was what made the conflict so bloody, and it was what sustained men and women when, in one spring after another for four long years, they faced the opening of yet another campaign season, praying that this one, unlike the last, would bring victory and peace.

While many of the stories in the following pages are of families unknown to most readers, others will be quite familiar, though often with a twist. That is how Sam Todd, Mary Todd Lincoln's Confederate brother appears in the text that follows, and it is how history's lesser-known families take center stage in one of the best-known stories of the war as we read the closing act.

It is also worth noting that this is not just the story of families enduring war in a vacuum. It is difficult to imagine how readers could truly understand what a mother's son suffers if we fail to examine what he experiences in battle. Similarly, a tale riddled with grief would belie mankind's ability to find humor in the horrors around them, which allows us to survive the emotional trauma that is war. And so there are sections that delve deeply into the complexities of well-known and lesser-known battles, and there are portions that laugh as well as cry with the veterans and the civilians at home. There are also pages that examine with care the wartime tensions that stressed the very relationships that helped Americans survive four years of hope, worry, hardship, joy, anguish, and redemption.

This, then, is the story of American families who fought for a land free of tyrants who would enslave them and trembled as they faced the fate that, as Hector foretold, is "born with us the day that we are born."

A brief word on formatting and other matters: I have not used the traditional [*sic*] to highlight misspellings in original documents because in a number of cases there were so many such references that I feared it would distract readers from the power of the author's point. I have also utilized a number of sources from the Internet to allow readers to enjoy the original documents themselves rather than keep that pleasure for historians who have the time and training to explore archives. In cases where I noticed that original letters were available both in books and online, I cited both options for readers. Finally, in sections where a significant portion of the story came from a couple of historical works, I cited those works at the beginning of the story and did not offer repeat citations, taking readers to the same source, throughout.

⋙ 1 ⋘

PREPARING FOR A WAR TO THE DEATH

Word of South Carolina's secession spread rapidly. The Palmetto State had been threatening to leave the Union for three decades, but when the moment finally came, most Americans didn't seem to know what to make of it. Four days before Christmas in 1861, the New York *Herald* reported that South Carolina's representatives departed Congress in "good humor" and in a manner "more like a departure of friends than of persons bound on a revolutionary mission." The New York *Journal of Commerce* (the precursor to *The Wall Street Journal*) wrung their hands at the coming loss of Southern business and hoped to avoid armed conflict. The editors chastised those threatening force, asking, "Shall we make war upon the South, and reduce them—if we can, which is more than doubtful—to slavery? We denounce African slavery. [S]hall we then make slaves of white men, our equals and our brothers?"

Wealthy Southern political leaders voiced similar concerns, with LeRoy Pope Walker, who hailed from one of Alabama's most politically connected families, scoffing at any mention of bloody resistance and famously offering to soak up all the bloodshed with a single handkerchief. South Carolina Senator James Chesnut, Jr. seemed to feel the need to see and raise Walker, offering to drink all the blood that might be spilled in this talked-of war.

But these public displays of calm belied an angry undercurrent that ran through homes North and South. The wealthiest Southern planters and Northern businessmen, all capitalists alike, may have understood the cost the war would bring. Patriarchs up and down the Mississippi River had voted for the Constitutional Union candidate in 1860, desperately hoping for some way to avoid a division that would destroy their investments and force them to choose between their country and their region. Standing by family, after all, offered few answers when so many of them from South Carolina to Mississippi had married Northerners, educated their children in the North, and vacationed in Yankeedom for decades.[2]

But the radicals in both regions, who either had little but dreams to lose or whose ideals inspired actions of principle rather than logic, welcomed war. In Massachusetts, transcendentalist Ralph Waldo Emerson, who viewed John Brown's 1859 raid on the Federal arsenal at Harper's Ferry, Virginia, as the work of an American martyr, advised a friend, "Declared war is vastly safer than undeclared war." In the coming months, as such things seemed increasingly likely, Emerson grew bolder, boasting that "Sometimes gunpowder smells good." Far to the south, a young Mississippi lawyer named William Nugent matched Emerson's cold confidence as he mused, "I feel I would like to shoot a Yankee."

For years—decades even—Americans had sought one compromise after another to settle their differences. This was, after all, how democracies worked. By the end of the 1850s, though, beatings occurred in the U.S. Senate, and a Wisconsin representative selected bowie knives when challenged to a duel by a Southern colleague.[3] It wasn't, as historian Bruce Catton once observed, that Americans could not compromise in 1861. It was that they no longer wanted to. Political leaders and wealthy elites may have hoped for peace, publicly insisting that secession did not necessitate war, but the majority of citizens at home seemed to realize what these events foretold, and they rushed, almost joyously, toward the looming violence, sensing its offering of cathartic release. For men like Louisianan Pierre Soule, who had been a Douglas Democrat once willing to compromise, the choice now seemed simple. When caught between "ignominy and revolution, I choose revolution," he said. Still, elites urged calm as exhausted patience snapped and swept the nation toward war. A Virginian, whose state would vote against secession later that spring until it changed its mind a month later, fretted over "the desire of some for change [and] the greed of many for excitement" that "seem[ed] to have unthroned the reason of men, and left them at the mercy of passion."[4]

Such passions also enveloped Mississippi that year. On November 30, just weeks after Abraham Lincoln's election as the country's sixteenth president, Mississippians decided that the Republicans now had enough power to elect a president without a single vote from a slave state. If they had such influence in 1860, Southern Democrats warned, just imagine the power Republicans could acquire in one presidential term. As Mississippians would soon explain in their declaration of secession, "utter subjugation awaits us in the Union. ... We must either submit to degradation ... or we must secede."[5]

Mississippi's 350,000 whites—most of whom may not have owned slaves but were linked by family, social, or economic ties to those who claimed among their property the 430,000 blacks in the state—sent delegates to a secession convention in Jackson in January 1861. Ten years earlier, they had gathered to ponder this same issue and voted, barely, to remain in the Union. This gathering in 1861, however, was about to vote otherwise.

Again and again, the state's elite white planters urged caution, but, caught between the prosecession radicals and a Republican president they did not trust, the convention members turned their backs on the previous compromises that many of them had drafted. Nothing else had worked, they argued. They were not destroying America with secession, they insisted. They were rescuing the only salvageable portions from self-destruction.

Arguments like these appeared in legislative halls, newspapers, taverns, churches, and dining rooms throughout the South. A Republican president threatened the power of the one party that protected the interests of slaveholders. The Free Soilers, the Northern political party that attacked slavery as an unjust threat to their free-labor principles, were foreign to the South, where many whites were accustomed to the strong class and racial structure that shaped their world. While the term "aristocratic" has been overused when describing the region, Southerners did value the deference, social mores, codes of honor, and romance that characterized their homeland. Their traditions were based more in race and class than in the modern capitalism personified by the new Republican Party, which not only failed to attract Southerners but also seemed to threaten all the white South valued. They scoffed at the rushed, urban pace of the modernizing North and challenged the influence of Republican ideas in the 1850s. But the election of 1860 indicated that Southern Democrats were outnumbered and could not stop these changes. And so, as Jefferson Davis explained, they were left with only two options.

One option was nullification, to reject the rules of the North. Davis insisted that this was unconstitutional: Members of the Union must abide by the laws of the Union. The other option was secession, and Davis argued that this was the only honorable option that remained to the white South. But he did not make this decision lightly.

"WE BUT TREAD IN THE PATH OF OUR FATHERS"

The magnitude of the failure to compromise resonated through a packed Senate chamber on a chilly January morning in 1861. After allowing four of his colleagues to speak first, Davis, the recognized voice of the South, rose slowly, suffering from the painful facial neuralgia that plagued him throughout adulthood. With a speech that would echo in Lincoln's call for "malice toward none" four years later, Davis explained that he and his constituents felt no animosity toward his Northern colleagues and those they represented.

Revealing the logic and reason that were the mainstay of his political career, Davis reminded his friends of a moment years earlier when Bostonians protested their forced return of fugitive slave Anthony Burns in the 1850s, and some had suggested that Massachusetts secede rather than enforce an unfair, immoral law. Davis had supported their right to do this, he reminded his audience, though he completely disagreed with their position on the fugitive slave law and had hoped Massachusetts would not leave. Still, the right of secession was one he could understand and support even while disagreeing on the immediate motives behind the action. Now he was making a similar decision. They might disagree; they may have failed to compromise. But he hoped his friends in the Senate would grant him the same understanding he had once shown. The man who had worn the uniform of an officer in the U.S. Army, who led the Mississippi Rifles to victory in Mexico, who represented the United States as Secretary of War and the state of Mississippi in the U.S. Senate assured his colleagues that he had not reached this decision easily. Like those who stood with him, their departure was not a celebratory one. But for Davis, it was the only logical decision when asked to compromise his, and, he would argue, the nation's, defining principles.

A key problem, Davis explained, was the antislavery wing of the Republican Party, whose candidate was about to become the first Republican President of the United States. Davis scowled at the party's insistence, as he saw it, in making "the theory that all men are created free and equal" the "basis of an attack upon [Mississippi's] social institutions." Furthermore, Davis added, "the sacred Declaration of Independence has been invoked to maintain the position of the equality of the races." Most Republicans would have challenged any description of their party as one promoting racial equality, but Davis believed that any interpretation of the Declaration along these lines was flawed. Racial equality, he insisted, was never an intention of the founders. The famous three-fifths clause in the Constitution, which addressed how the enslaved portion of the American population should be counted in terms of political representation, made this abundantly clear, Davis explained.

The first part of his position made clear, Davis reiterated the second half: In response to the attack on Mississippi's social institutions, an issue upon which he and his colleagues could reach no agreement, Davis insisted that only one honorable option remained. "Senators, we recur to the compact which binds us together," Davis stated.

We recur to the principles upon which our Government was founded; and when you deny them, and when you deny us the right to withdraw from a

Government which, thus perverted, threatens to be destructive of our rights, we but tread in the path of our fathers when we proclaim our independence and take the hazard. This is done, not in hostility to others, not to injure any section of the country, not even for our own pecuniary benefit, but from the high and solemn motive of defending and protecting the rights we inherited, and which it is our duty to transmit unshorn to our children.[6]

Davis added only that Southerners were aware of the great sacrifices made in abandoning the power and protection of the United States. But their "high and solemn motive" must override all fears for the future. Davis advised his Senate colleagues who remained with the Union to let the South go, warning that any effort to forcibly stop secession would "bring disaster on every portion of the country." He then clarified that he left without anger or hostility and offered his apologies for any wrong he had failed to correct, any ill will he had not mollified. With a final adieu, Davis rose from his desk while Vice President John Breckinridge and the remaining fifty-eight Senators, North and South, stood to honor the departure of old friends. Applause swept through the chambers, where men wept openly at what Davis's departure signified.

Years later, Davis would insist that the words he spoke that day were "not my utterances but rather leaves torn from the book of fate."[7] As his young wife watched him depart the Senate, she may not have been so sure. Varina Howell Davis was the brilliant second wife of Mississippi's newly former senator. A native of Natchez educated in Philadelphia with close ties to the Northern branch of her family, Davis was a rising Southern intellectual and well-known Washington hostess. She was also opposed to secession. She believed in a state's right to secede, but questioned the wisdom of the decision. Watching from the gallery with the other Senators' wives, Davis's loyalties were divided, and they reflected a complexity regarding secession that popular modern images have overshadowed.

Varina Davis feared the "whole thing is bound to be a failure" and had used her impressive political skills to persuade her husband of this during the previous twelve months. Talk of "disunionism," she admitted, was rampant in their Washington circle, and she feared that they would have to "quit here the 4th of March," following Lincoln's inauguration. She could not help fuming a bit, uncomfortable with the mob mentality that enveloped Washington. In November she warned against anyone who dared call "me a disunionist" and promised to "quarrel with the first person who said a word" against her stand.

During the war and in the ugly years that followed it, rumors surfaced that Varina Davis was never a true secessionist. That wasn't entirely fair. The fact was that she was more openly honest about her concerns than most Confederates, but her Unionist leanings were hardly rare among her social peers from Natchez to Washington. Her strong opinions would cause problems for Jefferson Davis, but they also allowed her to serve as one of his closest confidants. In the weeks following Lincoln's election, for example, she kept Davis abreast of the mood in the capital after her husband had returned to Mississippi to plan for the future. Amid the "settled gloom hanging over everyone," she wrote,

> Duf. Wallack has gone for Lincoln and is as fierce as a buck rabbit on Southern seceders—I say gone for Lincoln, he thinks he will make a strong, impartial, conservative President. Everybody is scared, especially Mr. Buchanan. Wigfall is talking to the bitter end. Hunter opposes secession. Jacob Thompson is prepared to go with the majority for everything. Toombs blathering about a resignation (in future). No one rings like the true metal so much as Constitution Browne who is enthusiastic and thoroughgoing, repudiates Mr. Buchanan's views openly, assuring secession responsibility.[8]

The Southern leadership in Washington had good reason to be conflicted. The process of secession might have been historically inspired and, at least as they saw it, Constitutionally defended, but now the South had to sleep in that bed of secession. At his Mississippi plantation, Brierfield, Jefferson Davis echoed the caution his wife saw in Washington. When asked by one of the leading fire-eaters, Robert Barnwell Rhett, Jr., for a statement for Rhett's journal, the *Charleston Mercury*, Davis urged patience. He hoped the Southern states would move as one, and he discouraged South Carolina from seceding alone. When he met with Mississippi's Governor John J. Pettus and several legislative representatives later that month, Davis clarified his opposition of secession as long as a peaceful resolution to their complaints was possible within the Union. When he returned to Washington in early December, however, it became clear to him that "no human power can save the Union."[9]

As other Southern states teetered on the edge of secession, Northerners like New York's William Seward, whom Lincoln would nominate as the next Secretary of State, believed that much of the South was Unionist and that, through patient perseverance, Northern leaders could reunite the national family. The trouble, though, was that they misjudged the South. As early as September 1860, before Lincoln's election, the New Bern *Weekly Progress*, a pro-Douglas paper, explained that North Carolinians' first loyalty was to their state and region. Although agreeing that secession was unconstitutional, the pro-Douglas press took on the role of the biblical Ruth: wherever North Carolina goes, so goeth its Unionists, "*right or wrong*, because all that we have and all that we hold most dear is here; and our native State having our heart's purest affections and affording to us all the protection we require claims our allegiance."[10]

As the secession crisis deepened that winter, Southern Unionists echoed Seward's caution and warned against any effort to force South Carolina back into the Union. Virginia papers railed against the Palmetto state for its rash decision, which could sweep the nation into "the vortex of revolution," and many Southern Unionists, especially those in the upper South, agreed. But Northern leaders misjudged the situation by assuming that this meant Southerners would side against a sister state if it came to war.

In Nashville, the *Republican Banner* explained "as much as we love the Union of these States, and as little as we sympathize with the schemes of those Southern men who have been plotting for years the disruption of the government ... we say 'let the Union slide' rather than attempt to preserve it 'forcibly.'" In Little Rock, the *Arkansas State Gazette* agreed. "South Carolina has gone; let her go; and wo to the administration, or power, that attempts to force her back into the Union against her will," the editors warned. "The Southern States may not be united now, but an attempt to coerce South Carolina will not only unite the Southern States, but the Southern people, as one man."[11]

Despite the efforts of leaders who urged caution, widespread, decades-old frustrations were sweeping the South into a revolutionary vortex. One day after Mississippi's departure, Florida left the Union. Alabama followed the next day, on January 11. On January 19, Georgia announced its decision to secede, and Louisiana left the Union on January 26. Texas announced its secession on February 1, the seventh state in seven weeks to leave the Union.

Although this revolutionary process may seem hasty, it is worth noting that South Carolina had seriously considered secession thirty years earlier; Mississippi had done the same ten years earlier. These were not rashly made decisions. True, radicals from seceded states urged others to join them, with dire warnings that abolitionists would inspire slave uprisings during this period of political uncertainty. But Southerners had heard these warnings before.

The difference with 1861 is found in the dramatic events that led to this moment. One of the most powerful of these was the recent evidence of Northerners supporting the radical abolitionist John Brown. Southern whites could not fathom how anyone could mourn his loss. He was, they insisted, the man who had barely been kept from achieving his October 1859 dream of a slave rebellion that would have massacred Southern men, women, and children in Harper's Ferry, Virginia.

Southern whites also feared the loss of representation in the national legislature and their waning influence throughout Washington. Their great fear was that Lincoln's election would continue to weaken the political influence they had enjoyed since the country's founding. Thus the white South listened that winter because the fears they had felt for years seemed to materialize one by one. The world they treasured above all others teetered on the brink of destruction, and, having tried compromise, election, and debate, secession, they concluded, was their only remaining option.

Northerners understood political frustrations but saw only spite in secession. From their perspective, Southerners had dominated every branch of the Federal government since the 1790s. Northern Democrats, Whigs, and Republicans felt they had made one concession after another to the slave South. In the Compromise of 1850, California may have entered the Union as a free state and, yes, slavery was outlawed in Washington City (as Americans then called the Federal capital), but the Fugitive Slave Act was a tremendous gift to the South, they argued. It clarified that Northern whites would, by law, aid in the capture and return of escaped slaves, and placed the power of a Federal law behind the act. This had been followed by the Dred Scott decision by the U.S. Supreme Court in 1857, which ruled that Congress could no longer legally limit the extension of slavery. Even this, Northerners complained, failed to appease the obstinate South.

When Senator John Crittenden, the failed Southern Democratic presidential candidate from Kentucky, offered one last compromise in January, Republican leaders were in no mood to deal. Crittenden proposed a constitutional amendment that would nullify the Compromise of 1850, return the nation to some of the terms of the old Missouri Compromise signed in 1820, and extend the 36° 30' boundaries to the Pacific Ocean. This was less slave territory than Southerners had hoped for in 1850 and far less than what the Dred Scott decision potentially allowed, but it was better than they now faced if they stayed in the Union.[12]

But Northerners like President-elect Lincoln believed the nation was incapable of settling the matter peacefully. Compromise was impossible, they argued, because any further concessions would cut into their principles, and these were principled men. Furthermore, the extension of slavery had plagued the nation with division from the start, and men like Lincoln believed that the country's survival required the death of the "peculiar institution." He advised against such proposals even before Crittenden had formally submitted his plan. "Entertain no proposition for a compromise in regard to the *extension* of slavery. The instant you do, they have us again; all our labor is lost, and sooner or later must be done over. Douglas is sure to be again trying to bring in his 'Pop. Sov.'" the prairie lawyer from Illinois warned. They must not return to Douglas's compromise of voting on slavery and freedom, as popular sovereignty had allowed with the Kansas–Nebraska Act in 1856, Lincoln insisted. "Have none of it. The tug has to come and better now than later."[13]

"I WILL COME AT YOUR BIDDING"

While politicians in Washington grasped for a peaceful solution to disunion, the seven seceded states agreed to send delegates to a meeting in centrally located Montgomery, Alabama. On February 4, 1861, the Southern Convention, as it became known, convened in the Alabama State House, a Greek revival-inspired structure that included a grand spiral staircase built a decade earlier by Horace King, a slave who was emancipated by an Act of the Alabama Legislature in recognition of his talents as an architect and engineer. Few who gathered there even mentioned it. To them, slavery was not wrong, and the recognition of King's talents had been wise. They mentioned no recognition of the irony of King's creation resting at the heart of the Confederacy's creation because they saw none.

As the delegates pondered the process of building a new nation, the task would have seemed overwhelming had they not been convinced of their rights and their obligations as members of a republic. They quickly went to work creating a body of laws to guide their countrymen. Reflecting the conservative nature of their rebellion and their desire to preserve American traditions, everything from their national flag to their constitution was strikingly similar to that of the United States. The delegates considered several candidates for their chief executive before they sent word to Jefferson Davis at Brierwood, asking that he serve as their first president. His role was quite similar to that of past American leaders, though he would serve for six years and was restricted to a single term in office. Davis reluctantly agreed to his appointment, preferring the idea of a field command but convinced that it was his duty to accept his new nation's call.

Varina Davis's shoulders sagged as she considered their burdensome future with her husband as President of the new Confederate States of America. But he had made a promise, and she was too well aware of his inability to bend when he had committed himself to a cause. While campaigning for Breckinridge several months earlier, Jefferson Davis had pledged his willingness to lead to a crowd gathered at Vicksburg. The promise blended his conservatism and sense of duty with the boldness that had made him an exceptional field commander and inspired the claim by *Harper's Weekly* that Davis was "emphatically 'one of those born to command.'" Having traveled the state for six weeks by that point, Davis had looked out on the crowd of fellow Mississippians and promised:

> If Mississippi in her sovereign capacity decides to submit to the rule of an arrogant and sectional North, then I will sit me down as one upon whose brow the brand infamy and degradation has been written, and bear my portion of the bitter trial. But, if on the other hand, Mississippi decides to resist the hands that would tarnish her star on the National Flag, then I will come at your bidding, whether by day or by night, and pluck that star from the galaxy, and place it upon a banner of its own.

Davis went on, poetically pledging to plant this banner "upon the crest of battle, and gathering around me Mississippi's best and bravest." He welcomed "the invader to the harvest of death."[14]

Varina Davis later claimed that when her husband received the message of his appointment as President of the Confederacy, he "looked so grieved" that she feared someone had died. It took Davis several moments to compose himself, and when he finally did share the news, it was "as a man might speak of a death sentence."[15] Granted, Davis had indicated on several occasions that he saw himself leading in the field, not in a Southern White House. But he never refused to be considered for the presidency. It's possible that the "death sentence" that Varina felt might have been her own.

She had watched the political world of Washington for nearly a decade and knew the loneliness that defined the tenures of her friends Jane Pierce and Margaret Taylor as first ladies. She also knew her own temperament. Varina Davis lacked the peace of a mediocre mind. Her education and years of private political debating had fostered strong, thoughtful opinions, which she rarely had the patience to suppress. She knew her time as First Lady of the Confederacy would be one of torture for herself and her equally obstinate husband. But she was duty bound, too, and in late February 1861, Varina Davis left to join her husband at

Montgomery to stand beside him as they received "the invader to the harvest of death."[16]

"FOR THE LAND OF CALHOUN"

In the coming months, the Confederacy scrambled to form and mobilize an army and navy to defend their borders in the possibility of war. On March 6, 1861, the Confederate Congress called for 100,000 volunteers for one year's service in their newly formed Confederate States Army, and from Austin to Charleston, Southern boys rushed to sign up. Preempting the politicians, fun-loving Tally Simpson and his friends at Wofford College in Spartanburg, South Carolina, had already organized into a company by the first week of February. The twenty-two-year-old boasted to his father that, "I am now Lieutenant Taliaerro Simpson, quite an honorable title for an unworthy junior." Like many volunteers, his enthusiasm helped to create popular images of youthful, brash South Carolinians racing to war. But Tally was more than just a romantic, naïve boy about to realize that the soldier's life little resembled what he had read or heard from the men in their rural South Carolina community. He was a thoughtful, reflective man, quick to smile, but also determined to "suit [him]self and not the community" in a life of his choosing. Days after Lincoln's election, he had been ready to go, though he did not believe it would come to war. Still, he insisted, he favored the idea of planning for armed conflict, if only to be prepared and "to show the North what we are willing to do for the land of [our] fathers and mothers, for the land of Calhoun, for 'the land of the free and the home of the brave.'"[17]

Tally's brother Dick, affectionately nicknamed "Buddy," did not quite share Tally's enthusiasm. The more thoughtful and the younger of the two siblings, twenty-year-old Dick Simpson briefly joined Tally's company, the "Southern Guards," before reconsidering. His dream was to be a lawyer, not a soldier. Their father, Richard Franklin Simpson, had served in the Seminole Wars of the 1830s and the U.S. House of Representatives in the 1840s before retiring from politics to focus on agrarian pursuits. He had returned to politics briefly to sign South Carolina's Ordinance of Secession, and both sons turned to their father for guidance and approval of their actions that spring. The senior Simpson, however, insisted that in this decision his sons must "be guided by their own sense of duty."

The Simpson family's anxiety was writ large across the Upper South. On March 4, Letitia Tyler, granddaughter of former President John Tyler, raised the new Confederate flag in Montgomery, just days after her grandfather departed the Washington Peace Conference he had helped to organize to find some solution to the mounting tensions. The very fact that the new Confederate government had already selected a president and his cabinet and even designed a flag indicated just how desperate the elder Tyler's efforts were. But they also reflected the mood of wealthy landowners and merchants across the region, especially in the Upper South. A month earlier, when 131 delegates representing twenty-one states gathered in Washington, Tyler had warned his fellow Southerners that if they failed "the conqueror will walk at every step over smouldering ashes and beneath crumbling columns."[18] Try as they might, the convention sank into the morass that had thwarted Clay, Douglas, Bell, Crittenden, and every major leader of the past thirty years who tried to find solid, lasting ground on which to unify the nation.

On the night of February 23, several delegates agreed to call on President-elect Lincoln, who had arrived at the Willard Hotel, where they were meeting. Their initial exchanges were pleasant, and several of the men were surprised by the rail-splitter's intelligence and grace. Virginian James Seddon finally challenged the pleasantries and complained to Lincoln of the North's "sins of omission—of your failure to enforce the laws—to suppress your John Browns and your Garrisons, who preach insurrection and make war upon our property!" Lincoln calmly reminded him, "I believe John Brown was hung and Mr. Garrison imprisoned. You cannot justly charge the North with disobedience to statutes or with failing to enforce them. You have made some which were very offensive, but they have been enforced, notwithstanding." When the New Yorker William Dodge tried to force Lincoln's hand, claiming that it was up to the President-elect "whether the whole nation shall be plunged into bankruptcy; whether the grass shall grow in the streets of our commercial cities," Lincoln smiled quietly, answering "Then I say it shall not," immediately clarifying what everyone in the room knew: The crisis was not that simple, and the convention was nowhere near a solution. But those gathering in Washington knew what their failure meant, and they persevered.

Three days later, delegates of the Upper South called on Lincoln again. Charles S. Morehead, the former governor of Kentucky who had served with Lincoln in the House, asked his old friend to consider withdrawing troops from all Southern states, arguing that this could preserve the peace. Lincoln sighed and told the men that this reminded him of a story from *Aesop's Fables*. In the tale, a lion falls in love with a beautiful woman and proposes marriage, but her parents will consent only if the lion agrees to have his dangerously sharp claws and teeth removed. Once this was done, Lincoln reminded his guests, "they took clubs and knocked him on the head."

William C. Rives of Virginia, the former Whig Senator and minister to France, had recently returned from revolutionary Paris, well aware that the same fate might lie ahead for America. He was frustrated by the telling of a child's tale in the midst of tense negotiations, and fumed that if Lincoln would not take a firm stance against coercion, it would almost definitely force his state from the Union. Noting the usually calm Rives's fury, Lincoln rushed to offer, "Mr. Rives! Mr. Rives! If Virginia will stay in, I will withdraw the troops from Fort Sumter." But Rives lacked the authority to make such a pledge. The moment of compromise would not last, but Lincoln had realized something important: While individual Southerners might want to compromise, the region as a whole could not achieve it. Lincoln could stop holding firm and adopt the role of the gracious conciliator, knowing that he actually risked nothing.[19]

As spring wore on, Lincoln maintained his "Sphinxlike silence," as Charles Francis Adams, the son and grandson of previous presidents and the future U.S. minister to Great Britain, observed.[20] The entire city seemed to be watching and waiting to see what Lincoln would do. He continued to avoid speaking publicly on the issue of slavery. Privately, though, Lincoln worked feverishly to avoid compromises on the issue.

While he promised his Southern friends that the North would not intervene with slavery where it existed, he remained convinced that any compromise on its extension would be devastating for the nation. In December, he had insisted that the "tug has to come and better now than later." In January, he clarified this, arguing, "If we surrender it is the end of us, and of the government. They will repeat the experiment on us *ad libitum*. A year will not pass, till we shall have to take Cuba as a condition upon which they will stay in the Union."[21] He even went so far as to support a vote by Republicans in Congress to pass a constitutional amendment protecting slavery where it currently existed. In truth, though, compromise was impossible. As he confided to his friend Alexander Stephens, who would soon be appointed Vice President of the Confederacy, "You think slavery is *right* and ought to be extended; while we think it is *wrong* and ought to be restricted. That I suppose is the rub."[22]

On March 4, 1861, two days before the Confederacy's call for volunteers, Abraham Lincoln officially became the sixteenth president of the United States. In his inaugural address, he clarified his hope to avoid conflict and reminded the South that compromise was up to them. He could not allow the South to remove his claws, so to speak, but he would not act with aggression. "In your hands, my dissatisfied fellow countrymen, and not in *mine*, is the momentous issue of civil war," Lincoln advised. "The government will not assail *you*. You can have no conflict, without being yourselves the aggressors. *You* have no oath registered in Heaven to destroy the government, while *I* shall have the most solemn one to 'preserve, protect and defend' it," he reminded the nation. Then, in a style that would define his presidency, Lincoln softened his tone. "We are not enemies but friends. We must not be enemies," he implored. "Though passion may have strained, it must not break our bonds of affection. The mystic chords of memory, stretching from every battle-field, and patriot grave, to every living heart and hearthstone, all over this broad land, will yet swell the chorus of the Union, when again touched, as surely they will be, by the better angels of our nature."[23]

Lincoln's contemporaries were rarely as pleased with his speeches as future generations have been, and the reactions that spring were no different. The *Richmond Times Dispatch* warned, "The Inaugural

Address of Abraham Lincoln inaugurates civil war, as we predicted it would …. The sword is drawn and the scabbard thrown away."[24] In Georgia, *The Atlanta Confederacy* was even more critical, describing Lincoln's address as "a medley of ignorance, sanctimonious cant and tender-footed bullyism." Louisianans seemed to agree. The New Orleans *Delta* reported, "If [Lincoln] is at all a man of his word, war is already virtually declared," while its competitor, the *Picayune*, warned "He would … send upon us obnoxious strangers enough to make mince pies of the southern people and cook them over their blazing dwellings." In Mississippi, the Oxford *Mercury* described the inaugural as a "bloody and brutal manifesto …. It amounts to a plain, open and unqualified declaration of war against the Confederate States and the South!"[25]

While much of the Deep South fumed, portions of the Upper South still called for patience. North Carolina's *Raleigh Banner* admitted that "portions of it, we confess, are well calculated to excite apprehensions on the part of conservative men of the South; yet, a reperusal will, we think, satisfy the unprejudiced mind that the rail-splitter will not, under any circumstances, attempt to split the heads of those who have thought proper to secede from the Union." Similarly, the *Chattanooga Gazette* advised Tennesseans to "suspend any formation of opinion" until the Lincoln administration had proved its intentions. "Mr. Lincoln … could not have spoken otherwise than he has, having taken the oath prescribed by the Constitution."

Just to the west, however, the *Nashville Union and American* insisted that "No man can read the Inaugural without coming to the conclusion that it is a declaration of war against the seceded States, and in less than thirty days, if its avowals are carried out, we shall have the clangor of resounding arms, with all its concomitants of death, carnage and woe." Even Virginia's conservative *Richmond Whig* warned that Lincoln's attitude toward "the seceding States will meet the stern and unyielding resistance of the united South."[26]

Northerners were not much more united in their responses. In New York, the *Albany Evening Journal* insisted, "No Message was ever received with greater favor." The editors were especially pleased with the balance Lincoln struck between being "equally firm and conciliatory."[27]

But the Democratic stronghold of New York City complained in the New York *Journal of Commerce* that Lincoln had announced "nothing less than a proclamation of war." Nonsense, responded the Republican New York *Times*. They declared, "the inaugural cannot fail to exert a very happy influence on public sentiment throughout the country."[28] In Kennebec, Maine, the *Weekly Journal* seemed as unaware of the anger rising across the lower South as the *Times*. The Kennebec editors applauded the President for meeting "the emergency with firmness and courage nobly blended with the spirit of conciliation and patriotism. He discusses the pending issues with a fairness, calmness and brevity which cannot fail to receive the approval of all friends of National perpetuity." The St. Louis *Democrat* (ironically, a Republican paper) agreed and insisted that the speech met "the highest expectations of the country .... Its effect on the public mind cannot be other than salutary in the highest degree." But in Chicago, the reaction in the Democratic *Times* confirmed the sense that Northerners were as divided as Southerners. "The whole [speech] seems to be a loose, disjointed, rambling affair," the *Times* complained. "Lincoln has resolved to force his doctrines upon the point of the bayonet .... It must be civil war within thirty days."[29]

The editors of the Chicago *Times* were not far off. All spring, as each state seceded, Southern forces had been seizing control of arsenals and other military resources in the new Confederacy. From their perspective, they now owned all government property within their state. But according to the U.S. Federal government, Southerners were illegally seizing U.S. property. Complaints were made, but since only U.S. property and not U.S. soldiers were seized, this kept the situation from coming to a head in every place but one: South Carolina, the state one politician quipped, was "too small to be a nation and too large to be a lunatic asylum."[30]

That spring, Major Robert Anderson commanded the Federal forces stationed at Fort Moultrie, located in the harbor of Charleston, South Carolina. His very presence was an example of the tightrope conservative Northern and Southern leaders had walked all winter. He had firm orders all winter to hold his position, but the War Department did authorize him to shift his base of operations to the more defensible nearby Fort Sumter if he deemed it necessary. Anderson had done just that the day after Christmas 1860, hoping that by moving to a strong position, he would discourage an attack that could ignite a war. Unfortunately, Anderson made his move just as representatives of South Carolina—at that point the only state that had left the Union—had traveled to Washington to secure the transfer of all Federal property within their borders to their new republic. They were furious over the timing of Anderson's actions, but there was little they could do.

Inside Sumter, thirty-six-year-old Theodore Talbot pondered his precarious state and that of the men serving with him. Talbot was a lieutenant commanding Company H of the 1st U.S. Artillery. The son of Kentucky Senator Isham Talbot, Theodore had spent his formative years traveling between his native state and Washington City, acquiring a superb education, and by the early 1840s Talbot was exploring the Trans-Mississippi West with John C. Fremont. The secession winter, however, brought those wandering years to a halt, leaving Talbot stuck inside Sumter.

In late November 1860, Theodore had explained to his sister, "The South, wearied of the persistent attacks of Northern fanaticism, feel that the moment has at length arrived when they must make a determined stand for their rights." The situation had pushed beyond the "mere question of Politics, in the ordinary acceptation of that term, to whether they will quietly submit to be despoiled of their property and their fair land made a second San Domingo," he wrote, referring to the Haitian slave rebellion of 1791. Talbot believed that many Southerners would "withdraw most unwillingly from our present compact. It remains to be seen," he challenged, "whether the Northern states will retrace their steps and abide by the compromises of that Constitution."[31]

By January, Theodore Talbot was trapped between his loyalty to the South and his duties as a soldier. He had tremendous faith in Major Anderson, insisting that "It [was] a positive relief to all of us to have a man here in command of Anderson's reputation." His predecessor, "Col. Gardner, [was] utterly incompetent to command a post under the most favorable circumstancy, [and] was peculiarly unfit at the present time." In the end, Talbot explained to his family, his oath of service had to guide his actions. Knowing that many of his fellow Kentuckians were as torn as he was, Talbot asked his mother to "Let my friends understand that wholly irrespective of the question as between the North & South we as military men and in obedience to our oaths must maintain the defensive until the wishes of the Genl. Govt are known. Even the So[uth] Carolinians ... acknowledge that we are in the right in this respect."[32]

But still the situation hovered in an awkward status quo. About the same time Lincoln delivered his inaugural address, Jefferson Davis placed General Pierre Gustave Toutant Beauregard in command of all Confederate forces in the Charleston area in the hope of maintaining more stability over the situation than he feared the local South Carolinians could offer. Davis had always pledged that the Southern states were exercising their right to leave the Union. Well aware of the vast industrial, agricultural, and military weaknesses of the seven Confederate states, Davis hoped to keep that promise and avoid war if at all possible.

President Lincoln did, too, but the situation was moving beyond his control. Secretary of State William Seward urged caution and conciliation, hoping that Unionist sentiments among planter elites would help quell the rebellion before it even started. To that end, Seward promised Confederate representatives in Washington (without the authority to do so) that the President would soon order Sumter's peaceful evacuation. As it appeared Lincoln would, indeed, evacuate the fort, pro-Union sentiments in the border states increased. As one North Carolina Union paper explained, "Let this policy be carried out, and we predict that the secession fever will die out in a short while, not only in the border States, but in those that have seceded." Tennesseans agreed, predicting that following Lincoln's actions and the end of secession fever, the Confederate states would "after a few years of independent existence, return to the glorious Union of our Fathers."[33] Seward's plan seemed to be working.

The trouble, though, was that even if Lincoln wanted to reinforce the fort, General in Chief Winfield Scott advised him that it was impossible. Across the North, however, Lincoln received increased pressure to do something. One paper mockingly posted advertisements on the President's behalf: "WANTED—A POLICY" while Lincoln remained frustrated by his limited options, all of which seemed wrong. As strongly as Seward advised moderation, Republican leader and German-American politician Carl Schurz advised taking the offensive. "As soon as one vigorous blow is struck," Schurz insisted, "as soon as, for instance, Fort Sumter is reinforced, public opinion in the free States will at once rally to your support."[34]

And then there were Lincoln's military advisors. The best generals in the army all told Lincoln it was impossible to relieve Sumter without starting a war, while Gustavus Fox, future assistant secretary of the navy, disagreed and advised the President of a plan to ship supplies and men to the fort while Sumter's own guns and naval warships provided protection. Of all the plans Lincoln heard that spring, he liked Fox's the best and agreed to it with a few alterations. Lincoln decided to only resupply Sumter with provisions; no additional troops, weapons, or ammunition would enter the fort. He also insisted that the warships accompanying the supply vessel maintain a supportive role, only entering the scene to defend the force. In his final attempt to avoid antagonizing Southern leaders, Lincoln decided to inform them of his plans to peacefully resupply the fort.

In just a few clever moves, the prairie lawyer had backed Davis into a corner. Southerners could not allow a foreign nation (as they defined the United States) resupply a fort within their own territory. But if Davis used force to stop the ship, he knew it meant that Lincoln had just made the South the aggressor in this conflict, the very position Davis hoped to avoid.

As Davis and his advisors pondered their options, they remembered that two months earlier Congress had voted to acquire control of forts in Confederate territory by negotiation or, if necessary, by force. They also knew that the rumors of a possible Federal relief effort, which had circulated across the South all winter, had helped to unify new Confederates against a common threat. Indeed, some argued that a fight for Sumter would force Lincoln into an aggressive stance and thus bring more states into the Confederate fold. Moreover, if Davis and the Confederacy wanted to command any respect as an independent nation, they had to prove that they could defend their own territory.

On April 9, with the support of his cabinet, Jefferson Davis ordered General Beauregard to demand the surrender of Fort Sumter before it could be resupplied. On April 11, Major Anderson responded to his former artillery student's request, explaining that he had orders to hold the fort. Anderson added, however, that he was so low on supplies that he would soon be forced to evacuate his position. The Confederates knew, though, that relief was on the way and if they were to address this threat to their sovereignty, they had best do it now. On April 12, at 3:30 a.m., Beauregard informed Anderson that he had one hour to evacuate Fort Sumter, otherwise Confederate batteries would open fire. As Anderson rejected these terms, an eerie calm enveloped Charleston harbor. Then, at 4:30 a.m., the Confederate bombardment began, and with it, so did America's Civil War.

Reaction was as Davis's advisors had predicted. Secessionists in Memphis demanded that Tennessee act: "*Now* we can have no political differences; *now* we can have no *Union* men; *now* we must have a united and harmonious South, giving counsel and courage to each other, to bear up the banner of *independence* fearlessly and onward." Virginia secessionists agreed, asking "When the tocsin has sounded and the gun is booming, shall Virginia turn her thumbs in silent motion as an old toothless woman? Is Virginia a suckling, powerless babe, then? Is she to be spit upon? Let her people answer."[35]

While Unionists initially urged caution, President Lincoln's next move forced them to act. On April 15, 1861, he called for a 75,000-man force to be raised to suppress the Southern rebellion. This required each state that remained in the Union to fulfill a portion of that number from their militias. Virginia's response was representative of much of the Upper South. Their state convention had voted down secession just eleven days earlier, but now they were being asked to march on fellow Southerners. Over the next several weeks, one by one, Virginia, North Carolina, Tennessee, and Arkansas voted to leave the Union.

Although the slave states of Delaware, Maryland, Kentucky, and Missouri remained, their support was anything but firm. As tensions rose and President Lincoln pondered the likelihood of Maryland's secession, which would place Washington City within the Confederacy, he sent out a plea for Federal volunteers to rush to the capital as quickly as possible. In response, Governor William Burton of Delaware explained that he had no state militia, and therefore could not fulfill Lincoln's request,[36] while Maryland's Governor Thomas Hicks agreed only to send troops in defense of Washington.[37] In Kentucky, however, Governor Beriah Magoffin took a stronger position. "I say, emphatically," Magoffin scowled, "Kentucky will furnish no troops for the wicked purpose of subduing her sister Southern states."[38] Missouri's response was harsher still, as Governor Claiborne Jackson's tirade shot through the telegraph wire: "Your requisition is illegal, unconstitutional, revolutionary, inhuman, diabolical, and cannot be complied with."[39]

While the border states debated their situation, Sumter, and especially Lincoln's call for troops, solidified the division between Union and Confederacy. Americans North and South responded with everything from glee to horror, from bombast to alarm. In Yazoo City, Mississippi, Kate Carney, enjoying a long stay in the comforts of her uncle's plantation, rejoiced when news arrived that Sumter was in Confederate hands. By April 18, she was even happier to learn that Virginia had left the Union and that Tennessee refused to meet Lincoln's request and had offered men to the Confederacy instead. As cannons fired in celebration in the Delta, Carney cheered, "Hurrah for Tenn." and pledged that if her native state did, indeed, secede, "I will no longer be ashamed of her."[40]

Similar revelry filled the streets of Chicago in late April, where a nineteen-year-old clerk named Willie Shepherd pondered his future. "This week has been one continual scene of wild enthusiasm and military movements, Processions, Parading, Bon Fires, Meetings, etc. all the time," he told his mother. "The principal streets of the city are thronged with men women & children, Soldier companies drilling, marching bands playing …" Sitting in his quiet room, Shepherd asked, "What do you think of my joining? … Be assured that if I go, the Christian's armour covers all the rest." Despite the ignorance of youth and the public enthusiasm that he realized "cannot be avoided," Willie carefully reflected on his duties. "Our two American principles of freedom and liberty must be preserved. Often when thinking of the great question of the day my heart jumps—sending a chill through my veins, inspiring my soul with courage to do anything in the cause of my country & liberty," he explained. "I *never had such feelings* before. It seems as though I must do something to rescue my Native land from destruction and ruin, though my efforts be ever so weak ... *If my country needs my services I shall go ...*"[41]

That same day, April 21, 1861, Confederate General Braxton Bragg, formerly of the U.S. Army, wrote to his old friend Henry Hunt, now in position opposite Bragg at Pensacola, Florida. "How strange are the mutations of life! ... A few short months since companions in army, and almost brothers in friendship, it is hard to realize the fact that we are in hostile array against each other." Bragg tried to explain his decision as well as his shock. "I would have taken an oath that my old friend Hunt could never be the instrument of oppression in the hands of a Black Repub[lica]n," Bragg swore. Line by line, he tried to explain his decision to Hunt in one last effort at peace and, quite simply, because Hunt's opinion of Bragg's character and that of the South mattered to him. "This is no movement of politicians ... Every class is represented in the ranks ... The people, en-mass, are the leaders—and every man is now united in the cause," he explained. "You may destroy us, but cannot conquer," he warned. "We have asked for peace, but shall not decline War."[42]

Hunt responded two days later, as awestruck by the turn of events as Bragg. "How strange it is! We have been united in our views of almost all subjects, public and private. We still have, I trust, a personal regard for each other which will continue, whatever course our sense of duty may dictate, yet in one short year after exchanging at your house assurances of friendship, here we are face to face, with arms in our hands, with every prospect of a bloody collision. How strange!" he repeated. Despite Bragg's assurances otherwise, Hunt believed "machinery [had been] employed to bring about this unanimity of opinion expression. I will be frank with you. A democrat of the President's school I now believe that the party was broken up simply to bring about secession, and unfortunately the course of events in the south has enabled the leaders to drag the people with them." He specifically blamed Jefferson Davis, and hinted at, but never specified, "things hitherto inexplicable in the administration of the War Dept. in the last eight years are now explained." He shared Bragg's concern that in the coming war, blood would "flow like water," but Hunt hoped for the day "if neither of us fall in the struggle—when we will meet again not merely as friends … but as fellow citizens of a great, prosperous, happy and united country."[43]

Despite the celebrations across the country, and contrary to the modern belief that Americans failed to recognize the bloody path awaiting them, much of the country shared Bragg's and Hunt's concerns. Northerners and Southerners were well aware of what war meant. Two weeks after Kate Carney had rejoiced over Virginia's secession and two days after she voiced her regret that Tennesseans had failed to hang their Unionist Senator Andrew Johnson, she became more reflective. It was May 3, and Carney heard drums signaling a steamer on the Mississippi River. It was the *Hope* carrying a company of volunteers among its passengers from Yazoo City. "Although I only know 3 that were members," Kate confided to her diary, "I could not but feel sad, when I wondered how many of that number would return to home & friends … What a depressed feel weighed down my heart, as their voices grew fainter & fainter as they rounded the bend in the river, and their shouts & cheers ceased to be heard. I could not for sometime shake off the gloomy feeling. I knew though their faces were wreathed with smiles it was a masque for sad hearts." Still determined in her faith in their cause, Carney prayed, "May God be with them & prosper our case that their blood may not be spilled in vain."[44]

Just down the river in Vicksburg, lawyer William Nugent shared her concerns. His deep reflections on the war are often overshadowed by his oft-quoted curiosity about "shooting a Yankee." In truth, though, he shared the nation's apprehensions about what war would bring. On April 15, he read of the "proclamation of war from the 'old rail splitter,'" and the signs of the "warlike spirit" across the North. "We are evidently in the midst of stirring times with the prospect of a long & bloody war ahead," he warned his young wife.

Two months later, with forces gathering in Virginia and having just received his appointment as Mississippi's Inspector General, Nugent again shared his concerns, as well as his deep conviction in the Confederate cause. "From present appearances this war will continue for some time and every man will have to take up arms in defense of his country. The North seems to be as united as we; and the struggle, unless we defeat the enemy at the Virginia battleground will be almost interminable," he worried. "It will take two or three decided victories to put us in an attitude to demand recognition abroad, and we need expect no assistance outside ourselves for some time. The sheet anchor of our hopes can only be the stalwart arms and brave hearts of our soldiers. They and they alone can achieve our independence."

Nugent had good reason for his sobering predictions. The North possessed 79 percent of the nation's rail lines, and, despite the South's reputation for being more agrarian than the manufacturing North, the Confederacy held only 35 percent of the national farm acreage and produced a mere 9 percent of nation's manufacturing output. The North had 110,000 factories to the South's 18,000, and the Confederacy would be forced to draw its ranks from a population of 9 million (compared to the Union's 22.3 million); 3.7 million of those Southerners were slaves the South would not arm.[45]

Still, Nugent was confident of victory, and he felt even more optimistic when news arrived of the Confederate victory at the first major battle of the war in July in Virginia. But, he prepared for a long war. "The Federalists were defeated and chased for miles," he boasted. "I notice, though, they are reorganizing and preparing *for a war to the death*." Still, Nugent insisted, "If God be for us, as I firmly and conscientiously believe his is—who can prevail over us."[46]

In distant Katonah, New York, John Jay shared Nugent's determination, but in support of a Northern victory that would destroy the slave system that was central to William and Ellie Nugent's Mississippi prosperity. Writing on the same day Nugent celebrated the Confederate victory in Manassas, Jay fumed over the Federal defeat. A long-time supporter of African-American rights and defendant of fugitive slaves, Jay knew that few Northerners shared his opinion that this war should be about much more than Union. He took heart, though, in his belief that "We have an agency at work for the abolition of slavery in the pending war more powerful than all the Conventions we could assemble." They must not, Jay argued, push too hard on the message of emancipation for fear of losing popular support. The wiser move was to allow the brutality of the war to convince the North. With fascinating insight, Jay argued:

> Every battle fought will teach our soldiers & the nation at large that slavery is the great cause of the war, that it is slavery which has brutalized & barbarized the South & that slavery must be abolished as our army advances as a military necessity — & that slavery must be either abolished or utterly paralized to enable us to conclude a peaceful settlement of this rebellion, in such a manner that the industry & prosperity of the North shall never more be imperilled by it...

He suspected that the Union would never abolish slavery on truly moral grounds, but rather for self-interest. Either motive satisfied Jay so long as the result was emancipation.[47]

David Hopkins, serving in the U.S. Navy, echoed Jay's ideas even as he disagreed with them. Writing on stationery emblazoned with a cannon, an American flag, and the message "No compromise with traitors," Hopkins assured his brother and sister in Ashtabula County, Ohio, that the war had nothing to do with slavery. "There are many wrongs to be sighted besides the one done to the Negro race. Sailors to day in both the Merchant and Naval Service of the U.S. are worse used than the slaves of the south .... I don't mean by this ... any apology for the 'Sacred Institution,'" he clarified, but insisted that this war was and must be about saving the nation. "The men who have struck this blow at our government are on to playing for a bigger strike than the right to hold ... or extend slavery. It is intended to be a death blow to our form of Government."[48]

"THE SAD REALITY OF WAR"

As Americans debated the issues of the war, they also debated the significance of the battle Northerners called Bull Run and Southerners called Manassas. Their comments indicate what many Americans suspected from the very beginning: A single fight would not settle their feud. As they pondered this, recruits continued to fill the ranks of both armies, and they settled into the habits of soldiers. As Oliver Norton of the 83rd Pennsylvania Infantry wryly explained, "The first thing in the morning is drill, then drill, then drill again. Then drill, drill, a little more drill. Then drill, and lastly drill. Between drills, we drill, and sometimes stop to eat a little and have roll-call."

Writing from Virginia, Dick Simpson may have lacked his brother's enthusiasm for the martial life, but he did answer his country's call. "I never wished to be back [home] as bad in my life," he wrote from the 3rd South Carolina Infantry Regiment's camp. The early summer found him musing on his responsibilities as a soldier, confiding to his aunt, "I felt right funny creeping through the woods with my rifle ready to shoot—to shoot what? Why, my fellow men. But I believe I could do it with as much grace as I could eat an apple pie." Still, he admitted "All I wish is that the wars were over, and I could see you all … once more." When the fighting began at Manassas on July 21, the Simpson brothers and the 3rd South Carolina were not in the heart of the battle with Jackson on Henry Hill or preventing Sherman from crossing at the Stone Bridge, but they saw enough to proudly claim a part in the Confederate victory and boast that, "The fight was terrible, but southern valor never waned." A few days later, Tally Simpson insisted, "We are now much better prepared than before and are anxiously waiting for an attack."

By August, though, Dick reported that the soldier's life was mostly marching and misery. "During the battles"—which were actually small skirmishes—"and the time between we … had very little sleep and very little to eat. Sunday evening when we went in pursuit, we were double-quicked until we were almost dead. The next morning we marched out in a rain (very hard one) to Centreville to collect spoils, but when we were about half way our company was sent back about 2 miles to bury the dead … but we found them all buried, so we returned," complained Simpson. "We then started again for Centreville, staid there until dark, and returned at night through mud such as you have [never] seen …. We had to wade creeks and any other thing that came in our way." When the exhausted South Carolinians finally reached a stopping point for the night, they had "no tents and such muddy men you have never seen before; we were wet to the skin …. We soon built us a fire and in our wet clothes we laid down on the wet ground and went to sleep. I had nothing but an oil cloth for bed and cover. The next morning, although we had been on our feet the whole of the day before and slept very little that night, we again started to we didn't know where."[49]

Dick could have been describing any camp, North or South, where men drilled and marched and learned that the soldier's life was far less glorious in reality than in legend. Still, for Confederate soldiers, the news was generally good. The Southern victory at Manassas in July was followed a month later with a victory at Wilson's Creek, Missouri, which secured a Confederate stronghold in the southwest portion of the border state. For Union soldiers, just as weary from unrelenting drill, the defeats damaged morale. Writing from Bird's Point, Missouri, in mid-August, Willie Shepherd missed Kenosha as badly as Dick Simpson missed his beloved South Carolina. Shepherd had yet to experience battle, but he noted that "as each day falls into the arms of the silent night nearing us to the great strife—The sad reality of war and its fearful effects is deeply impressed on my mind and I shudder at the thought of the death and destruction that must certainly attend it." Despite his sorrow and concern, Shepherd's faith in the cause remained strong.

The mood was a little different, though, in Washington. By autumn 1861, Southern spirits soared from their battlefield victories while Northern spirits plunged. As the weeks rolled through September and into October, Union and Confederate troops near Washington City took up defensive positions along the Potomac River, particularly at the various fords where forces could cross. Among them was Brigadier General Charles P. Stone, who commanded a 6,500-man division known as the Corps of Observation on the Potomac Line near Poolesville, Maryland, 30 miles from Washington City.[50]

During the first few days of October, Stone received reinforcements in the form of Colonel (and U.S. Senator) Edward D. Baker and his California Brigade (comprised of the 1st, 2nd, 3rd, and 5th California infantry regiments). Confusing everyone, these were predominately made up of men from Pennsylvania who were fighting under the name

"California Brigade" to ensure, per Baker's wish, that the West Coast was represented in what was assumed would be the center of the fighting. To complicate matters further, Baker was not a Senator from California; he represented Oregon. Still, the name brought to mind America's far western regions and, for General Stone, Baker's California Brigade brought his total strength by early October to about 10,000 men.

Opposite Stone was South Carolina Colonel Nathan "Shanks" Evans. He commanded the 7th Brigade of the Confederate Army of the Potomac (which later would become the "Army of Northern Virginia"). He was already famous for his influential role in the Confederate victory at First Manassas and for his love of whiskey, which an aide kept in constant supply. Evans commanded about 2,800 men opposite Stone's 10,000. Originally this did not worry him too much. Stone's mission was clearly just one of observation. By the second week of October, however, Union Brigadier General George McCall established Camp Pierpont at Langley, Virginia, with 12,000 men about 25 miles east of Leesburg. Evans was now between these forces, which made him uncomfortable, and when some small fighting occurred upriver from him at Harper's Ferry on October 16, Evans left his position at Leesburg without orders and marched southward to a more secure location.

When he reported this decision to Beauregard, Evans received a biting reprimand and promptly returned to his original position. His absence, however, had sparked the interest of the Federals. General George McClellan, commanding forces in the area, ordered General McCall to make a reconnaissance-in-force, taking his entire division to Dranesville, which was about halfway to Leesburg. McCall was to stop there and then move forward with a smaller force to see what Confederate strength was around Leesburg. By the time McCall did this, Evans was back in position in Leesburg, convinced that he was going to be attacked by a strong Union force.

Complicating an already complicated situation, McClellan did not like that McCall was as exposed as he was, so McClellan had him recalled back to Langley on October 20. McClellan also informed General Stone (opposite the river from Evans) that McCall was nearby in Dranesville—which he was, but he was preparing to leave per

McClellan's orders, an important detail that McClellan never shared. Stone would later explain that he spent the entire day of October 21 positive that McCall was just a few miles away with 12,000 men ready to assist him if necessary. By then, though, McCall's men were actually marching away from Stone's position.

Following all of this movement, McClellan decided to reassess the Confederate position by having Stone conduct a "slight demonstration." He ordered Stone to move a force down river, entirely visible to the Confederates. At Edwards Ferry, Stone ordered General Willis A. Gorman to move a portion of his brigade—two regiments of New York and Minnesota infantry—and to use some artillery fire to drive the Confederates back a bit from view while two companies of Minnesotans crossed the swelled river on flatboats.

Despite all of this movement, there was no plan for attack. It was only a feint to see what, if anything, the Confederates would do and to convince them to abandon their position. By dusk on October 20, Evans had not taken the bait and was holding firm. So, having inspired no response, Stone pulled his troops back—but not until he did one last thing. While the Confederates were focused on this "slight demonstration," Stone ordered about twenty men of Company H, 15th Massachusetts commanded by Colonel Charles Devens across the river further upstream just after dusk. They crossed at Harrison's Island, a small strip of land about 2 miles long and 300 to 400 feet wide lying midstream in the river opposite Ball's Bluff, which rose 70 feet above the Potomac. Captain Chase Philbrick led the expedition since he and his men were already familiar with the area, having explored it on a similar movement two days earlier.

After crossing the river, they moved up a small trail that wound to the top of the bluff. From there, Philbrick led his men down a cart path, through a large clearing, into a section of woods, and then into an open field. When they were about a mile from the river, they made a simple but important mistake. In the distance, just barely visible in the moonlight (there had been a full moon two days earlier), they mistook a row of trees for a row of tents in a Confederate camp. Compounding the error, Philbrick failed to send anyone forward to verify the "discovery." Instead, the force crossed back over the Potomac to report their find to General Stone.

Stone decided he had an opportunity—"a very nice military chance," he called it—and he sent 300 men commanded by Colonel Charles Devens of the 15th Massachusetts to raid the camp, return, and report. Devens's force crossed in the early morning hours of October 21. About a hundred men from the 20th Massachusetts who would secure the bluff supplemented them. Very early into their expedition, Devens's men discovered there was no Confederate camp, but Devens had the authority from Stone to stay if he drove the Confederates easily from this mythical camp or if there was no threat. Devens decided to stay and see if he could secure some small advantage for all of their efforts. He sent word back to Stone, who approved of Devens's decision. Thus what was to be a small raid had evolved into a reconnaissance of the area to assess Confederate strength near Leesburg.

To ensure success, Stone ordered the rest of the 15th Massachusetts across the Potomac to assist Devens. By this point, though, unbeknownst to Stone, portions of the 15th and 20th Massachusetts had already come into contact at about 8:00 a.m. with Confederate forces and brief skirmishes had ensued with portions of Captain William Duff's 17th Mississippi. The Battle of Ball's Bluff had begun.

Around 9:00 or 10:00 a.m., Colonel Baker entered the scene. Baker was on the eastern shore of the Potomac with the majority of Stone's force and noticed a fair amount of activity in camp. Curious, he went to Stone's headquarters to inquire about the movements and see what he might do to help. Stone explained the situation and his decision to expand it to a reconnaissance in force, mistakenly confident that General McCall was in nearby Dranesville should Stone require assistance.

As the men spoke, Stone decided to order Baker over to the bluff to assess the situation and report back if he thought they should cross more troops over for an advance or withdraw those already there. While Baker moved upriver to carry out these orders, he ran into a messenger on his way to tell General Stone that Devens's small party had run into a force and that skirmishing had started. Baker took it upon himself to order all the troops he could find across the river. Realizing the logistical challenge this created, he then spent the next four hours looking for boats and overseeing the river crossing. All the while, the forces gathering on Ball's Bluff had no one in overall command. Baker's error was a simple one. He should have delegated the issue of transportation to a junior officer while he continued across the river and carried out his orders to command the forces on the bluff. But it was early in the war, and it was an easy mistake for a green officer to make.

As Baker worked feverishly on the wrong side of the river, the battle raged. The morning's fight involved a series of skirmishes separated by quiet lulls as inexperienced junior officers tried to make sense of the confusion around them. The situation continued like this until about 3:00 or 4:00 p.m. when Confederate forces had pushed the Federals back to the bluff. It was here that Baker, who had finally arrived, tried to organize the men into a defensive position that took the shape of a backward "L." Contrary to wartime and postwar accounts of the battle, the Union forces were not simply running away and dashing headlong into the Potomac. Baker managed to seize temporary control of a bad situation, and although the position he established was not ideal, it would force advancing Confederates into a Federal crossfire as they approached the river. Indeed, that is exactly what happened when Colonel Erasmus Burt's 18th Mississippi moved forward and failed to see the Federal right wing, which was concealed by sloping ground and a wood line. When the Union forces opened fire, one Mississippian described it as "the best directed and most destructive single volley I saw during the war." More than half of the 18th Mississippi's eighty-five casualties suffered that day came during that single volley.

The remainder of the afternoon was "made up of charges," as one Union soldier recalled, and they were not particularly well coordinated. Gradually, though, the Confederates wore the Federals down. It was during one of the final assaults, most likely led by the 18th Mississippi, that Colonel Baker was mortally wounded. A captain in the 20th Massachusetts saw Baker shot while rallying his men, and the young captain noticed that Baker managed to get up and resume control, only to be struck again by several shots. It was now late in the afternoon of October 21, and by 5:00 or 6:00 p.m., Evans, who had done a superb job of shuttling forces into the fight, sent 700 fresh men of the 17th Mississippi forward for one final assault. As Evans had hoped, they were too strong for the exhausted Federals, weakened by the loss of Baker, and their line broke. As one Confederate recalled, "A kind of shiver ran through the huddled mass upon the brow of the cliff, it gave way; rushed a few steps; then, in one wide, panic-stricken herd, rolled, leaped, tumbled over the precipice."

A number of the men drowned trying to get back across the swelled river. Some made it to Harrison's Island, only to be gunned down there. Official reports record the death of twenty-nine Union soldiers at Ball's Bluff, but the actual total, which includes the deaths noted in postbattle medical reports, regimental rolls, and by locals who buried the bodies that continued to wash up on the banks of the Potomac, is closer to 250 men. The Confederates lost forty soldiers.

Ball's Bluff, and especially Baker's death, became the battle that unraveled the patience of the North, or certainly of Northern politicians. On October 24, three days after the battle, General George McClellan reported that "the disaster was caused by errors committed by the immediate commander [Baker], not General Stone." But this simple statement did little to satisfy the anger of Northern leaders trying to understand why they seemed to be losing a war that, on paper, they should have won six months ago. The situation was compounded by the fact that the defeat was an embarrassing mess. Prominent Northern men had been captured or killed, including a U.S. Senator. The elite 20th Massachusetts, whose officers came from some of the most prominent families of Boston, had their Colonel William R. Lee and Major Paul Revere (grandson of the Revolutionary War hero) captured by Confederates, along with about a dozen others. A young, prominent officer in their ranks by the name of Oliver Wendell Holmes was among those severely wounded.

"THE SIMPLE QUESTION IS WHETHER A FUGITIVE SLAVE SHALL BE SURRENDERED TO A REBEL."

Equally problematic was a strange turn of events that brought the divisive issue of slavery into an already contentious situation.

During the Union retreat from the bluff, a few slaves had escaped with the rushing Federals, and on November 24, two other men, runaway slaves from Maryland, showed up in the camp of the 20th Massachusetts, which was still in position near the Potomac. Per standing law at this time, Maryland being a loyal slave state, the slaves were returned to their owners by Stone's orders. A number of men of the 20th, some of whom came from staunch abolitionist families and had the political connections to make waves, disagreed with that decision. One of two young lieutenants wrote Massachusetts Governor John Andrew about the matter, and Andrew in turn wrote letters of inquiry to the commanding officer of the 20th Massachusetts, Lt. Col. Francis Palfrey, and to Secretary of War Simon Cameron.

While this occurred, Stone was made aware of the two runaway slaves who escaped with the Federals rushing back from Ball's Bluff. Jack and Bob McCoy may have run away or simply may have been caught up in the chaos, but their families remained enslaved in Virginia. The McCoys, worried that their families would suffer retribution for their escape, informed Stone that they actually wanted to return to slavery. Already dealing with the fallout of his defeat at Ball's Bluff, the death of Colonel Baker, and the other controversy involving the Maryland slaves, Stone carefully noted the details of the McCoy brothers' case, their request to return to Virginia, and the fact that his actions were in accordance with standing law. He allowed them to return to their life of slavery in Virginia.

An enraged Governor Andrew sent additional letters of protest and copied them all to Secretary Cameron. But Stone's real problems came from the rage his actions inspired in Massachusetts Senator Charles Sumner. In a December 1861 speech on the Senate floor that dripped with sarcasm, Sumner observed that, "Brigadier General Stone, the well-known commander at Ball's Bluff, is now adding to his achievements there by engaging ably and actively in the work of surrendering fugitive slaves. He does this, sir, most successfully. He is victorious when the simple question is whether a fugitive slave shall be surrendered to a rebel."

Stone, already angered by what he saw as politicians' interference with his earlier decision to return runaway slaves, was becoming increasingly sensitive to the public media mess over Ball's Bluff and the recent martyrdom of Colonel Baker. Sumner's Senate speech pushed Stone over the edge. On December 23, Stone wrote directly to Sumner, accusing him of "a slander and a falsehood" and declaring him a "well known coward." It was a terrible mistake. Sumner was a controversial but respected senior Senator. He was also famous for the brutal caning he had suffered by South Carolinian Preston Brooks in May 1856 in response to Sumner's slanderous comments about Brooks's family and their defense of the slave system.

Following that famous "Caning of Sumner" and the House's failure to agree on any censure of Brooks for the attack, several of Sumner's then-fellow Senators—including Ohio's Ben Wade, Michigan's Zachariah Chandler, and then-Senator Simon Cameron—swore they would meet any such future force with equal or greater force. Indeed they had promised "to carry the quarrel into the coffin." It was not an idle threat. They were men who had risen to power through their own raw efforts. They were forces of nature who had a haunting memory of a moment when they failed to respond to violence with greater violence, and they swore it would never happen again. Indeed, shortly before the war, when the enraged Georgian Robert Toombs challenged his senate colleague Ben Wade to a duel, Wade responded: "rifles at twenty paces, with a white paper the size of a dollar [coin] pinned over the heart of each combatant."

Wade, Chandler, Cameron, and Sumner remained just as determined, if not more so, than they had been before the war began to fight force with force, and now they were in a perfect position to carry out their pledge. Just before Stone had fired his angry response to Senator Sumner, calling him a "well known coward," all four men had played a role in organizing the new Congressional Joint Committee on the Conduct of the War.

Organized in the wake of Ball's Bluff, the committee first met on December 10, 1861.[51] Wade served as chairman, and his chief ally was his fellow Republican Senator Zachariah Chandler of Michigan. Both men were leading radical Republicans, hard-spoken and long-standing opponents of slavery and any "softness" toward the South or Southern sympathizers. The only Senate Democrat on the committee was Tennessean Andrew Johnson, who was so embittered toward his former colleagues now in the Confederacy that he worked quite well with the radicals on the committee. The representatives from the House included Republicans John Covode of Pennsylvania, George Julian of Indiana, and Daniel Gooch of Massachusetts, with Julian the most determined radical in that group. Gooch was not as well known as some of the others, but he added dedicated legal skills to the group's efforts. The only Democratic House member was Moses Odell of New York. He often disagreed with his colleagues, but he, too, had a reputation for hard, dedicated efforts in their investigations.

Originally created to investigate defeats at Manassas, Wilson's Creek, and Ball's Bluff, the committee quickly expanded its role to one that investigated anything that seemed to threaten the Union war effort. The problem for Stone was that his exchange with Sumner occurred right after the committee was formed, in full vigor. The committee members came down on the Democrat, a West Pointer, with a vengeance. During a two-month period from the end of December through the end of February, they met with thirty-nine witnesses, many of whom were never at Ball's Bluff but reported second- and third-hand information about what happened there. Most of the testimony was given in secret, and the questioning was prejudicial, with leading questions and unchallenged hearsay accepted from known enemies of Stone. Stone was never allowed to offer any testimony in his own defense.

On January 27, in the middle of these inquiries with "witnesses," committee members Chandler, Julian, and Gooch met with the new Secretary of War, Edwin Stanton, to present their findings to date on Stone. The following day, Stanton ordered Stone's arrest. George McClellan, to his credit, convinced Stanton to at least allow Stone to defend himself, and on January 31, Stone stood before the committee.

When Wade informed Stone of the evidence against him, Stone—who was only aware of the investigation, not of the arrest warrant—asked to see the evidence, but Wade refused to share it, thoroughly baffling Stone. The situation remained in an awkward stalemate for the next week, during which time Stone, still unaware of the warrant, attended a White House reception on February 5. Three days later, Stone opened his door to find his old friend Brigadier General George Sykes and several soldiers holding the warrant. For Sykes, the arrest of his former commanding officer from Old Army days was "the most disagreeable duty" he ever had to perform.

Stone spent the next 189 days in jail, even though charges were never filed against him. Adding insult to injury, a mix-up in the travel arrangements left the young lieutenant escorting Stone with insufficient funds to cover what were supposed to be prepaid tickets, and a disgusted General Stone had to loan him the money to cover the trip. When Stone arrived in New York, he wrote to everyone imaginable who might have been able to help, and more than 700 prominent friends in Massachusetts signed petitions on his behalf. But the controversy continued, and Stone languished in jail at Fort Lafayette for the next six months.

As soldiers settled into winter quarters and civilians prepared for a series of long, cold months with their loved ones far from home, the committee continued to do its work. Their actions remain a puzzle to this day. The irony is that these were well-intentioned men, determined to end the enslavement of fellow human beings and to save the nation they dearly loved. But they also represented a dangerous challenge to the Union war effort.

The leaders of the committee were free-labor, self-made radicals who viewed regular officers as potentially disloyal Americans whose sympathies were especially damnable because they had been educated at and were employed at the public expense (conveniently forgetting that committee members also served at the public expense). Stone, as a West Pointer and veteran of the Old Army, was in their eyes more closely linked to an "aristocratic" and Democratic South than to his native North. Wade, Chandler, and Julian in particular all spoke out strongly against the military academy and regular Army officers. In part, this was the result of the perception that so many West Pointers resigned to join the Confederacy (although that number was smaller than it seemed at the time). As Wade argued, "I do not believe there can be found an institution on the face of the earth ... that has turned out so many false, ungrateful men as have emanated" from West Point. Chandler agreed, informing a friend that half of the Old Army had been comprised of "downright traitors & 1/2 of the other sympathize with the South."

Stone was the antithesis of the free-labor, self-made man. The committee believed his failures at Ball's Bluff were the result of (unproven) Southern sympathies and judged his return of runaways to slavery as an inexcusable sin. Compounding this was Stone's unwise and violent disrespect of Sumner, an abuse these men had sworn to return ten fold should the opportunity arise. Stone was doomed—but so too, in many ways, was the Union—to months if not years of the distracting and yet entirely well-intentioned interference that is such a fundamental characteristic of democracies at war.

As 1861 came to a close, the Committee on the Conduct of the War continued their investigations, determined to revive the Federal war effort. At the same time, Union and Confederate families endured the long, cold winter and ushered in a new year filled with hope and fear. The Union's eyes were now all on a man the press called the "Young Napoleon:" General George Brinton McClellan. He was a star of the Old Army and had secured some of the few, if minor, victories the North could claim. Now the President had called on him to take command of all Federal forces and lead the newly organized Army of the Potomac in the field. Despite Lincoln's worries that McClellan would be overwhelmed with his duties, the bold West Pointer insisted, "I can do it all," and the North prayed he was right.

But as the months ticked by and it came time for the armies to break winter quarters and resume the campaign season, Wade, Chandler, and their supporters suspected a traitor in their midst. They saw in McClellan another man educated at public expense, another Northern Democrat, and another commander opposed to embracing emancipation as a war aim. Suspicious, they called McClellan before them to investigate his failure to act immediately against Southern forces. When McClellan responded that he lacked sufficient transportation and bridge crossings, and that he needed to be sure there was a line of retreat for his forces should that prove necessary, the committee frowned. Chandler asked: "General McClellan, if I understand correctly, before you strike the rebels you want to be sure of plenty of room so that you can run in case they strike back." "Or in case you get scared," Ben Wade added. After a frustrated McClellan left the room, Wade asked Chandler what he thought "of the science of generalship." Chandler declared, "I don't know much about war, but it seems to be that this is infernal, unmitigated cowardice."

By early spring 1862, Confederate hopes soared with dreams that this year would bring the victories that would secure foreign assistance and true independence. The Union, on the other hand, seemed primed to flounder between a general who could build an army but not use it and politicians who, despite their determination to win, seemed to only push the nation toward defeat.

⇒ 2 ⇐

A WAR FOR UNION AND FREEDOM

While politicians fumed in Washington that winter, the home front remained quiet as families endured the first holiday season of the war without their loved ones. Mary Felicia Loughridge sat down on Christmas Day 1861 in Falls County, Texas, to write to her husband, James Rodgers "J. R." Loughridge, a first lieutenant serving with the 4th Texas Infantry Regiment in Virginia. She took pleasure in sharing this day with him, if only on paper, and she offered thanks that he was healthy despite the sickness in camps across the Union and the Confederacy. But then sadness rose to the surface, and her words came out like a sigh, "This is the dullest Christmas that I have ever witnessed," she complained. There was "no firing of guns nor any thing of the kind." All she could picture were "the merry words and … the genial smile of friends now far far away enduring the … hardships and trials of war oh how those thoughts make my heart ache and my eyes fill with tears." She took comfort in their faith, but she couldn't help complaining that "the longer we are separated the worse I want to enjoy the blessed privilege of walking the long road through this world by your side my hearts treasure."

Determined to remain strong, Felicia promised J. R. that despite her sorrow, she and their girls were making the best of things. Mary, their four-year-old, "was up this morning early examining her stocking," for signs of Santa's generosity. Felicia had warned her that shop shelves offered few of the treats Santa used to bring. Mary pondered the possibility that, as Felicia had explained, "she would get nothing" in her stocking because "Santaclause had gone to war." To this, Felicia boasted, Mary declared "that she was willing to do with out his candy and raisins if he would help to whip the yankees so her Pa could come home."[52]

Several months later and a little further east along the Mississippi River, William Nugent shared Felicia Loughridge's frustrations. It was the spring of 1862, and he had grown tired of his role as inspector general of Mississippi and enlisted in Company D of the 28th Mississippi Cavalry that March. It was a move that said more about Nugent's notions of responsibility than his faith in Confederate victory. "Nothing but a love of country & sense of duty would have reduced me," he told his wife, "[to] my present mode of life …. The prevailing impression seems to be that the war will soon be over—will last no longer than six months—and will be concluded with the coming campaign. I presume we all wish such a hopeful result" he mused, but warned "the wish is father to the thought I fear." Still "'Hope on, Hope ever' must be our motto, and diligence our watchword—By determined action and prompt responses to the calls of our country we will yet whip the Yankees, and thus vindicate the position we have taken."[53]

In the North, the winter had closed under clouds of depression and suspicion. Political and military leaders scrambled to understand how America's standing army could be defeated at Manassas Junction, Virginia, by a newly recruited band of southern rabble, and how the same thing could have happened a second time at Ball's Bluff. As the armies rested and reorganized in camp, Washington City practiced its well-worn trade of gossip to pass the winter. Congressmen's wives gathered over tea and stuck to their favorite topic: the President's wife.

Mrs. Lincoln impressed no one. To be fair, neither of the Lincolns had made good impressions when they arrived in the U.S. capital in 1861. Lydia Child, a leading abolitionist and humanitarian reformer, grimaced with distaste each time she saw Mr. Lincoln, admitting that "I never see old Abe's *picture* without thinking that his lanky neck looks as if he was made to be hanged." His clothes did not drape properly, his frame lacked the Grecian symmetry that the Western world craved in their leaders, and although he seemed friendly and sociable, many Northerners suspected that it was only his country charm combined with the political divisions of 1860 that had won him election. They worried that he lacked the intellectual fortitude to lead the nation. As months went by, though, Mr. Lincoln had grown on people. Word leaked out about his incredible work ethic, characterized by sixteen-hour days. Even Child came to acknowledge that, "with all his deficiencies, it must be admitted that he has grown continually …. I think we have reason to thank God for Abraham Lincoln."[54]

In those same months, however, Mrs. Lincoln's reputation sank lower, if that was possible. She possessed the narcissist's habit of self-indulgence, self-absorption, and a cruel willingness to use people in any way necessary to find the security that had eluded her youth. It is a dangerous trick to psychoanalyze the dead, basing judgments on limited medical reports and having no ability to interview the patient. Still, historians and contemporaries alike generally agree that Mary Todd Lincoln's narcissism left her prey to manipulators who seemed to fill her insatiable need for glorification and love.

Her troubles began at an early age. As one biographer explained, "At less than a year, [Mary] had been abruptly weaned and had lost her place as the youngest to a first son. When she was four, a baby brother died. At five she lost part of her name," when her parents gave the latest baby Mary's middle name, Ann. "At six," the list of tragedies continued, "her mother died, and … at seven a stranger absorbed her father's affections," and at eight, that stranger, Elizabeth Humphreys, became her stepmother. Mary's maternal grandmother had taught the Todd children to despise Elizabeth from the start and, by all accounts, she made no effort to change their opinion. While Mary's misfortunes were not uncommon for the mid-nineteenth century, she did suffer more than most of her peers, year after year, and lacked the love that might have sustained her through those awful times and far into the future.[55]

By the early spring of 1862, having lost a child years earlier and, more recently, her husband's attention to an all-consuming war, Mary found herself in a whirlwind partly of her own creation and partly the result of the disasters that seemed to follow her. Upon arriving in Washington, it seemed the First Lady had, with help from several unsavory characters who had befriended her, managed to embezzle or misuse government funds for fictitious improvements to the White House and its gardens. This group of male friends included the well-known lawyer Daniel Sickles, who had killed his wife's lover in broad daylight and then walked free, thanks to the nation's first use of the temporary insanity defense. Mary's other Blue Room compatriot (named for the spot where they all met for hours on end) was Henry Wikoff, whom contemporaries described as exciting and dangerous and whom P. T. Barnum claimed trained him in the entertainer's essential art of deception and trickery. Wikoff was also known as "a world renowned whoremonger and swindler" who once kidnapped a tobacco heiress and then had the nerve to publish an account of it.

In an example of astonishingly poor judgment, Wikoff became Mary Todd Lincoln's closest confidant. During the previous December, he convinced her to give him an early draft of Lincoln's annual address to Congress. When portions of the President's address then appeared in the *New York Herald*, for which Wikoff served as an informant, Mary was horrified, not from guilt but from the social embarrassment, especially when the public demanded a formal investigation. When President Lincoln realized that his wife might, indeed, be the source of the leak, he convinced the congressional committee to cease their inquiry, but the rumors refused to die.

Unfortunately for the President and the First Lady, the scandal broke amidst reports circulating through the North that Mary's half-brother had been the sadistic warden of Libby Prison, in which so many Union soldiers had suffered after the Battle of Bull Run. By early February, newspapers and parlors were filled with theories about Mary's embezzlements and the Todd family's genetically cruel nature. Talk even escalated to accusations that the President's wife was a Confederate spy. She was, after all, leaking state documents to the press, the socialites claimed, while their friends nodded, silently smiling with relief that they were not the targets of this season's gossip.

Their husbands, though often assumed to be above feminine gossip, joined in. The most caustic report came from Oregon Senator

James Nesmith, who, following an East Room reception, described Mrs. Lincoln to his wife as "weak-minded" and displaying a "sorry show of skin and bones." Unable to leave it at that, Nesmith claimed, "She had her bosom on exhibition, a flower pot on her head." It seemed to him that the woman who would "cook Old Abe's dinner and milk the cows" now wanted to "exhibit her milking apparatus to public gaze."[56]

The Lincolns ignored most of the gossip. The President was too busy with political and military matters to grant it much attention, and Mary was secure in her faith that she was misunderstood by the jealous and the weak who clung to her husband. But even that self-created cocoon could not protect her from everything.

The knowledge of high infant-mortality rates in nineteenth-century America often leads to the false assumption that earlier generations came to expect the loss of their children; that they developed a numbness to the small tombstones that dotted their churchyards. Granted, there was an expectation that one must find some way to, as ministers advised, persevere and accept God's will rather than try to explain it. The Lincolns had wrestled with this in 1850 when they lost their son, Edward, named for Senator Edward Baker, who died at Ball's Bluff. They barely survived that heartbreak, and when two more sons fell gravely ill that winter of 1862, it brought both parents to their knees, especially Mary.

The doctors thought it was typhoid fever. No one was entirely sure, but the symptoms were all there: fever and sweats followed by intestinal pain that could bring grown men to tears. It was awful enough to see adults suffer from the disease, but when it attacked nine-year-old Tad and eleven-year-old Willie Lincoln, their small bodies twisting in pain, the Lincolns could focus on little but their boys. Contaminated drinking water was the most likely source of the disease. In the 1860s, the White House water came from the Potomac River, which also served as a general dumping ground for the district as well as passing ships. Abraham and Mary suffered helplessly as they wiped their sons' brows and felt their soft hands clench as pain wracked their small bodies. Doctors tried to break the fever with Peruvian bark, beef tea, and every other remedy they could think of, but nothing seemed to work.

As Willie grew worse, he called for his friend, Bud. It seemed like yesterday that Bud and Holly Taft, the sons of Federal patent examiner Judge Horatio Nelson Taft, and the Lincoln boys had thundered through the White House on one of their adventures. President Lincoln loved telling the story of the day he found the boys pondering the execution of their toy soldier, Jack. Lying in his Zouave uniform of deep reds and blues, the soldier-prisoner was a little dirty. A thoughtful gardener had just interrupted Jack's burial by suggesting that the boys seek a pardon for Jack, whose sin was falling asleep on picket duty. The boys loved the idea, the only honorable solution for such a dishonorable crime. They rushed to see the President, who set aside his work, as he so often did for his children, and listened carefully to the boys' case. Nodding in agreement, Lincoln took out a sheet of White House stationery and wrote a simple, life-saving decree:

> The doll Jack is pardoned.
> By order of the President
> A. Lincoln.

Jack survived about another week before the destructive nature of boys reared its head again, possibly in discussions in their fort atop the White House mansion's roof. It was Julia Taft, Bud's and Holly's teenage sister, who found Jack hanging from a bush in the garden. As Tad Lincoln explained soberly, "Jack was a traitor and a spy," and so was hanged for his crimes.

But death became all too real that February, and in the evenings, it was often Bud Taft whom the President found curled up asleep next to his feverish friend. When Lincoln encouraged Bud to go to bed, the boy explained, "If I go he will call for me." Night after night, Lincoln would let Bud fall asleep and then carry him to a bed in another room.

The exhausted President would then spend the rest of the night with his fading boy. Such a perceptive man as Lincoln must have been struck by the irony that Willie was the liveliest of his sons. Robert was reserved, while Tad's immaturity and tendency to take childish pranks from amusing to annoying caused most adults to avoid him. But Willie possessed his father's inner light. It was Willie who had developed the habit of walking down to the White House stables to read battle reports to the staff and debate the commanders' decisions. Nearly everyone who met the boy marveled at his maturity, his intellect, and the humor he inherited from his father. Night after night, the Lincolns sat with their sons, desperately willing them to live. By some miracle Tad survived, but Willie, the brightest of them all, slipped into a coma and died on February 20.

Mary Lincoln's free African-American seamstress and confidant, Elizabeth Keckley, washed and dressed Willie for his funeral, his mother unable to look at the boy once he was gone. With the duties of parenthood left to the President and Keckley, Lincoln's shoulders slumped under the devastating loss. Wrestling to understand the inexplicable decision of an all-powerful God, Keckley heard Lincoln murmur, "My poor boy, he was too good for this earth. God has called him home. I know that he is much better off in heaven, but then we loved him so. It is hard, hard to have him die!"

Keckley understood Lincoln's pain. She had purchased her freedom and her son's in the 1850s, watched with fear and pride as he joined the Union Army, and then wept when news arrived that he had been killed in battle. A powerfully independent woman, Keckley would sustain her faith in the war and its promise of freedom by founding the "Contraband Relief Association" later in 1862, an organization dedicated to helping poor free blacks and former slaves seize the opportunities that emancipation offered.[57]

But now, as they prepared for Willie's funeral, Keckley could only share President Lincoln's suffering as she watched him, head in hands, as sobs shook his body. After some time, he managed to gather himself and tried to return to his work, but when Lincoln entered his office, he said to his secretary, John Nicolay, "Well, Nicolay, my boy is gone—he is actually gone!" and then Lincoln burst into tears again before he managed to shut the door behind him.

Four days later, heavy, cold rains slashed the White House as a small, private gathering arrived to pay their respects to the family. Mary Lincoln could not bring herself to leave her bed; in fact, she refused to enter the room where Willie died as well as the Green Room where he was embalmed, and she would not look at a single item of Willie's belongings ever again. Even Bud and Holly Taft were banned from her sight; indeed, they were banned from the White House entirely. Mrs. Lincoln's decision confused Willie's young friends, who were grieving over the loss of their dear friend, their expulsion from his home, and the realization that adults could not protect them from everything. Nor was their young friend Tad any help. After his recovery, he took on Mary's mannerisms to the point where he would throw himself on the floor and scream if any of the Taft children attempted to come near him. Heartbroken and lost, they and their mother eventually left for her family home on Long Island, far from the pain that seemed to permeate the White House and all who came near it.

Mary wanted her son remembered, but she would have none of those memories around her, would allow none of it to touch her, and she seemed callously unaware of the additional pain she caused by her behavior. The President could exhaust himself with work, allowing the distraction of the suffering of other mothers' sons to focus him on the task of Union. He could focus on the peace that he hoped would bring an end to the season of death that had taken hold of the nation. But for Mary, narcissistic suffering seemed her only cure, as she stayed in mourning for the next twenty months, forcing everyone around her to adapt themselves to her loss.

"TO PART NO MORE IN THIS WORLD"

One week before Willie died, Felicia Loughridge sat down in her Texas home and wrote another letter to her husband in Virginia. It had all of the usual updates about the farm, but she slipped and revealed her sorrow as she asked if there was any way he could get a furlough and come home for the summer. She would soon learn that summer was a soldier's busiest season, but in these naïve early months Felicia hoped for the impossible, as did their girls. As the evening light faded and she closed her letter, Felicia added notes and hand-drawn kisses, just as J. R. did in his letters, from the girls. Little Ella's messages were simple, but four-year-old Mary added more details. "I love to kiss the kisses that you send to me because your hands have been on them and because I think you have kissed them. I pray for you every night. [C]an you get a furlough and come home to see us this summer I do want see you so bad .... good by my sweet Pa here is a kiss...."

Before folding the letter, Felicia confided to her husband that "sometimes I dream that you are sick and lying in my arms but I nearly always dream of seeing you well and hearty. I do [not] ... want you to think that I believe there is any thing in dreams for I do not," yet clearly it helped her to share them. As she finally forced herself to say goodbye, she wrote, "Good night love. I hope we will meet soon to part no more in this world and to spend a useful happy life together." Amid all of the death and the heartbreak that too many families had already endured, the Loughridges clung closely to one another despite the miles that separated them. Maybe, just maybe, they would be among the fortunate families who would survive the war intact.[58]

Meanwhile in Richmond, Confederates were fascinated by rumors of a ship in their vicinity, the *Virginia*, that was made of iron—or at least covered in it. The doubters noted that the *Virginia* was really just the old USS *Merrimack*, a ship retreating Union forces had scuttled as they abandoned Norfolk at the beginning of the war. Worse, the *Merrimack*'s engines had been condemned before it was sunk and left in the harbor. But the optimists embraced this challenge and noted that this made its resurrection as the CSS *Virginia* all the more impressive. Indeed, some had heard that the local Tredegar Iron Works had designed a secret weapon for the new ship, a beak-like ram that attached just below the waterline to the *Virginia*'s bow that would inflict deadly blows to the North's outdated wooden ships.

Her commander was equally inspiring. Captain Franklin Buchanan had turned his back on an illustrious career in the U.S. Navy when Upper South states began seceding following the crisis at Fort Sumter and President Lincoln's call for volunteers. Buchanan received his appointment as a midshipman in 1815; by the 1840s, he commanded a sloop-of-war against Mexico; and by the 1850s, Buchanan was leading Commodore Matthew C. Perry's flagship on his famous expedition to

Japan. A contemporary described Buchanan as "a typical product of the old-time quarter deck," who was as "indomitably courageous as Nelson and as arbitrary. I don't think the junior officer or sailor ever lived with nerves sufficient to disobey an order given by the old man in person." In the chaotic spring of 1861, the heroic Buchanan assumed his native Maryland would secede, and so, determined to play a role in the coming war, he offered his services to the Confederacy.

But Maryland failed to secede, and suddenly Buchanan—the grandson of a signer of the Declaration of Independence and the father of the U.S. Naval Academy—found himself on the sidelines with no country to serve. In what must have been a monumental moment of humility, Buchanan contacted U.S. Secretary of the Navy Gideon Welles to revoke his resignation. Buchanan explained that he "never was an advocate for secession …. I am as strong a Union man as any in the country … I have had a horror of fighting against the 'stars & stripes.'" But Welles refused to listen. He had, as Welles told his son, "no time for pampered officers who deserted their flag when their loyalties should have upheld it."[59] Welles's official reply summarized that with brutal brevity: "By direction of the president, your name has been stricken from the rolls of the navy." Infuriated and determined to receive a commission, Buchanan looked South, but then he still hesitated, having already made the mistake once of acting in haste. He delayed his commitment to the Confederacy until after their first victory at Manassas, but then he gave himself whole-heartedly to the Southern cause. Once he did, Confederate Secretary of the Navy Stephen Mallory tapped the old salt for command of the CSS *Virginia*.

Buchanan's leadership on March 8 signaled the wisdom of Mallory's decision. Confederate crews had just completed work on the ironclad, and Buchanan decided there was no test quite so effective as the real thing, so he sailed the *Virginia* down the Elizabeth River to engage Federal warships resting in Hampton Roads. Witnesses said the Southern technological marvel looked like the roof of a house, floating downstream with the current. She was not, as they say, yar; on a calm day, the *Virginia* could boast only 15 knots. But what she lacked in grace and speed, the *Virginia* held in sheer power.

On that bright morning, the *Virginia* sank one of the Union Navy's old wooden ships, the *Congress*, with a flurry of broadsides while the Federal sailors could only hurl back solid shot that bounced off the *Virginia*'s iron shell. She rammed the *Cumberland*, leaving a hole so large a man could drive a horse and cart through it, or at least one sailor claimed he could. As the *Cumberland* sank and the *Congress* became engulfed in flames, the three remaining ships, all made of now clearly outdated wood construction, tried to flee, but they ran aground in their haste. What saved them was the *Virginia*'s draft, which was so great she could not get within range to actually hit the stranded Federals. That night, resting near shore as repairs were made, Confederate sailors cheered their victory, though, like most in this war, it was tarnished with a family tragedy.

A few hours earlier, when Buchanan had seen the *Congress*'s white flag of surrender go up, he sent a crew over to the conquered Union ship to discuss terms of their surrender. Moments later his brow furrowed, first in confusion and then in shock as he realized that Federal shore batteries were firing on the Confederate forces crossing to accept the *Congress*'s surrender. When Buchanan sent a second ship under a white flag to clarify the situation, the Federal battery fired on that vessel, too. Adding insult to injury, when Buchanan decided to personally return fire with a musket, a Federal round struck him, inflicting a serious injury that pulled him from the rest of the fight. Before relinquishing command, a furious Buchanan ordered his crew to fire "hot shot" into the *Congress*, which set the Federal vessel ablaze as two red-hot solid iron balls lodged into her wooden stern. Caught in those flames was Buchanan's younger brother, McKean Buchanan, who had remained loyal to the U.S. Navy and served as paymaster aboard the *Congress*. The *Virginia*'s crew spent the night watching the *Congress* burn while their Captain was taken ashore where doctors tended his wound. Buchanan may have worried about his brother and hoped that he had left the ship before flames engulfed it. First in his mind, though, were his duties to the Confederacy. As it had for so many families and the country itself, loyalties to their flags had trumped loyalty to their clan.[60]

"HIS BLOOD CHILLED AT THE TERRIBLE SIGHTS"

Far to the west, or what was then the American West, warming weather indicated the approach of Mars's season as the armies prepared to reengage. The spring grasses and drying roads could sustain the men and animals and allowed them to travel with relative ease. The first key battles of the war had been in the East, but in early 1862, the focus shifted to Kentucky and Tennessee. A different breed of generals operated here, some of whom would prove brilliantly decisive in the war. That spring brought the talents of Ulysses S. Grant, William Tecumseh Sherman, Albert Sidney Johnston, and Henry Halleck (once he found his true calling, that is) to national attention.

President Lincoln had recently assigned Halleck, or "Old Brains" as he was known in the Old Army, to cool the boiling pot of Missouri, which seemed half in the Confederacy and half in the Union. The bulging-eyed, bookish New Yorker had run away from his family farm as a boy. When he arrived at West Point, New York, years later, he so impressed U.S. Military Academy superintendent Dennis Hart Mahan that the taskmaster allowed young Halleck to teach classes while still a cadet. Military service in the Mexican War later proved that Halleck was a capable field commander, and his lectures and writings showed his genius for military thought. But it was in the 1850s in California that Halleck's true talents as an administrator surfaced. By 1861, he was a Democrat with strong Southern sympathies, but the New Yorker remained true to his Union roots and those of his wife, Elizabeth, who was the granddaughter of America's ultimate Union man, Alexander Hamilton.[61]

Ulysses Simpson "Sam" Grant was Halleck's opposite in almost every sense. Grant had impressed no one with his intelligence during his years at West Point, though he did reveal a talent for horsemanship and an unparalleled perseverance that allowed the underprepared student to graduate twenty-first of thirty-nine cadets in the Class of 1843. He performed well as a junior officer in Mexico, but where Halleck thrived in the 1850s, Grant seemed to collapse. Homesick for his bride and children, bored to death on isolated Army posts, and accused of finding a dangerous level of comfort in the bottle, Grant resigned his commission and rejoined his young family in Galena, Illinois. He was the kind of man who always did better with his wife, Julia Dent, at his side. Their love and relationship is legendary, as is Grant's devotion to his children, but in those years before the war, it seemed as if the Fates had given Grant so much in terms of family that no fortune remained for the rest of his life. He failed at one venture after another, and he failed with conviction.

When the war began, his townspeople looked to their veteran friend to finally find his calling and command a company of local men, but Grant refused to join them. He trained the men, but he was reluctant to embrace the rush for war, just as he had originally opposed the Mexican War in 1846. But, once again, Grant resigned himself to the reality of the conflict and slowly rose from colonel of the 21st Illinois to command of the District of Southeast Missouri by the spring of 1862. The same quiet perseverance that had helped him survive the rigors of West Point proved equally useful in command. It remained to be seen, however, how much leadership and responsibility the quiet officer with the shaky past could handle.

William Tecumseh Sherman had grown up with better connections than Grant, but 1862 found him facing an equally questionable future. The loss of his father in Sherman's Ohio youth led to his upbringing in the prominent Ewing family, in which he received a strong education and excellent social opportunities but no emotional security. His army years in the 1840s, during which he participated in the oft-overlooked wars against the Seminole, exposed him to hard fighting and revealed his talents as a commander. The mid-1840s found the gruff redhead moving from one Southern post to another, and it was here that Sherman developed a deep but troubled love for the South and its people. That passion was followed by a rocky relationship when Sherman married his foster sister, Ellen, in 1850. They spent the rest of their lives squabbling over Sherman's refusal to fully embrace Ellen's Catholic faith and her desire to never leave the family's Ohio roots. Sherman's next decade mirrored much of Grant's experiences. While Sherman had the connections that allowed for more impressive ventures during his years with the Old Army, and later as a bank manager in San Francisco, he was plagued by a geographically and emotionally distant wife, as well as by insecurities that had haunted him since his youth.

By 1861, Sherman's family life and finances were as shattered as the nation, though his work as commandant of a Louisiana military school brought him some satisfaction. In the end, despite his love of the South, he could not bring himself to leave the Union when Louisiana seceded. Like Grant, Sherman eventually—and hesitantly—returned to army life. He fought well at First Manassas as a brigade commander, but failed miserably when he was thrust into command of the Department of the Cumberland later that year. Panicked under the weight of his responsibilities, Sherman was soon replaced when Lincoln moved him to the staff of "Old Brains" Halleck. Sherman's fears continued, though, as did his debilitating waves of depression, and Halleck sent Sherman home on extended leave to rest and recuperate. The time in Ohio seemed to only heighten his insecurities, and when Sherman finally snapped at inquisitive reporters asking about the Union Army's failures, rumors flew that he teetered on the brink of insanity.

Peace returned when Sherman reported to a low-pressure, low-profile assignment in Benton Barracks, Missouri. The pace allowed Sherman's troubled soul the time, purpose, and distance from the Ewings that he needed to recover. It also brought him into contact with a similarly troubled soul who found the same peace and sense of purpose in war: Ulysses S. Grant.[62]

Opposing Halleck, Sherman, and Grant in the West was a man whom contemporaries presented as the South personified. Albert Sidney Johnston actually had New England roots, but he was raised in Kentucky and later claimed Texas as his true home. Like his opponents in the West, Johnston was trained and educated at West Point, where he showed a flair for mathematics and army life. It was also during those days on the Hudson that Johnston demonstrated a lifelong habit of favorably impressing almost everyone he met. He was the kind of cadet that other cadets admired, and he became the kind of commander men sought to serve with. Southerners admired his leadership during the Black Hawk War as well as his decision to resign his commission to return home in 1834 to care for his invalid wife. Following her death, Johnston served in the

Texas Army during Texas's war for independence, and he rejoined the U.S. Army a decade later to participate in America's war with Mexico. By the time another ten years had passed, Northerners had also come to embrace Johnston as one of the finest commanders the nation had ever produced. The editors of the national *Harper's Weekly* offered a lengthy description of Johnston as perfect in habit, mind, manner, acquaintances, and bearing, but it was his commanding officer, General Winfield Scott, who captured Johnston best: "Colonel Johnston is more than a good officer—he is a God send to the country thro' the army ...."[63]

Like Grant and Sherman, Johnston entered yet another war with hesitation. He had a strong loyalty to the Union, but his identity with the Lone Star State trumped that, and by the fall of 1861, Johnston was in Richmond meeting with his close friend, Confederate President Jefferson Davis. Davis entrusted Johnston with the management of a massive territory that ranged from the western Appalachians to Indian Territory. From his headquarters in Bowling Green, Kentucky, Johnston set about planning to defend Confederate borders that were almost indefensible. The flow of the eastern rivers acted as natural barriers to Federal offensives, but in the West they seemed to welcome Union forces as prepared highways of invasion. Still, this was Johnston, hero of the Texas Revolution, the Mexican War, and countless frontier engagements. Davis and the Confederacy had faith in the talents that made Johnston perfectly suited for his challenging task.

The Union and Confederate commanders of the Western Theater may have been experienced officers in the spring of 1862, but the vast majority of the soldiers serving under them had little experience with battle, and those who did had seen only minor skirmishes. Among them was Willie Shepherd, the nineteen-year-old Chicago bookkeeper whose devotion to the cause of Union kept him in the ranks despite his homesickness. As a member of the First Illinois Light Artillery, Shepherd was not entirely green in 1862. He had one small fight at Fredericktown under his belt, which had been quickly followed by the Battle of Belmont, both in Missouri in the fall of 1861. They did not give him extensive experience, but it was enough to make an impression and quickly harden the men in the ranks. A letter Shepherd wrote following Fredericktown was filled with scattered details as the young, thoughtful clerk tried to process what he had just experienced. Memories of the chaos included flashing scenes of a colonel leading his men while eating an apple, while another insisted on calming his skittish troops by drilling them in the manual of arms until they settled enough to successfully push forward.

Shepherd marveled at the brutality that destroyed one life while another was preserved only through trickery. "One poor fellow," he told to his mother, "was shot while crossing a rail fence and dropped *there* remaining on the fence all night. Another lay on the ground shaking his leg and groaning sadly—but on being questioned as to his wound said he was unhurt—but uses that means of saving his life—rather than take the chances of retreating up the hill. One lay in the grass and waved a white flag—asking for quarter and entreating our men to save his life—thinking us a band of blood thirsty men—fighting only for the sake of shedding human blood."[64]

When Shepherd returned to the battlefield the next morning, his "blood chilled at the *terrible* sights." Some of the men lay "with hands folded across the breast" so that they "seemed to be—but sleeping—yet cold and rigid in the embrace of the Great destroyer." But others left signs of "fearful struggles as their lifes blood bathed the sod in a scarlet hue—One man had received a shot in the head causing the brain to run out on the grass; *yet breathing*—Oh—I shudder at the *thoughts* occasioned; much more the *sight* of such a living death—Another had been eaten by the hogs—till the face was but a mass of bones—Never did I think of—or realize the horrors of a battlefield till that morning— and I hope for *no more* to convince me of the *truth*."

Despite his initial shock, Shepherd adjusted to the horrors of war quite quickly. He pondered the destruction of civilian homes, observing how Union soldiers retaliated against locals who failed to inform the Yankees that they were walking into a trap at Fredericktown. Sympathizing with the soldiers, Shepherd explained to his family at home that the men "were so incensed against the people; to think they should allow us to be taken in such an ambuscade … that they were almost wild—about a dozen of the most prominent secession homes were burned—during the night."[65] By the end of October, Shepherd showed signs of the hardening that would help him survive the relentlessness of war. His focus shifted from death to small matters like a "*secesh* rifle" he sent home, the happy news of heavy, warm pants just distributed to the men, and winter coats on the way.

The first week of November brought more fighting at a large battle at Belmont, Missouri, but Willie emerged unscathed again despite the intense fighting. "The musket shots were just right at one time and we had given up all hopes of ever getting away of alive—for the bullets whizzed by the hundred every half minute …. I have been examining my clothes to find a bullet hole but cannot—I *know* several balls passed my head within twelve inches …." That fight was their largest to date, and Willie claimed "Old Mexican soldiers say they never saw such a fearful struggle."[66]

As Shepherd and his fellow Union soldiers marched through Tennessee three months later, thoughts of their first two great battles rushed through their minds. During the previous fall in Missouri, Ulysses S. Grant had discovered that the enemy "had as much reason to fear my forces as I had his," and the men serving with Willie Shepherd had made as similar discovery. He never stopped hoping the war, which he declared a "*fearful reality*," would end, but Shepherd remained steadfast in his faith in the Union and his obligation to serve.[67]

The beauty of the South overwhelmed Shepherd as they continued into Tennessee. "Trees are budding—through all the forests and *some* that *bear flowers* are an airy cloud of pink and white which truly look beautiful. While nestled in the carpet of fresh grass we find all the wild flowers so common to our own woods in 'America.'" But just after he finished that thought, reports swept through camp that a "considerable force" of Confederates was just 3 miles from them. "I cannot think that the rebels will attack us," Shepherd wrote to his sister on April 5, "yet they *may*."[68]

That same day, Henry Morton Stanley, a private in the 6th Arkansas Infantry, camped with his fellow soldiers in line of battle just a few miles from Willie Shepherd. Stanley and his compatriots were tired, cold, and hungry. When they left Corinth, Mississippi, on April 2, they had received three days' rations and planned to attack Union forces on April 4. But weather, as always, had failed to cooperate, and the inexperienced soldiers had enjoyed their rations on the first day's march while they unburdened themselves of the heavy knapsacks, blankets, and other gear that weighed them down. Now, hunching their shoulders against the rain, they were learning a hard lesson in soldiering. Sitting near Stanley, Private Rufus Daniel summarized the situation: "we got all wet."[69]

Stanley was hardly the bold adventurer that the world would later recognize for his famous greeting—"Dr. Livingston, I presume"—delivered when he tracked down the famous British explorer in Zanzibar. Indeed, Stanley had resisted the early rush to arms that remains the stereotypical image of Southern men in 1861. It wasn't until Stanley received an anonymous gift of a woman's petticoat, a symbol of cowardice that was commonly used to inspire men to Civil War service, that he joined the "Dixie Greys," whose ranks were dominated by planters' sons.

His place in that company belied Stanley's early roots, captured in the title recorded at his christening: "John Rowlands, bastard." After bouncing from one distant relative to another, his extended family committed Stanley to a workhouse when he was six. By the age of fifteen, he had had enough and ran away. He resurfaced three years later when the *Windmere* docked in New Orleans, and Stanley jumped ship without a penny to his name. He worked as a grocer's clerk until a planter named Henry Hope Stanley befriended the young man and became the father John Rowlands never had. By 1860, Henry Morton Stanley, as he now identified himself, was living on Henry Hope Stanley's plantation in Cypress Bend, Arkansas. It was nearly two years later that the young Stanley, an orphan of his birth family and his nation, sat in the mud awaiting his first test of battle to defend the family and the nation he had made his own.

Years later, Stanley admitted that at dawn on Sunday, April 6, "many wished, like myself, that we had not been required to undergo this discomfort before" being hurled into battle. Sitting next to him, seventeen-year-old Henry Park picked some violets from the ground, hoping that "the Yanks won't shoot me if they see me wearing such flowers, for they are a sign of peace." Stanley liked the idea and did the same, despite the mocking laughter that rumbled around them. A short time later, the Dixie Greys moved forward in line and entered the battle of Shiloh, or Pittsburg Landing as many Confederates would remember it. Stanley recalled an "explosive burst of musketry [and] the air ... pierced by many missiles, which hummed and pinged sharply in our ears, pattered through the tree-tops, and brought twigs and leaves down on us." Next to him, the violet-picking Henry Park whispered with surprise, "Those are bullets."

The fighting began in the predawn hours of April 6 when several companies from Colonel Everett Peabody's 25th Missouri discovered Confederates camped just a few miles from the Union position at Pittsburg Landing. Shortly thereafter, the Missourians, along with some Michiganders, spent the next several hours making their way down a country road trying to ascertain the rebel strength. The men stumbled along in wagon ruts just barely visible in the half-moonlight. As they continued through the thick southern air, they came to prefer the ruts to the sinking Tennessee mud that lined the roads.

Near dawn they finally made brief and surprising contact with Alabama cavalrymen, along with some Mississippi infantry. The early exchanges had brief moments of intense fire but remained fairly sporadic as the green troops adjusted from the lessons of drill to actual combat. A young Confederate, Private Thomas Duncan, watched, horrified, as a bullet tore through one of the Mississippians' throats, and then gasped as a flying piece of wood, likely loosed by the infantry volley, cut into his left eye while a bullet slammed into his thigh, bending the saber blade that saved his leg.

Albert Sidney Johnston and his staff were eating breakfast when they heard the fighting around Duncan. With the sun just barely visible in the sky, Johnston met briefly with his immediate subordinate, Pierre Gustave Toutant Beauregard, to review their battle plan. Then Johnston mounted his horse, Fire-Eater, and moved toward the sound of the guns. By the time the sun was disappearing, thousands of American boys lay dead and thousands more were hobbling off the field. The Confederates had rushed forward in a series of long lines, one wave after another crashing into the Federal positions on that beautiful spring day.

For years, Grant and Sherman would insist that, contrary to popular opinion, they were not surprised by the Rebel attack, only by exactly when it had come. Other commanders crafted themselves into heroes, especially Union General Benjamin Prentiss, while civilians spread the legend of a cherubic drummer boy name Johnny Clem who symbolized the nation's own youth shattered on the field at Shiloh. Veterans would speak of soldiers' wounds clouding a watering hole on the battlefield that they renamed Bloody Pond, as though by giving it a grand title they could find meaning in all of that death.

Ironically, all of these were wrong. There was no Johnny Clem, nor was there a bloody pond in 1862, and it was Union Colonel Everett Peabody who was the hero of the day. Northerners would celebrate Prentiss as the man who held Confederate attacks back until Grant could organize his shocked forces into defensive positions. In fact, Prentiss was only following Grant's orders to avoid engagement with the rebels, which Grant hoped to postpone until all Federal forces in the area had gathered and then they would move on to take Corinth, Mississippi. But while Prentiss followed orders to the letter, Peabody, like many of the Federals, had heard enough movement around their position to know that rebel forces were in the area. He had the foresight to organize a group of Missourians and Michiganders to reconnoiter ahead of their position on the morning of April 6. Granted, Peabody violated orders and caused an engagement when he did this, and Prentiss held him responsible for it. But in the end, it was Peabody's decision to probe the Confederates, and the small engagement that ensued, that forewarned the Union's Army of the Tennessee. Unfortunately, no one would remember it that way for well over a century because Peabody's premonition that he would not survive the battle proved accurate, and he and a number of his other supporters were not alive to refute Prentiss's claims. Union Brigadier General W. H. L. Wallace, who actually organized much of the meaningful defense of the area that horrified troops would name "The Hornet's Nest," didn't survive the fight either. With their deaths, and the North's need for a hero, Prentiss claimed that it was he who rallied the surprised Yankees and held the Union line on that bloody April day.

For the men in the ranks, though, the claims of heroics were pointless; it was chaos alone that had filled their hours at Shiloh. During the fighting, young officers had tried to lead their troops and maintain some sense of order, but within hours there was so much smoke and noise that it was difficult to separate friend from foe. Years later the dark, powerful American writer Ambrose Bierce, who served in the 9th Indiana Infantry Regiment, recalled the confusion. "A few inaudible commands from an invisible leader had placed us in order of battle. But where was the enemy?" Bierce asked. "What protected our right? Who lay upon our left? Was there really anything in front?"[70]

Young Willie Shepherd remembered similar confusion in his Illinois artillery battery. On April 8, he wrote to his parents to tell them he was alive, but he struggled to find words to explain what he had experienced. This was not his first battle, but its magnitude seemed to overwhelm the Wisconsin boy, just as it did the nation. "Sunday was a terrible day," he told his family. "The enemy drove us to the river bank, when night put an end to the fighting. On Monday ... we turned the enemy and now hold our former position," he explained, adding, "We are confident of victory." But then his fears overwhelmed his confidence and he blurted out, "I cannot describe the *terrible* slaughter that has been made on both sides." Two days later, Shepherd tried to explain more in a letter to his father, but again Shepherd admitted "I cannot describe the *fury* of the engagement during the two days—and very much doubt the ability of *anyone* to do so. To say that *it was terrible* would be a very tame description of the bloody conflict."

Haunted by the recurring visions of the battle—he referred to "seeing" or "sight" three times in four sentences—Shepherd insisted, "the only true idea of this horrible fight could be gained by a sight of the field on which we fought for two days. Dead and wounded soldiers by the hundreds, Federals and rebel, side by side .... The horrible sights we were obliged to behold on every side were enough to chill the blood of the most vile murderer. Fredericktown, Belmont, and Donelson—cannot be compared with it. God grant that we may never be called to see the *lightest* of it again."[71]

The horrors of Shiloh touched families rich and poor, powerful and inconsequential. One of the most notable victims that April was Mary Todd Lincoln's brother, Sam. Three of her brothers and two brothers-in-law were in the ranks that day, but Sam's saga captured the confusion that so many families endured in the days following the battle. The Todds and the Lincolns knew that Sam was a private in Company H of the Crescent Regiment from New Orleans. But in the days following Shiloh, as the siblings all surfaced, Sam remained missing.

Sister Elodie in Selma, Alabama, had been receiving fairly regular letters from Sam, and his silence after the battle had her worried. Capturing the frustrations of mothers, sisters, and wives across the country, Elodie fumed that "Really these battles and rumored battles keep me miserable all the time .... It [is] utterly impossible to keep posted as to the whereabouts of my Brothers. When I think of [those] I perhaps may never see again ... I feel as tho' I could bear no more." And then her brother, David, confirmed their worst fears. Having found the doctor who witnessed Sam's death, David was so stunned and devastated that he could barely bring himself to share the news with the family. "The report has been here for several days," he wrote, "but I could not believe it as no one has seen him either dead or even wounded .... I cannot describe the grief of his widow ...."

Slowly, the Todds pieced together Sam's experiences at Shiloh. The Crescents had arrived on the field around 8:00 a.m. near Owl Creek. As they marched up Purdy Road, Sam was horrified when he witnessed his first death as a shell tore through the ranks and took off most of their drummer's head. Still, the officers managed to reorder the ranks and the men continued forward. About noon they came across the abandoned camp of the 6th Iowa, and the boys broke ranks to root through the Yankee tents for food. They hadn't eaten in three days. Having marched from Corinth on five crackers apiece, they named the spot where they collapsed for a brief rest one night "Camp Starvation."

If Sam had briefly recovered from the loss of the drummer boy, the grim reality of war surfaced again as some of the men entered a tent and discovered a decapitated Union soldier, his head resting on his hands just below the gaping hole where his chest had been. The scene stunned them into some semblance of order, but they continued to wander around the camp as no one seemed to know what to do with the Crescents for nearly two hours. Then, in the timeless hurry-up-and-wait-fashion of all armies, they were rushed into the fight at about 2:00 p.m.

A general had told them to "Go on, my brave boys. Charge them and the victory is ours …. Shoot low, shoot low," but Sam's colonel was not entirely sure where the enemy was, which made any charge difficult. The Crescents were as confused as Ambrose Bierce's 9th Indiana had been. A soldier with Sam remembered, as they rushed toward the Hornet's Nest, that "the field was literally strewn with dead and dying …" while another recalled "balls and bomb shells whizzed over our heads and burst in the air or carried away tops of trees."

Somehow, Sam survived all of this and greeted dawn on April 7 with terrible memories of the previous day and the embarrassed exhilaration of survival. But the Crescents were not as fortunate on the battle's second day, and as Federal forces pushed back from the river to reclaim the ground they lost on April 6, Sam was lost in the rush. When a friend spotted him again, Sam appeared at the top of a hill, stumbling forward. The spot where the ball had entered his back was relatively small, but its exit had ripped a hole in the thirty-two-year-old Todd, who struggled to remain on his feet as his intestines spilled out of his body. Some of the Crescents rushed to his side and carried Sam to an ambulance, but it was already full. There was a spot on the next ambulance, but in the end it held no relief. Sam died in that crowded, filthy wagon, surrounded by strangers. With odd efficiency after days of chaos, the doctor who found Sam's body gathered his personal effects for his family, and a group of strangers buried President Lincoln's brother-in-law in a ditch on the side of a road. Sam Todd had been in the Confederate Army for four short weeks.

Sam's death captured the fratricidal nature of the war. In Georgia, the *Macon Daily Telegraph* insisted that he "died in defense of his country against the hireling invaders whom the husband of his sister, Mrs. Abraham Lincoln, sent to desolate our country and dishonor our people." In New Orleans, the editors of *The Delta* agreed, arguing that Mary Lincoln's brother had "fallen by the hands of her husband's mercenaries."

It seemed that no one was to be left untouched by the battle. It was the largest in American history to that point, with more casualties than all of America's previous wars combined. For the South, the excitement following Confederate reports of victory on April 6 was crushed as subsequent telegraph messages relayed one problem after another. They lost one of their most experienced commanders, Albert Sidney Johnston, who was the key to so many Southern hopes for victory. Then reports flooded in that their army in the West was falling back. They had sacrificed Nashville, Bowling Green, and all of Tennessee, and now their rebel sons retreated back to Corinth. By the end of April, New Orleans fell, and the western Confederacy shuddered as Union forces pushed in from all sides.[72]

"MAD ENOUGH TO EAT A YANKEE RAW"

As exhausted Confederates retreated toward Corinth, their compatriots in Virginia tramped up the James River Peninsula. A month earlier, they had abandoned their positions along the Potomac River and begun to consolidate their strength around Dumfries. The move forced Union General George Brinton McClellan to revise his plans for a spring attack, and his daring new idea involved a complex amphibious landing at the tip of land between the James and York rivers. It left the Union capital thinly defended, but McClellan—nicknamed "The Young Napoleon" for some of his early victories against a still little-known Confederate commander, Robert E. Lee, in western Virginia—was certain of victory. His men shared his confidence, having grown to love the man who rebuilt their tattered confidence that winter following the disaster at Bull Run.

But when they landed at Yorktown, the Confederate commander, General John B. Magruder, had far more men than McClellan's intelligence sources had reported. Or at least he seemed to. The Rebels had the old Revolutionary War town protected by tens of thousands of troops well supported by artillery. McClellan halted his advance, despite his army of 70,000 men with an additional 30,000 Union soldiers about to arrive, to reassess the situation.

In fact, Magruder had only 17,000 men. A great patron of the arts, the theatrical "Prince John" paraded his men in loops while commanders shifted guns from one location to the next. It was an exhausting performance, but the results were brilliant. McClellan sat for four weeks, pondering how best to approach the seemingly overwhelming forces between him and Richmond.

With those men was a brigade of Texans, South Carolinians, and Georgians. Their commander, who led a single regiment until March, was John Bell Hood, already recognized in the army for his bravery and passion, tempered with a willingness for self-sacrifice that endeared him to his men. The core regiments of this motely crew, known as Hood's Texas Brigade, were the 1st, 4th, and 5th Texas infantry regiments, recruited predominantly from the East Texas counties that were populated with families who had immigrated from the Old South. Indeed, most of these men were born in Virginia, Tennessee, Alabama, and North Carolina and had visited their extended families along their journey to the "seat of war" in Richmond. In an army known for stereotypes of chivalry and Old-South charm, the Texans were more famous for their wild, western habits as Indian fighters whose skin had become as bronze as their enemies' during their years of extended combat. The Texans enjoyed their reputation as wild, ill-disciplined fighters, and their commanders reflected the unit's love for bold individuality—a troubling trait in an army. But somehow it worked for the Texans, making them march farther and fight harder than many other units.

Their favorite officers embodied the brigade's eccentric independence. John C. Upton, commander of the 5th Texas, refused to wear a traditional uniform, preferring to march into battle in "an old pair of pants, a dilapidated pair of cavalry boots, and old cotton shirt, a slouch black hat [and] a huge saber, with a pair of six shooters—looking less like an officer than any of his men."[73] And then there was Captain William "Howdy" Martin, commander of Company K of the 4th Texas. Known for his dislike of the traditional military salute, he had replaced it with a Texas "howdy" for each man he came across, a trait that belied his inner fire. One of the kindest souls in camp, Martin was also known for rowdy "sermons" when he would leap atop a stump or, on one occasion as the men were leaving Texas, "on an old goods box under a hickory tree ... long, angular, with a voice like thunder ... he would shake his long hair [as he spoke] and look like he was mad enough to eat a Yankee raw." The men loved his fire and his empathy for their adjustment to a long year away from home and their loved ones. Like Hood and Upton, Martin exemplified the Texans, who wondered, as they broke camp that spring, if they would live up to their tenacious reputation.

In camp with the Texans at Yorktown that April was a twenty-year-old private named Valerius Cincinnatus Giles, better known as "Val" to his friends in the "Tom Green Rifles," Company B of the 4th Texas Infantry. Giles had frozen for much of that winter with his fellow Texans as part of an ironic Confederate effort to blockade the Union, at least along the Potomac River. Despite those hardships, he was sorry to leave their winter quarters when the retreat was ordered in early March. The men had constructed cabins that reflected their independent spirit. Some of the messes, as the cabins and the mates in them were known, had wooden walls. Others benefited from brick construction, much to the frustration of a local farmer who lodged formal complaints about the disappearance of his chimney. A few had glazed windows, and one sparkled with the domestic charm of green blinds. And then there was the one that was too small to hold all of the men assigned to it. The soldiers in that mess took a vote and relegated the two failed architects who had mismeasured to spending the remainder of the winter in a chilly tent outside.

When spring came, Giles and the Texans accepted the need to leave their winter home to protect Richmond, but they hated the lack of wagons that required them to abandon supplies that would benefit the Union forces sure to find the camp. In carefully laid-out plots, they buried shovels, tents, clothing, cook pots, and utensils. When men from the 1st Massachusetts Infantry discovered the plots a few weeks later, they were respectful of the Confederate graveyard. Units on both sides had suffered terrible losses that winter from disease as men from wide-ranging counties and states exposed each other to a variety of new diseases, too often failing to maintain the basic sanitary conditions in camp that might keep them from becoming ill. Indeed, the Massachusetts men had discovered a coffin warehouse in the Texans' camp, where twelve coffins were awaiting their guests, while an order for another twenty-four for a single regiment waited to be filled.

But then they noticed that the warning signs that dotted the graveyard seemed odd, predicting devastation to those who dared disturb the silent slumber of these "men." And it was all so neatly arranged—so very different from the worn and poorly organized cabins that dominated the rest of the camp—that the Yankee soldiers became suspicious. Daring the spirits, they began to dig and found the supplies that the Confederates had so carefully hidden.[74]

By that time, though, the Texans were well on their way South. And by early April, they were defending Yorktown from an astonishingly unaggressive McClellan. As Joseph E. Johnston, the Confederate commander of the Army of Northern Virginia (the Southern forces in that area) knew, he could not hold off the Federals if they chose to advance, but they refused to do so. As Johnston observed, "no one but McClellan could have hesitated to attack."[75]

While McClellan's and Johnston's forces waited in their standoff, the men became used to each side taking shots at the other as opportunity afforded. But by the first week of May, Johnston suspected the Federals were about to make their move and ordered the Confederates to withdraw northward toward Richmond. The Texas Brigade had the dubious honor of serving as rear guard for the entire Army of Northern Virginia. They marched at the end of a line of tens of thousands of men in the spring rains, which meant that the Texans were slogging through gooey mud that clung to their legs and tested their balance. As Giles complained, "Virginia is covered with beautiful glades, lovely valleys, rolling plains and open woodland, but both armies would sneak off to a swamp or big thicket to fight their battles! Eltham's Landing … was fought in a hole. Gaines' Mill, a little later, was some better, yet we had to wade a lagoon waist-deep before we reached the battlefield. Manassas was a pretty decent sort of place for that type of business, and I suppose that was the reason they fought two battles there."

By the end of June, the Texas Brigade, along with the rest of the Army of Northern Virginia, had fought in several engagements, and now they marched under a new commander of the Army of Northern Virginia. At the time, his soldiers weren't so sure about General Robert E. Lee.

He certainly had an impressive family name. He was the son of "Lighthorse" Harry Lee, one of George Washington's cavalry commanders. A hero of the Mexican War, he had gone on to be a respected superintendent of his alma mater, the United States Military Academy. But when the Civil War began, he lost the Battle of Cheat Mountain, Virginia, in 1861 and spent the next year as President Jefferson Davis's military advisor, overseeing the construction of defenses around Richmond.

When Joseph E. Johnston was severely wounded at the Battle of Seven Pines on June 1, 1862, Davis appointed Lee as Johnston's successor. Initial reactions were lukewarm. As one North Carolina woman summarized, "I do not much like him, he 'falls back' too much … His nick name last summer was 'old-stick-in-the-mud' … There is mud enough now in and about our lives, but pray God he may not fulfill the whole of his name." The soldiers called him "the king of spades" and "Granny Lee," but they wouldn't be laughing long. Lee believed the key to Confederate victory was in launching aggressive attacks and then maintaining that momentum. Only then could Confederates hope to counteract the Union's numerical advantages in manpower and supplies.

By the end of June, Lee was putting his plans into motion. His army stumbled at the Battle of Mechanicsville on June 25, when the aggressive Thomas J. "Stonewall" Jackson, now famous for his daring operations in the Shenandoah Valley, was uncharacteristically slow and failed to coordinate his attacks with Confederate General A. P. Hill. But Lee tried again two days later at Gaines's Mill.

The situation was perfect. For the first time, and quite possibly the last, Confederate forces outnumbered their aggressor. The Union Army was straddled across the Chickahominy River, leaving one third of its men on the north side with their backs to the water. Lee focused on this portion, which was Union General Fitz John Porter's V Corps, and placed the Confederates in the rare situation of outnumbering their opponent: 60,000 to 65,000 Confederates faced 34,000 Union men. Months later, the Committee on the Conduct of the War would investigate McClellan's motives in allowing his men to be caught in a situation too much like Ball's Bluff, where they were pinned against the Potomac, but the truth of the matter was that McClellan was preparing to retreat southward to the James River. Porter's positioning protected the rest of the Army of the Potomac until they could move. Lee may not have realized that McClellan was already abandoning the Confederate capital, nor did Lee realize just how sizable his numerical advantage was. But he seemed to sense that the Federals were in the perfect position of vulnerability and that the time to strike was upon them.

Still, if war proves anything, it's that nothing is assured. With his men ready and in position—a six-division attack, one of the single largest assaults he would ever lead—Lee ordered the attack forward on the morning of June 27. But his trusted Jackson stumbled again. Then the attacks that did begin as scheduled ran into the challenging terrain that covered the western and central portions of the battlefield. Finally, Lee's picture of the battle in his head was about 90 degrees off from the way the forces were actually laid out, forcing him to shift his lines when he finally realized the situation, which cost additional valuable time. All of this offset the Confederates' numerical advantage with uncoordinated attacks that struck up and down the Union line. By late afternoon, nearly 100,000 men were engaged in some of the most intense fighting of the war, but nothing had yet been decided.

It was here that Lee's brilliance first became apparent. It wasn't that his plans were always the best; nor were his commanders. But he could often sense where to place units and which officers to leave to their own initiative, and this ability proved key to his victories. Val Giles and the rest of the Texas Brigade proved key that day, too, as they led the dusk assault that finally broke Porter's V Corps' line. It was only one of seven devastating days of fighting, but Gaines's Mill convinced "The Young Napoleon" to abandon his drive for Richmond. The months of retreating, fighting, and digging in had saved Richmond and made veterans of some of the units that would sustain Lee and the Army of Northern Virginia for three more bloody years.

"AS ALL GOOD PATRIOTS SHOULD ACT"

Thirty-six-year-old Andrew Erskine was on the field at Gaines's Mill with the Texans that hot June day. The Virginia-born surveyor was the fifth of ten children and had moved to Texas with his family as a boy. At the age of fourteen, he helped defend their home from a Comanche raid, and three years later he joined the Texas Rangers to do more fighting. By the age of twenty-one, in 1847, he decided it was time to settle down. He married Ann Johnson and worked on his father's cattle ranch for a while, and then he moved his family to Mill Point on the Guadalupe River near Seguin, Texas. There he purchased a gristmill, ran a ferry owned by his father-in-law, and over the years he and Ann added a sawmill, cotton gin, and purchased and operated an inn with its own stage stand. They had six surviving sons, and never quite got over losing their seventh, Powell, when he accidentally drowned in the Guadalupe River.

When the war began, Andrew contacted a local politician about organizing a company, but it went no further than that. Perhaps Andrew decided not to go because he had such a large family depending on him, or perhaps, in his mid-thirties and a veteran of the Texas border wars from his Ranger days, Andrew felt he had done enough for his community. Whatever the case, Andrew was not among those who rushed off to war in the spring of 1861.

But the following spring of 1862, as Mary and Ella Loughridge wrote notes and drew kisses for their father and Mary Todd Lincoln and Elizabeth Keckley mourned their lost boys, Andrew Erskine felt the call to serve. His brother-in-law, Thomas Ignacious Johnson, who was already in the Texas Brigade, came home to Seguin on recruiting duty, and when he left town on April 20, Andrew, his brother, Alexander M. Erskine, and two of their nephews had joined "Ig" Johnson in Company D of the 4th Texas Infantry Regiment.

Andrew Erskine lacked the youthful enthusiasm that Tally Simpson and Willie Shepherd felt when they left home for war. Unlike many of the young men in the ranks, Andrew Erskine had been in battle, though on a far smaller scale than anything he was about to encounter. Still, he sensed the challenges that awaited all of them. It was an overwhelming sense of duty that drove Andrew Erskine into the Confederate Army that spring. As he and the new recruits traveled toward Virginia, he tried to explain this to Ann:

> You must feel quite lonely and low spirited, my dear wife ... but you must bear it bravely as I know you can. You know I left you and my sweet darling boys and my comfortable home because I deemed it my duty, and because I thought that the public expected me to go. I was too proud to remain at home when everybody in the country able to bear arms had left to go in defense of the bleeding and suffering country. I believe that God will spare me to return home to you, my dear wife, and my dear boys.

But Andrew Erskine had seen enough suffering in this life to know that there was a chance he would not return. "Let me ask you as a favor to me," he continued,

> to be cheerful and not brood over the possibilities of my being killed in battle, but always think that I am soon to return to you and that we are to spend many happy days together yet. Don't stay at home by yourself, but spend a good part of your time with your mother.... Always think I am acting as all good patriots should act and that although it may seem to you hard that I should leave you and my little boys alone, remember that no one could say hereafter to my children, 'Your father did not aid in gaining the independence of the Southern Confederacy.'

As he closed yet another long letter, Andrew was comforted by the thought "that I am now folding you in my arms. Would to God that it were so."[76]

The Erskine brothers, Ig Johnson, and their nephews caught up with the Texas Brigade in Virginia at the end of May 1862, and shared the terror and rush of their first great battle at Gaines's Mill. The day after the fight, Andrew tried to describe the battleground to his wife, but a week later he had to try again as he himself struggled to comprehend the site. "I never had a clear conception," he explained, "of the horrors of war until that night and the morning. On going round on the battlefield with a candle searching for my friends" the night of June 27, "I could hear on all sides the dreadful groans of the wounded and their heart-piercing cries for water and assistance. Friends and foes all together." On the following morning, Erskine was equally horrified. He awoke "on the field and [saw] the mutilated condition of men and horses. Oh! The awful scene …. May I never see any more such in life." Still, it was important to him that his sons understand what war was, and what their father and their neighbors were sacrificing for their nation. "Tell them about the big battle," he instructed his wife.[77]

One of those injured on that awful field was J. R. Loughridge. He was leading Company I of the 4th Texas, not far from Erskine in Company D, when he fell. Badly wounded in the arm, Loughridge first made his way to a field hospital, and then, in mid-July, he received orders transferring him again—only this time, he was going home. It was not permanent; it was simply a furlough to recover and then return to the front. But by some dangerous miracle, Felicia and their daughters' prayers had been answered. J. R. Loughridge got his furlough for the summer.[78]

"I WOULD SAVE THE UNION"

While soldiers engaged in the unavoidable reality of war that spring and summer of 1862, Abraham Lincoln was busy wielding a different weapon in his effort to aid them. That April, he signed into effect the District of Columbia Emancipation Act. Using his power as President, Lincoln struck a strong, but limited, legislative blow at the "peculiar institution." And, as with so much that he did, no one was happy.

The President walked a tightrope when it came to the issue of slavery. The institution appalled him. Eventually, he would explain his position clearly: "I am naturally anti-slavery. If slavery is not wrong, nothing is wrong. I can not remember when I did not so think, and feel."[79] But in 1862, the master politician masked his views as he did many of his opinions. If he leaned too closely to those who opposed the idea of owning a human being, he risked offending constituents who insisted that slavery was protected with Fifth Amendment property rights outlined in the Constitution. Thoroughly disagreeing with the Fifth Amendment defense, Lincoln often reminded his opponents that the word "slave" appeared nowhere in the Constitution, mainly because the document's primary author, James Madison, was so conflicted by the institution. The Virginia slave owner who became utterly convinced of the necessity and majesty of the Bill of Rights could not bring himself to free his slaves, but he also refused to force his personal slave to return to Virginia with him when the Constitutional Convention ended.

Seventy years later, Lincoln shared Madison's qualms, though never as a slave owner. The institution disgusted Lincoln too much for that, but he and Madison had lawyers' minds, and Lincoln challenged anyone to prove that the founders ever supported the idea of listing human beings as property in the Constitution or in the Declaration of Independence. "No man is good enough to govern another man," Lincoln argued in 1854, "*without the other's consent*. I say this is the leading principle—the sheet anchor of American republicanism."[80]

But during the first year of the war, Lincoln feared pushing too hard in this direction. Plus, he respected the state laws that protected slavery where it existed. This crossroads of faith, as it were, had left him in the camp of conservative Republicans and old Whigs, who believed in free labor and free men but who also hoped to end slavery legally by limiting its extension, hoping that the inefficient labor system would wither and die on the vine. This compromise of conscience had helped win Lincoln the election in 1860, but it did not prevent secession.

Ever since that victory, Lincoln had moved step by carefully placed step across the political tightrope of slavery. Much of the system fell in the purview of the state, not Federal, courts. If Lincoln moved too aggressively, slave owners would cry foul, challenge his presidential decree, and most likely prevail, thanks to the conservative nature of the courts whose justices had a long record of pro-Southern rulings. While the President preferred to move cautiously, radical Republicans had insisted on moving more quickly from the very beginning of the war.

In August 1861, Congress passed the First Confiscation Act, which treated slaves like cargo seized on an enemy vessel. Linking captured slaves with the law of prize, Congress would pass a Second Confiscation Act in July 1862, giving Union commanders the right to not only seize slaves working for rebellious forces, but to free this confiscated human property. Reform-minded generals like John C. Fremont and David Hunter took similar action in 1861 and early 1862, only in their case they emancipated confiscated slaves through the power of martial law.

Lincoln understood what they were trying to do, but the zealous reformers wore on him as much as the irrational fire-eaters. Neither side seemed concerned with the laws that kept their democracy from crumbling into chaos. In Lincoln's mind, martial law did not allow commanders to permanently seize a home that they occupied while a battle raged. When the soldiers left, Lincoln explained, the property returned to its owners' control, and those owners could later appeal to the Federal government for damages. Similarly, the law of prize applied to enemy ships at sea, not "cargo" on land. Ever the realist, Lincoln revoked Fremont's and Hunter's orders, which were based in these flawed interpretations of the law, and the President generally ignored the confiscation acts for similar reasons. Then he braced for the withering storm as abolitionists howled in response.

But Lincoln did take action where he thought he could legally, or where he thought he could at least test the issue. In November 1861, Lincoln devised a plan to gradually emancipate slaves in Delaware, one of the small border states that had remained in the Union. The President called for the immediate emancipation of all slaves over thirty-five years old, the gradual emancipation of those age thirty-four and younger, and a $700,000 package of U.S. bonds that Congress would grant the state to compensate their slave owners for "property" losses. Lincoln had been clear on his personal opposition to referring to a human as "property," but the realist in him was determined to find some solution that might inspire other states to follow suit. The more states that agreed to the program, he reasoned, the more the demand for slaves would fall, further driving down slave prices and inspiring others to leap at the compensation option before they suffered a complete loss.

But the slave owners cried as loudly as the abolitionists when Lincoln released his plan. Slave owners did not want Lincoln's compromises on what they saw as one of their fundamental Constitutional rights. Other politicians in Washington balked at the high cost of compensation, despite the President's reminder of what the war itself was costing. As 1861 came to a close, no one subscribed to Lincoln's plan of reason, and he refused to subscribe to others' plans of passion.

One opportunity remained, and that was to repeal slavery legally. State law, which Federal law did not yet have the power to trump, protected the institution where it existed. But Lincoln could strike a blow in Washington, D.C., which lay under Federal jurisdiction, and simultaneously test the white North's tolerance for emancipation. As the Massachusetts senator and abolitionist Charles Sumner had reminded him, the largest slave owner in the United States was the President himself, because he "holds all the slaves in the District of Columbia."[81] Lincoln was never convinced by Sumner's dramatics, but he recognized the wisdom in the observation and, in the spring of 1862, Lincoln acted on it.

The District of Columbia Emancipation Act, signed into law on April 16, 1862, officially ended slavery in the district, immediately freeing 3,100 Africans and African Americans. In the only case in American history, it also allowed the Federal government to compensate all slave owners still loyal to the Union up to $300 for each slave the law emancipated, totaling nearly $1 million (roughly $24.7 million in 2013 dollars). Additional Federal funds, up to $100 per person, were allotted to freed men and women who chose to emigrate from the United States.

Word of the new law flew through the district's black communities. One African-American man recalled relaying the news to two women he knew. As he finished reading the report from the *National Republic*, one of the women broke down in tears of joy while the other declared, "that Jesus has done all things well." The man, writing to his friend in Maryland, had only one regret and prayed "Would to God that the Law applied also to Baltimore but a little patience and all will be well."[82]

But would all be well? Four months after signing the District's Emancipation Act, Lincoln publically refused to take any action to end slavery elsewhere. Clear proof of this came in his published response to abolitionist Horace Greely's public letter to the President titled "The Prayer of Twenty Millions," which again called on Lincoln to free all the slaves. Greely was the editor of the New York *Tribune*, which first carried his letter before it swept across the nation. He insisted that emancipation would strike a blow at the Confederacy, and warned that many who had supported Lincoln's election in 1860 were "sorely disappointed and deeply pained." In a nine-point letter, Greely excoriated Lincoln for failing to force his generals to enforce the Confiscation acts and for being too easily swayed by "the counsels, the representations, the menaces, of certain fossil politicians hailing from Border Slaves States." He even questioned the President's commitment to American freedom and democracy.

Lincoln refused to take the bait, but he offered a response in Washington's *Daily National Intelligencer* on August 23, 1862. "As to the policy I 'seem to be pursuing,' as you say, I have not meant to leave any one in doubt. I would save the Union," Lincoln answered with powerful simplicity. "If I could save the Union without freeing any slave I would do it, and if I could save it by freeing all slaves I would do it; and if I could save it by freeing some and leaving others alone I would also do that." In the end, the matter of slavery would come into play if and only if it could save the Union, and Lincoln would save it "the shortest way under the Constitution."

But, in truth, as Lincoln crafted that response to Greely, a draft of the Preliminary Emancipation Proclamation lay in his desk. He had already decided that ending slavery was key to saving the Union. But he had also decided, long ago, that he didn't like extremists and their emotionalism. Captured best in an address he gave in the 1840s, Lincoln hoped for the "happy day … when, all appetites controlled, all passions subdued, all matters subjected, *mind*, all-conquering *mind*, shall live and move the monarch of the world …. Hail fall of Fury! Reign of Reason, all hail!" He refused to be swayed by emotion or public taunts, especially from abolitionists, whom he had come to characterize as "almost fiendish." Lincoln knew that he had to offer a calm, reasoned, legal plan if he was going to convince the majority of white Northerners to support emancipation. The abolitionists had not sold Americans on their cause; radicals rarely did. The nation favored conservative reform; moderated change. And he offered just that four weeks after he responded to Greeley's letter.

Lincoln had been waiting for a victory. Grant was conquering whole sections of the Confederacy in the West, but he was overshadowed by McClellan's defeats in the East, as well as the losses of the Union commanders chasing after Confederate General Thomas Jonathan "Stonewall" Jackson in Virginia's Shenandoah Valley. When McClellan abandoned the peninsula, Lincoln hoped that General John Pope's Federal army might be able to stop Lee at the Rappahannock. Instead, the armies clashed on the same ground where they had met thirteen months earlier, and once more Union forces limped home from Manassas. The second fight along Bull Run had gone no better than the first for Lincoln. And now he watched in horror as Lee and his Army of Northern Virginia, riding their momentum from Second Manassas, or Second Bull Run as it was known in the North, invaded the Union.

Proving that every rule has its exception, George McClellan, whose force had just left the peninsula, raced after Lee and actually forced a confrontation at Sharpsburg, Maryland, before the Virginian had his army in place. Normally, this would spell disaster, but once again Lee managed to get most of his army together before McClellan managed to attack.

Lee's and McClellan's men had been snipping at each other all along the route to Sharpsburg, but it was there, beginning in a cornfield owned by a man named Miller, that they engaged in a battle that changed the course of the nation. Hour after hour after hour the men pushed back and forth along their lines in a battle that would be named for the waterway, Antietam Creek, that flowed nearby. As the sun rose overhead, the intense fighting shifted to a sunken road where so many men would perish that it became known as Bloody Lane. And then, as if the death toll weren't awful enough already, Union General Ambrose Burnside, whose glorious sideburns belied a shy, overwhelmed commander, sent thousands of men to their deaths in piecemeal fashion across the bridge that would mockingly take his name. They were decimated for hours by a tiny band of Georgians who eventually granted the Federals victory, but by that time the position had lost its value.

As the sun had set behind the old Dunker Church on September 17, nearly 23,000 men had been killed or wounded or had gone missing in a battle that remains America's bloodiest single day. And those casualties did not include the survivors who would succumb to wounds in the weeks and months to follow, or those forever changed by that autumn day. Among them were the men of the 1st Texas Infantry regiment who helped bring Miller's cornfield to national attention.

Involved in the early phase of the fighting, "Hood's Brigade," still known for their second and favorite commander, John Bell Hood, had advanced into the cornfield along with the rest of their division, which Hood now commanded, in "Stonewall" Jackson's Corps. Hood's men, which still included Val Giles, moved forward with the horrifying beauty of well-led veterans embarking on the destruction that defined their purpose. They fought magnificently, with the 1st Texas reaching the northern edge of the field, but Union Major General Joseph Hooker's I Corps checked their advance. Then the fighting shifted from daring to desperate. Watching as his men counterattacked, Hooker was more horrified than relieved by his success. "Every stalk of corn in the northern and greater part of the field was cut as closely as could have been done with a knife, and the slain lay in rows precisely as they stood in their ranks a few moments more. It was never my fortune to witness a more bloody, dismal battle-field."[83]

The men of the 1st Texas had the unenviable glory of reaching the furthest point of the advance, where they were then surrounded and cut off from the rest of the brigade. J. M. Polk of Company I declared the air "full of shot and shell" as the men, "in an open field with no protection" had not chance of surviving. "I didn't take time to load my gun," he explained, "for there were plenty of loaded guns lying on the ground by the side of the dead and wounded men, and they were not all Confederates: the Blue and the Gray were all mixed up." Polk's commander, Lieutenant Colonel P. A. Work, was trying to make sense of the fight when one of his officers, Major Matt Dale, approached to report on the unit's condition. "The roar all about us of nearby small arms and of artillery more distant was so deafening that the Major, in making his report, had to place his mouth to my ear," Work recalled. And then, midsentence, Dale collapsed by Work's side, killed instantly by the fire raging around them.

When Work did finally extract his regiment from the field, he discovered that he had lost 186 of his 226 men. No one remained from Company F, while Company A had but one survivor. Company C could offer the macabre boast of two soldiers, and Company E had three. Company M, though, had the best survival rate, if one could call it that: Eleven of its members survived Miller's Cornfield. While the rest of the regiments of Hood's Brigade suffered fewer casualties, the unit still reported 64 percent overall losses. When General Lee asked Hood that night what happened to his "splendid division," Hood's sad, heavy eyes spoke of their suffering. My men, Hood answered, "are lying on the field where you sent them, sir …. My division has been almost wiped out."[84] Their families at home did not yet know about how many of them would receive devastating news in the coming weeks. So many of the surrogate families that the men had created since they left home were shattered that day. War had forged bonds of brotherhood that sustained the soldiers through disease and death, and as they looked around their shattered ranks that awful morning, the men's weighty sorrow matched Hood's.

When time and grief allowed, some of the men sat down to try to put to words what they had experienced. It was important to them that the families at home understood what the men endured. And it was important that they knew how their loved ones had fallen.

Alexander Erskine was among them as he scratched words onto a rough sheet of paper: "Oh how desolate is my sad heart at the loss of that brother twice endeared by the hardships and perils we have passed through together." A month earlier, Ann had received a similar letter, explaining that her brother, Ig, had been lost at the battle of Second Manassas. It had been fought as the family celebrated her thirty-sixth birthday. "You cannot imagine," her husband had lamented, "how lonely and sorrow-stricken I feel and how little fit I am for anything," as he tried to comprehend, for himself and for Ann, that Ig Johnson was gone. And now, similar words echoed from another letter as her brother-in-law told her that her husband was gone. "But if my heart is so sad, what must yours be, my sister, deprived of a husband and a friend …. Our dear one suffered no pain in death … he was shot through his temples."

Alexander apologized that they had not even been able to go back to bury Andrew's body, knowing how this would upset Ann. The problem, however, was that there was just so much death, the Confederates had been forced to leave the field in Union hands, and Alexander himself was too badly wounded by a ball that tore through his left arm, while two others struck him "slightly" on the side, to go after Andrew himself. Still, he knew his pain was only relative to what his sister-in-law felt as she read his letter the moment it arrived in far off Seguin. There in Texas, as the words she had most feared blurred on the page, Ann Johnson Erskine realized that she was alone in the world. She had lost her father-in-law and her father earlier that year to the normal ravages of life that continue regardless of war. Then came the loss of Ig in August and now Andrew's death at Antietam. Autumn 1862 found her a widow with six sons under the age of thirteen and a massive family enterprise to maintain.[85]

"WE ARE IN A TERRIBLE WAR THAT HAS GOT TO BE FOUGHT OUT"

Antietam came in a series of waves, and the Texans had only been in the first phase of the fighting. As they fell back, the horror of Sharpsburg shifted to other units that included Irish-American brothers Sergeant Cornelius Gillen and Captain Daniel Gillen, who served in the 69th Pennsylvania Infantry regiment, known for its large German and Irish representation. The late morning of September 17 found them marching out of the East Woods as they advanced through the southeast corner of Miller's Cornfield. As the men moved forward, their officers reminded them to stay in formation, but it was nearly impossible due to the scene of utter destruction all around them.

Irish-born Captain James O'Reilly, a company commander, carefully picked his steps, "lest I should trample the fallen foe." Mangled bodies, some of them possibly Texans, lay amid the broken corn stalks, and the wounded's cries for help and water overcame some of the Pennsylvanians, who broke rank to leave in the hands of dying men the canteens they knew they would miss. Continuing on, the men crossed Hagerstown Pike and advanced into the West Woods, eerily quiet as South Carolina and Mississippi soldiers held their fire until the Federals came into perfect range. When they did, the roar of rebel muskets, quickly followed by devastating artillery fire, sent a wall of lead through the 69th's ranks. As the Union troops returned fire and the engagement intensified, they could barely see through the smoke from the guns, and many of them failed to hear II Corps commander, Major General Edwin V. Sumner, ordering them to fall back. By the time the men of the 69th Pennsylvania realized what he wanted, it was too late. Confederates were overwhelming them.

The Gillen brothers managed to stay together through most of the fight. Either finally hearing Sumner or simply realizing that falling back was their only option, they led Company I of the 69th Pennsylvania toward Hagerstown Pike. As they approached the edge of the West Woods, cannon sent solid shot careening through the lines, rushing past the lucky few while hitting others, including Cornelius "Neal" Gillen. With his leg nearly cut in two, he fell to the ground. Daniel led the rest of their company to temporary safety across the Pike. Then he insisted on returning to Neal's side, where the two men spent an excruciating night amid the cries of dying men, wounded horses, and the demons that haunted them all.

As the sun broke on September 18, Confederates captured the two men, though Neal was allowed medical care by a Union surgeon who tried to save him by amputating his leg. Neal battled for his life for another week, and then joined the list of those who died too long after a battle to be counted by anyone but their families. And while Daniel technically survived, he was never the same. Reports indicate that he suffered a mental or emotional breakdown in the weeks that followed. His symptoms were described as "nostalgia" or "soldier's heart" since there was no psychological term for it then, though the symptoms were well known in the ranks by that point. When Confederates released Daniel Gillen from Libby Prison in Richmond in early October, he kept right on walking, never rejoining his regiment or the war that had destroyed him.[86]

As powerful as the stories of the 1st Texas and 69th Pennsylvania are, they were not unique to the bloody carnage that inspired one soldier to describe Sharpsburg as a "landscape turned red." As President Lincoln received the casualty reports, he was relieved that McClellan's army had thwarted Lee's invasion but frustrated that the Confederates had escaped to Virginia. For families at home, though, the battle had more personal significance. They read the casualty reports, their fingers directing their eyes down the columns of casualties that ran one, two, even three pages, calling out names for the neighbors who could not read the reports themselves.

In Washington, President Lincoln demonstrated his uncanny ability to focus on the big picture, as a successful commander must, despite the devastating losses. When he heard that McClellan had stopped Lee at Sharpsburg, he telegrammed back, "God bless you, and all with you." But in the very next sentence, Lincoln added, "Destroy the rebel army if possible." The rational man inside him knew that Antietam, despite its magnitude, would be just one step in a long, bloody war that would only get worse. Indeed, while Antietam seemed to nearly break the Army of the Potomac's backbone, despite their limited victory, Lincoln thought they, and the nation at large, still failed to comprehend the scope of the struggle before them. Later that fall he complained:

> The fact is the people have not yet made up their minds that we are at war with the south. They have not buckled down to the determination to fight this war through; for they have got the idea into their heads that we are going to get out of this fix somehow by strategy! That's the word—strategy! General McClellan thinks he is going to whip the Rebels by strategy; and the army has got the same notion .... They think there is a royal road to peace, and that General McClellan is to find it. The army has not settled down to the conviction that we are in a terrible war that has got to be fought out .... We must change the condition of things ....[87]

Determined to help the nation realize the gravity of their situation, or maybe to save the Union despite them, Lincoln announced, five days after the battle of Antietam, by Presidential Proclamation, that all slaves still in bondage in Confederate-held territory as of January 1, 1863, would be forever free. If the North refused to voluntarily grasp what was required of them, he would force the issue himself while also destroying the one thing that threatened the perpetual destruction of the country. As he had explained to Horace Greely and the nation as a whole just one month earlier, his paramount goal was the Union, the Union, the Union.

Contemporaries despised the proclamation and howled at levels that match the praise Lincoln receives for emancipation today. Abolitionists sneered, "Where he has no power Mr. Lincoln will set the negroes free; where he retains power he will consider them slaves."[88] Southern slave owners raged, and in Richmond, Confederate President Jefferson Davis declared that he had "profound contempt" for the creators of the proclamation, which was "the most execrable measure recorded in the history of guilty man." Their only comfort, he claimed, was that now everyone could see "the complete and crowning proof of the true nature" of Lincoln and the Republicans.[89]

In some ways, they were all right. The Proclamation freed only those slaves in Confederate-held territory. A slave in Federal-occupied New Orleans was not free; nor was a slave in Maryland, Kentucky, Missouri, or Delaware, the border states that had stayed in the Union. Lincoln dared not touch the institution where it could further divide the fragile North. But the Proclamation brought other bold changes, including the fact that it allowed African-American men to serve in the Union Army, not just as laborers but as soldiers. And from this point forward, every slave in every inch of land that the Confederates held on January 1, 1863, would be free as soon as the Union Army could get to them, or the slaves could get to the army.

True, the reasoned Lincoln, who despised emotionalism, proclaimed his ideas in a style that one historian claimed had "all the moral grandeur of a bill of lading." Now was not the time, though, for the thoughtful emotion Lincoln had inspired at his inaugural address a year ago. Nor did he draw from the well that would capture the heartbreak of thousands in his address at Gettysburg a year later. This was a legal act; one that Lincoln knew would inspire some celebration, but also one that would incite far more rancor and possibly more rebellion. And he handled it with the ordered thoughts that were necessary for the citizenry to fully grasp the changes that the Proclamation wrought.

The war was destroying America, and Lincoln knew that although slavery was not its only cause, it was at the heart of the Union's destruction, and it would remain there, like a deadly virus, slowly killing the country unless they could kill it first. Lincoln did not want inspirational words to be confused; he spoke with cold clarity to ensure that every letter of the Proclamation would be understood and implemented with the power of the presidency. Its words bolstered the Union Army's ranks with African-American volunteers. It inspired slave desertions from farms across the South, leaving women and families without slaves to work the fields at a time when Confederate husbands and fathers, sons, and brothers were too busy fighting to tend to the crops themselves. Most importantly, it placed the end of human bondage at the heart of the American Civil War. By the fall of 1862, it was already doubtful that England would openly support the Confederacy. But now, with Europeans generally opposed to slavery, Southern leaders watched the mood in Europe shift even further away.

In the North, Lincoln knew the backlash would be harsh, and in some ways he was right. In the fall elections, Democrats gained thirty-two seats in the House and two governorships, and they won the majority in the legislatures of Illinois, Indiana, and New Jersey. Ohio Congressman Samuel Cox crowed that the election had handed down a new amendment: "Thou shalt not degrade the white race by such intermixtures as emancipation would bring."[90]

Despite this, though, Democratic advances came in areas that had always offered strong support for the party. Republicans gained five seats in the Senate, and their losses in the House were less than the majority party had suffered in off-term elections in the past twenty years.

Both sides could claim victory, and they were quick to do so. More importantly, though, the election signified that Lincoln may have led the nation to the realization that they were "in a terrible war that has got to be fought out." And he may have helped them realize that now was the time to make the change that had escaped their forefathers. The time had come to crush the system that had plagued the city on the hill since its birth. But as Christmas 1862 approached, the terrible war was far from over, and the suffering that filled American homes, North and South, only marked the end of the beginning.

⇒ 3 ⇐

YET ANOTHER SEASON OF WAR

In January 1863, the quiet of the Confederate winter encampment at Fredericksburg, Virginia, broke as sergeants ordered companies into line to prepare for the attack. The men were barely assembled before the fight began, and they stumbled across the snow-covered ground on limbs that responded slowly after weeks of rest. Tally Simpson's South Carolina company was on the far right of their line when the enemy's fire swept across their flank. As his comrades fell back, Simpson tried to hold his position, along with his friend "Old Miller," but a ball smashed into Simpson's mouth and nose, "which staggered me for a while," he admitted. Undaunted, Simpson and the rest of 3rd South Carolina Volunteer Infantry Regiment redoubled their efforts and reorganized the line. "All the men were in high spirits" and revived from the "dull monotony" that had pervaded their winter quarters. Spotting enemy forces across from them, Simpson heard "some one hollow ... to attack the 'Seventh'. The effect was instantaneous." Men rushed to join the forces on each side and the fighting escalated as they struggled for every inch of the field "with terrible energy." Hearing the cry "charge boys, charge," Simpson and his fellow soldiers "all made one simultaneous rush upon the scattered and well-worn ranks of the foe and drove them back," but darkness came and brought the fight to an end before they could capitalize on their success.[91]

The next morning broke with a bitter chill and revealed fresh ammunition covering the ground throughout the camp. Grinning as they emerged from their messes, the South Carolinians scooped up handfuls of white powder, packing it tightly as they moved into position. The well-placed shots of the previous day's fight had allowed the 3rd South Carolina to capture the 7th South Carolina's Lieutenant Colonel Elbert Bland, but the enemies of yesterday decided to combine forces today and focus their fury on 15th South Carolina. The Palmetto boys ducked and threw with a fury until the 15th collapsed under the veteran snow-ballers of the 3rd and the 7th and offered their surrender. But the men decided to reorganize and combine their efforts again, and so it was that the 3rd, 7th, and 15th South Carolina continued onward toward the 8th South Carolina's position.

Remembering the lessons of Marye's Heights from the previous month, they refused to directly assault the 8th, which had benefited from a hilltop encampment all winter. Instead, the attackers, "by a skillful manoeuvre," Simpson boasted, divided their force, with a portion attacking the 8th's right flank. As the 8th shifted their attention to the movement on their side, the remainder of Simpson's Palmetto band assaulted the hilltop defenders and quickly secured their surrender. Thrilled with the results, the victors invited the 8th to join them and attack the nearby Georgians of Thomas R. R. Cobb's brigade, who were already busy in a separate fight against the notoriously brutal Texans of John Bell Hood's old Brigade.

The pattern continued like that for hours, with victor and vanquished joining bands after one fight to focus their combined fury on the next target. By the end of the day, brigades were assaulting other brigades with more than a thousand men on each side commanded by junior officers. Large bands of grown men whipped hard-packed snowballs at each other as icy powder stung their faces, sides, and legs. Simpson's force was eventually overrun, but he boasted that he nearly saved their regimental colors until "a dozen men … thoroughly whitewashed me." Fortunately, he escaped his captors and returned to his camp uninjured, declaring the last two days' battles "the greatest snow balling I have ever witnessed."

All of the men involved in the snowball fights of January 1863 agreed that they were some of the best days of an awful war. Well, all of the men except for Augustus Dickert of the 3rd South Carolina. Somehow, in the midst of "battle," he earned the wrath of a "wild-eyed Georgian" who failed to understand that the snowball fight was all in good fun. When Dickert realized that there was no way that he, "a boy of seventeen years old and never yet tipped the beam at one hundred [pounds]," could successfully fight "that monster" who gave Dickert "the horrors," Dickert decided his only salvation lay in "continual and rapid flight." And fly he did. Dickert raced toward the safety of his camp, which "seemed a perfect [mirage], now near at hand, then far in the distance," past the ongoing battle, snowballs flying and men brawling, until he dove into his "tent, more dead than alive, just as I felt the warm breath of my pursuer blowing on my neck. I heard, as I lay panting, the wild-eyed man say, 'I would rather have caught that d—n little Captain than to have killed the biggest man in the Yankee army.'"[92]

The snowballing in the Confederate camp that winter represented a feverish rejection of a melancholy the men could not shake. Their days were filled with cold marches back to camp from an even colder series of hours spent on picket duty and quiet moments spent in rough cabins where the men wrote letters home that reflected their struggle between depression and determination, followed by desperate wishes for a rare letter in reply. The trouble was that this was their second Christmas in camp far from their families at home. These were veterans of a full season of war. Two years ago, they had thought one battle would show the North their resolve and secure their independence. Since then, these soldiers of the Army of Northern Virginia had won one victory after another, but still the war continued. The fighting confidence was high, and their morale should have been much higher than that of the Federals, so accustomed to defeat that year, who camped across the Rappahannock. But even among the victorious Confederates, morale wavered and sank. They worried about their families at home, who suffered through months of sacrifice and now faced another cold winter with less wood for the fire, less food for the pot, and fewer men at home to keep the farms running.

On Christmas Day 1862, Tally Simpson had sat dejected in camp, longing for the cheerful sounds of his family at home. The "very stillness" had forced him into reflections on the previous December when "many thousand families" were "gay and joyous ... drinking health to the absent members of their families," and praying for the men's homecoming. "[B]ut today," Simpson mourned, these families

> are clad in the deepest mourning in memory to some lost and loved member of their circle. If all the dead (those killed since the war began) could be heaped in one pile and all the wounded be gathered together in one group, the pale faces of the dead and the groans of the wounded would send such a thrill of horror through the hearts of the originators of this war that their very souls would rack with such pain that they would prefer being dead and in torment than to stand before God with such terrible crimes blackening their characters. Add to this the cries and wailings of the mourners—mothers and fathers weeping for their sons, sisters for their brothers, wives for their husbands, and daughters for their fathers—[and] how deep would be the convictions of their consciences. Yet they do not seem to think of the affliction and distress they are scattering broadcast over the land. When will this war end? Will another Christmas roll around and find us all wintering in camp? Oh! that peace may soon be restored to our young but dearly beloved country and that we may all meet again in happiness.[93]

A year at war had tempered the enthusiastic cavalier. In 1860, Tally Simpson was the young buck elected lieutenant by his classmates in Wofford College's newly formed militia company in Spartanburg, South Carolina. He was the complete opposite of his logical, legal-minded sibling Dick. Just thirteen months earlier, Tally had promised his worried aunt that even if war came, which was doubtful, there would be "one or two little outbreaks in some uncertain communities," and there might be "some fighting about the division of territories, but a civil conflict is not to be apprehended."[94] Now Dick was home, his chronic illness in camp forcing him first out of the infantry and then from the cavalry. Tally remained in Virginia, and although friends and cousins were in his regiment, it was not the same as being with family at home. The war seemed endless, despite victory two weeks earlier at Fredericksburg, and Tally could not shake from his mind the images of those missing from his wartime family. The men of his regiment had bonded like brothers under the pressures of war, and now too many of them lay buried on distant fields, never to be seen again.

What set the winter of 1862–63 apart from the previous year was not the men's high morale, nor even their faith in victory. It was their ability to swallow their loneliness and their fears and continue to fight because, quite simply, they believed it was their duty. They believed in what they were fighting for. Each side defined that differently, but an astonishing number of men remained determined that, come what may, they must defend the principles on which their country was founded.

This was how, like so many Americans that winter, Simpson could shake the gloom from his head and quickly change the tone of his letters, asking about friends at home and reminding his family to write, even if little mail seemed to make it to him. Within eight weeks, on February 26, 1863, and still in camp in Fredericksburg, he admitted that the day was "as disagreeable as it can be." Having spent the morning on wet, cold picket duty, Simpson was happy to be writing around a warm fire, but he was still frustrated by the scarcity of food and comfort. "It is as hard living now as I have ever experienced—a little bacon and flour with a little sugar and rice occasionally," he grumbled to his sister. "A morsel of old cow would taste as good as 'ginger bread.'" Complaints of weather and food were followed by concerns about the plight of Vicksburg, Mississippi, about which Simpson was "fearfully alarmed." He knew Union forces were "moving heaven & earth to reduce that point of all points to us, and if they succeed, the moral effect produced thereby upon the mind of the northwest will be much more serious than a great many will imagine."[95] But then Simpson's mind swung to playful thoughts about the perfect young belle his aunt and cousin had found for him to marry when he returned home. Life, it seemed, would go on.

"SIMPLY A SLAUGHTER-PEN"

Across the Rappahannock, Union forces, so recently defeated, were too focused on their own misery to find much hope in Vicksburg. It had been a rough few months, starting with their Pyrrhic victory at Antietam in September. They had stopped the Confederate invasion of Maryland, but at a horrifying cost, which photographers documented for their families at home in state-of-the-art studios. Then came the December disaster under Major General Ambrose Burnside, who replaced the "Young Napoleon" as the new commander of the Army of the Potomac when President Lincoln's patience with George McClellan finally wore out. Burnside had resisted his promotion by the President and was hesitant to initiate yet one more battle in 1862 before settling into winter camps. But Lincoln insisted that the North needed a victory. It would brush aside the gloom that followed Antietam and the criticisms of emancipation, he argued, and plant the seeds of optimism that would sustain the Union into the next year.

Unfortunately for the North, Burnside had an excellent sense of his own limitations. He may have been a solid commander at lower ranks, but he was correct when he told the President that he was not the man to lead the Army of the Potomac. Burnside's campaign toward Richmond, which crossed the Rappahannock at Fredericksburg, seemed destined to prove that very point.[96]

The army was delayed leaving Washington, and then they realized that the pontoons, which were required to build the supplemental bridges for the army's river crossing, had been accidentally left behind. Then, after additional delays, Burnside finally decided to launch what would turn out to be one of the greatest disasters in American military history. On December 12, he ordered nearly half his force to cross the pontoon bridges, which had finally been built by Union engineers while under constant fire by Confederate sharpshooters in the buildings and homes along the Fredericksburg waterfront. The next morning, brigades began to move through the historic town's streets. The buildings offered some protection, but the roads clustered the men into massive blue targets that attracted artillery fire from Confederates on Marye's Heights, a gentle hill that rose behind Fredericksburg and overlooked the town.

Below the rebel cannon were rows of Longstreet's infantrymen, all dug in on the gradual slope, with the lowest ranks enjoying the protection of a sunken road and a stone wall that ran across the upper third of the heights. It was a nearly impregnable position, but one that inspired Burnside's determination. He would send Sumner's men there to keep Confederate General James Longstreet's First Corps from moving to support Stonewall Jackson's Second Corps, which was being attacked by Union General William Franklin's Left Grand Division on the far left of the Union line. It was that simple. Sumner's men weren't trying to drive the Confederates from their position. They just needed to occupy their attention. And once they had it, the Union men would have to fight valiantly enough to keep Longstreet's First Corps from rolling the Federals back through town and into the Rappahannock and then moving to help Jackson.

As Sumner's men moved into position to carry out this plan on the morning of December 13, 1862, they scowled at the morticians who scurried through their ranks, trying to secure just a few more sales. The tradesmen promised soldiers that should they fall in the battle that had already begun, their bodies would be recovered, embalmed, and shipped home to their loved ones in pristine condition—"sweet as a nut," one man boasted. Some of the soldiers ran the men off, but others took comfort in the card pinned to their coat or the cold metal disc hanging from their neck that guaranteed an embalmer's service, knowing that they had a chance of being reunited with their families in death, if not in life.

The veterans of the Peninsula, Second Manassas, and Antietam pushed forward, block by block, even as Minié balls careened through their ranks, tearing heads and limbs from bodies. When they finally reached the base of the heights, the soldiers realized that they would have to cross a millrace, which would again bottleneck their forces into tight blue targets for the Confederate defenders. Some of the men crossed the small waterway on their own while others used the small bridges, all of them knowing that even if they did make it across unharmed, they would be among the unfortunate souls who would have to advance across a hundred yards of open ground into constant infantry fire coming from Confederates protected by a stone wall.

One of the units engaged in this portion of the battlefield was the famous Irish Brigade of the Army of the Potomac. The Irish- and American-born sons of Irish immigrants who dominated the ranks of this unit had earned early fame at the first Battle of Bull Run. Only the 69th New York had participated in that fight, not the entire brigade, but they had handled themselves well, and the New York press had offered rare praise for the brawling Irishmen, who usually earned the ire of the city's Republican paper, *The New York Times*. In the fight that summer of 1861, the soldiers' skill in battle made it clear that they weren't just brawlers; they were disciplined soldiers, and their bloody struggle against the Confederates in the Sunken Road at Antietam just a few months earlier further solidified the Irish Brigade's reputation as a unit commanders called on in tough situations.

As the Irish Brigade crossed the millrace, they suffered nearly thirty minutes of fire and an unknown number of casualties—no one took the time to count until after the fighting was over. Once they all finally reached the other side, they took a moment to dress their ranks. Thick clouds of smoke from the raging battle blocked the early afternoon sun. Members of the 63rd, 69th, and 88th New York, along with the 28th Massachusetts and the 116th Pennsylvania, the regiments that comprised the Irish Brigade, pushed past the protection of a small swale in the ground and advanced up the hill. Several brigades had preceded them, and the evidence of their brutal fight lay all over the ground.[97]

Advancing with the 116th Pennsylvania, Private William McCarter checked the veterans on his left and right. McCarter had joined the 116th Pennsylvania just a few months earlier, and now he watched with fascinated fright as officers and men fell all around him. He continued to push up the hill until a spent round struck his shoulder and then another sliced through his kepi, "leaving it dangling at my ear by a solitary thread." Undeterred, McCarter loaded and fired his weapon again and again until a round tore through his right arm, which fell limp by his side. McCarter collapsed on the ground unconscious.

Nearby, Major John Dwyer of the 63rd New York looked behind him to check on his men and was stunned to see that "the dead were piled in heaps" all around him. St. Clair Mulholland of the 116th Pennsylvania watched with similar shock as a round tore through Lieutenant Garrett Nowlen's leg and another ball struck Lieutenant Robert McGuire in the chest, knocking him to the ground, gasping for air. When Mulholland turned again, he saw an orderly sergeant's head whip around, spraying blood from a gaping hole, but Mulholland barely had time to be horrified before a Minié ball cut through his right calf and sent him to the ground.

One of the tragic ironies of that day was that some of the men shooting at the Irishmen in blue were fellow Irishmen in gray. Decades later, veterans and writers would tell stories of the Irish Confederates weeping at the thought of their countrymen suffering at their own hand, and some insisted that the rebel Irish even refused to fire. But the 24th Georgia's Irish-born Colonel Robert McMillan, who commanded the Irish rebels at the stone wall, insisted that they knew exactly who was opposite them and that they fought with joy.

Many of the Confederate Irish resented their fellow immigrants' willingness to serve the Union cause, which the Southerners saw as similar to the United Kingdom's refusal to allow Ireland to leave Britain's rule. When McMillan saw the green flag of the 28th Massachusetts, he shouted to his men, "That's Meagher's Brigade! .... Give it to them now, boys! Now's the time! Give it to them!" Years later he swore that "never did men better respond to a call."[98]

The results of Sumner's efforts to hold Longstreet's attention were horrifying. Fourteen Federal brigades charged up Marye's Heights. Combined with the losses suffered in the attack by Franklin's Left Grand Division, which also failed, the Federals suffered 13,000 casualties, as many as they had at Antietam, only here there was not a glimmer of victory. Adding insult to injury, the Federals were disgusted to learn that the well-protected Confederate defenders suffered only 5,000 casualties. The Irish Brigade took 45 percent losses, an astonishing level considering that most units break at about 20 percent casualties. Among those who fell were fifty-five officers, a crushing blow to the brigade's leadership.

Father Corby, the chaplain of the 88th New York, insisted that "the place into which Meagher's brigade was sent was simply a slaughter-pen." Brigade staff officer Captain David P. Conyngham agreed, declaring "It was not a battle—it was a wholesale slaughter of human beings— sacrificed to the blind ambition and incapacity of some parties," referring to General Burnside and, quite likely, to President Lincoln.

Colonel Robert Nugent of the 69th New York summarized it best. Fredericksburg, he wrote, was "a living hell from which escape seemed scarcely possible."[99]

Nugent's sentiments were carried to Irish homes as those who survived the battle tried to explain it to their families. On December 14, 1862, the day after the battle, Captain William J. Nagle of the 88th New York vented his fury at the waste of the fight and its impact on his faith, and that of his fellow soldiers, in the war. Two weeks later, his father published Nagle's letter in the New York *Irish-American*, summarizing the mood of much of the Irish Catholic community in the North. Nagle spoke well of his commander, General Meagher, but complained about the utter waste of the battle and its devastating effect on the ranks. "Irish blood and Irish bones cover that terrible field to-day," Nagle wrote, "The whole-souled enthusiasm with which General McClellan inspired his army is wanting—his great scientific engineering skill is missing—his humane care for the lives of his men is disregarded. We are slaughtered like sheep, and no result but defeat ...."[100] Summarizing the situation best, one soldier wrote, "As for the remnant of the Brigade, they were the most dejected set of Irishmen you ever saw or heard of."[101]

"WHAT A WEAK AFFAIR I AM"

They were not alone in their misery that December. As the second Christmas of the war drew near, families across the North were disgusted with a conflict that was supposed to have been decided in a single battle. Granted, 1862 had brought some victories in the West, but it seemed that these had only inspired the South to fight harder in the East. Part of that determination, Yankees grumbled, had been inspired by the Emancipation Proclamation, and unskilled workers and Democrats alike across the North complained bitterly about the labor competition they believed that slavery's end would bring. As the men sat in camp that winter, they missed their savior, "Little Mac," and wondered if their misery would ever end.

One of them was Wilbur Fisk. He was twenty-one years old when the war began and was sharing his self-taught knowledge as a teacher to a small group of school children in Tunbridge, Vermont. That spring, he and some friends stopped at the local post office for news of the looming conflict when the old postman, tears streaming down his face, announced that the war had come. "We boys," Fisk recalled, "did not take it so seriously as he did. We were ready to shout hurrah because now there would be a chance to teach the South a lesson."[102]

Despite the postman's gloom, as well as that of his parents—"who followed their soldier boy to our railroad station at South Royalton" and watched with shoulders stooped as the train "took him from their sight"— young Private Fisk was full of the same dreams that had inspired Tally Simpson to rush to arms in South Carolina just a few months earlier. Fisk joined Company E of the Second Vermont Volunteer Infantry regiment.

Also like Simpson, Fisk spent that first winter in camp stunned by the rough conditions and battling sickness, but he grinned proudly as he described the semibasement that he and his messmates dug for their rough cabin, which provided additional protection from wind and rain. They even managed to raise their beds, creating extra space to store wood, and then they built a fireplace with a chimney, though they also discovered that when two of the men who slept on the floor curled a little too close to the warm fire one night, the entire mess awoke suffocating from smoke. But on the whole, they were confident that first winter; their letters were filled with optimism and bravado. Fisk told his readers, who were growing in number ever since he had signed on as a regular soldier-correspondent for the *Green Mountain Freeman*, that his unit hoped they would "prove ourselves worthy sons of Vermont, and inherit the title of Green Mountain Boys, with all its historic luster ...."[103]

By 1862, Fisk continued to express public confidence, but privately he was just as conflicted as Tally Simpson. The war was unlike anything Fisk had ever experienced. The challenges seemed endless. And the horrors were just frequent enough to interrupt any deep sleep he managed to get. He broke down that winter.

Fisk wrote his last correspondent letter of 1862 on September 10, just one week before the Battle of Antietam. But after sending it off to the *Freeman*, Fisk and some fellow soldiers succumbed to a case of chronic diarrhea, and they were sent to a hospital near Washington City. By January 1863, Fisk's condition had improved, though he still suffered lingering symptoms, and he was living in the hospital's convalescent camp.

A few weeks later, when Fisk tried to draw his pay, he discovered that he was on the rolls as a deserter. He had either ignored or never received orders to return to his regiment, and Fisk knew he needed to get there to clear his name. But when he left the convalescent camp in the capital, instead of traveling south to report to his unit, Fisk went north, all the way to New England. He spent a month at a training camp in Brattleboro, Vermont, before continuing on to his family's farm in Tunbridge. A few days later, his parents assumed Fisk returned to camp in Brattleboro, but instead, he went to Lawrence, Massachusetts, to find Angelina Drew, a young woman with whom he was in love and who was working in the cotton mills there. In a bizarre turn of events over a matter of weeks, the rule-abiding, highly ideologically motivated volunteer had deserted his unit. Twice, if that was possible.

As February ticked by and Fisk continued to be marked absent in camp, he floundered in Massachusetts, wrestling with his conscience. He desperately wanted Drew to marry him, but he was unable to bring himself to ask her, believing that "should Angie accept me as her husband she will be surprised to find what a weak affair I am." Also troubling him was the loss of his first cousin, Edgar Dinsmore, a sergeant in the 9th New Hampshire cut down by a Confederate volley two months earlier at the Battle of Fredericksburg.[104] Edgar and Wilbur were raised just miles from each other and had grown up playing and fighting, as Wilbur recalled years later, in the fields that connected their fathers' farms.

Edgar had rushed to arms when the war began, but returned from the First Battle of Bull Run a changed man. He still believed in the Union cause, but he feared the South could never be defeated. "They were so united, so determined, so bitter in their hatred of the North [that Edgar] believed they would never yield to them," Wilbur explained. But Edgar was equally certain that the Union must be saved, and he had re-enlisted in the late summer of 1861, only to fall just before Christmas the following year. His mother would send men on three trips to Virginia to locate Edgar's body and bring him home. They never could find him.[105]

And so it was in the early spring of 1863 that Wilbur found himself unable to move forward and rejoin his unit, but also unable to go home to Vermont with the war unfinished. By February 25, he still struggled, knowing that "the wear and tear of my nervous system in consequence of my dangerous position as a deserter and my anxiety and wakefulness which I cannot overcome is making sad havoc with spirits and feelings and physical enjoyment." He negotiated with God, believing "if God will grant me the full restoration of my health and physical vigor perhaps I can show myself more of a man than she had known me yet."

But, no matter what he did, Fisk found himself unable to make a move. It may have been that he could not bring himself to return to his regiment, knowing that doing so would ensure his role in another brutal season of battles and disease. Maybe Wilbur had simply lost faith in himself. Perhaps he faulted himself for being sick in the hospital and unable to fight in Fredericksburg, unable to somehow help his cousin, Edgar. Or perhaps he lost faith in the Union when its salvation came at such a terrible cost. Whatever the cause, Fisk spent most of February wrestling with his conscience, unable to move forward and unwilling to go back.

And then, quite suddenly, something snapped. It may have been building gradually, but the change seems to have occurred over a two- to three-day period. Fisk found a way through the darkness, and the timing indicates that while his family at home could not seem to calm Fisk's soul, Angelina Drew did. She had more faith in Fisk than he realized. Indeed, she had more faith in Wilbur Fisk than Wilbur Fisk himself did, and by the end of February, just days after he confided to his diary that he feared that Drew would discover his weakness and that anxiety and ill health were breaking him down, Fisk and Drew eloped. Within just a few days after that, Fisk had reached his regiment.

His return to the ranks wasn't entirely smooth. Fisk promptly found himself in the guardhouse awaiting a court-martial trial, but he benefited from an astute captain's reminder to their politically aspired colonel that Fisk was a correspondent with the influential *Green Mountain Freeman*.

Fisk's commander realized how public the case might become and released Fisk with the understanding that the readers at home would hear nothing of the melancholy that had nearly broke Fisk—and thousands of others—that winter when he continued his role as a soldier correspondent.[106]

Fisk kept his promise. But he did try to help those at home understand the puzzling nature of war. Just a few months after his return to camp and following the Chancellorsville Campaign in May 1863, Fisk told his readers,

> It is difficult to realize in the time of an action, the extreme peril one's life is in. Death there seems of less consequence than anywhere else, one gets so used to it. Let a railroad accident happen, or a factory tumble to the ground, mangling a great many, and terrifying numbers more, and the whole country shudders, but the same number may be killed and maimed in a brisk skirmish, and the affair is very "brilliant." Such is the acknowledged difference, and it well that it should be so. But when the excitement is over and we go back to camp and see so many comrades whose society was our pleasure, missing, we feel very keenly the loss we have sustained.[107]

Throughout the winter of 1862–63, men like Wilbur Fisk and Tally Simpson struggled to comprehend of the brutality of the war. Some men in the ranks could not find sense in it at all, and they deserted or refused to reenlist when their terms of service expired. But others, like Fisk and Simpson, emerged from that winter determined to fight until they were victorious, however long that would take. They had moved beyond the early excitement for adventure in 1861 and their bewilderment at the cruel irony of war in 1862, the period Fisk tried to explain when he claimed that, "Bullets play curious freaks sometimes."

As the spring of 1863 approached, Simpson took strength from the letters he exchanged with his family in South Carolina, just as Fisk found peace in the new family he built with Angelina Drew. That peace helped him continue his role as a translator of sorts for his community at home, publishing letters with renewed vigor that explained the war and why it was necessary. His own struggles so mirrored those of his townsfolk that his renewed faith was all the more inspiring. The letters that he published, while never speaking of his breakdown, captured the concerns and losses that so many home front families had endured and Fisk's new found purpose in the war inspired similar faith at home.

"THE VALLEY FORGE OF THE WAR"

Just as Wilbur Fisk emerged stronger that spring, so too did the entire Union Army. It was an astonishing achievement considering how low the men's spirits were in the Federal camps that winter. Desertions from the Union Army had reached epic proportions. An estimated 58,000 officers and men had gone absent with or without leave from the Army of the Potomac, and by March desertions for the entire Federal Army approached 125,000 men.

President Lincoln knew that the most well-known punishment for desertion—execution—was not feasible. Several months earlier, in November 1862, he had met with a group of women from the U.S. Sanitary Commission, a federally approved private organization that supplemented the often insufficient medical care and overall support that the government provided soldiers with. The women were shocked by Lincoln's aversion to executing men for desertion. They suggested that he enforce the penalty, which may seem an odd argument coming from this group, but they theorized that if the men were in the ranks where they needed to be when a great battle came, it could be won with such overwhelming force that it would bring the end of the war and cause far fewer deaths than if the war simply dragged on. Lincoln sympathized, but he insisted that this would never work: "You can't order men shot by dozens or twenties. People won't stand it, and they ought not stand it." Instead, he argued, he needed true fighters leading his armies. Only they could inspire the men and help them understand that there was only one way to bring peace, and that was through a victorious conclusion of the war.

The trouble, of course, was finding the right commander. In January

1863, General Burnside decided to attempt one last push toward Richmond. The skies had been free of rain for weeks, making such a plan reasonable despite the time of year. But the Union forces had just barely begun moving when the skies opened with such a downpour that their operation, if one could even call it that, became known as "The Mud March." Within two days, reports were flying into headquarters of wagons stuck in ankle-deep mud and mules sunk to their ears. The men, losing shoes and boots in the muck, noticed with rage, and then dejection, the Confederates across the Rappahannock who had come out to watch the debacle and mock their enemy, waving signs that directed, "This Way to Richmond," while another broadcast, like the headlines that were soon to follow, "Burnside Stuck in the Mud."[108]

On January 22, two days after he had ordered the march to begin, Burnside wisely cancelled the operation and returned the men to winter quarters. He then wrote a letter to Lincoln, accepting full blame for the mess, and Burnside sent copies of his admission to newspaper offices across the North.[109] Such humility was refreshing in the wake of McClellan's arrogance, but it hardly lifted spirits. Burnside was a decent man, but he was not the leader Lincoln needed.

If desertions were worrisome to the President in November, they were disastrous by January 1863. On Christmas Day 1862, the same day Tally Simpson confessed his doubts to his family in South Carolina and mourned the loss of too many friends, Major Rufus Dawes sat across the Rappahannock from Simpson in the 6th Wisconsin's camp wondering the same thing. For the Union man, though, the problem was compounded by the fact that their army had no faith in their commander. Dawes predicted that this winter would be "the Valley Forge of the war," the great test to see if, like George Washington's army, these men could survive the winter and emerge better trained and capable of victory.[110] But where was their Washington? An officer in the 140th New York looked about camp and saw an "entire army struck with melancholy ... The mind of the army, just now, is a sort of intellectual marsh in which False Report grows fat, and sweeps up and down with a perfect audacity and fierceness." Another New Yorker agreed: "From want of confidence in its leaders and from no other reason, the army is fearfully demoralized."[111]

Lincoln knew he had to act, and in January 1863, he accepted Burnside's offer to resign, but then astonished many by appointing a man whose headquarters had been described as "a place to which no self-respecting man liked to go, and no decent woman could go. It was a combination of barroom and brothel." This was Major General Joseph Hooker, whose aggression and confidence had led newspapermen to nickname him "Fighting Joe." He was certainly bold. The forty-eight-year-old West Point graduate had tiptoed across the line of insubordination more than once with his political maneuverings in camp and with his friends in Congress, and he had even told a reporter that what the country really needed was a dictator.

By January, President Lincoln was desperate enough to take a gamble on Hooker. Lincoln informed Hooker that he knew of the soldier's reputation for political maneuvering and backstabbing, his loud criticisms of Lincoln himself, and his less-than-savory habits in camp. Hooker's appointment, Lincoln explained, had come despite these, not because of them. "I have heard," Lincoln added in a late January letter, "of your recently saying that both the Army and the Government needed a Dictator … Only those generals who gain successes, can set up dictators. What I now ask of you is military success, and I will risk the dictatorship."[112]

Several men, including Lincoln's personal secretary, John Hay, supported Lincoln's gamble. Hay had seen enough to wonder if the rumors of Hooker's intemperance and philandering were just that—rumor—and others suspected that Fighting Joe might just be the commander the North desperately needed. Within days, Hooker's actions in camp confirmed their opinions. "My men shall be fed before I am fed," Hooker announced, "and before any of my officers are fed." The quality of food soon improved, too, and systems were set into place to ensure that both quality and quantity of fresh bread, vegetables, and meat would remain stable. Hooker revised the payment system to ensure that soldiers who had not been paid in months received their back wages and that all future payments would come on time. Hooker also convinced the President to grant deserters amnesty if they returned to camp, and he dropped charges against those awaiting trial. Then he developed a furlough system to allow those who had remained in camp a brief visit home before the campaign season began.

Hooker appointed Jonathan Letterman (whose talent and foresight would eventually have him recognized as the "father of battlefield medicine") in charge of the medical department in the army, which led to dramatic and lasting improvements in camp conditions and the men's health. Fighting Joe reorganized the army and designed corps insignia that inspired unit pride among the men. Watching the impact of these changes, even commanders who didn't particularly like Hooker had to admit that the army's spirits had improved dramatically by the late spring of 1863. Sergeant Edmund English of the 2nd New Jersey summarized their astonishment as he looked around camp: "I do not think it possible that such a change could have taken place for the better as has been effected in the short space of two months. From a dissatisfied and almost mutinous mob, we have become a good and well-disciplined army second to none."[113] Wilbur Fisk agreed, and his letters to the *Green Mountain Freeman* ensured that the men's renewed faith in themselves, in their commander, and in the war itself spread to their families at home. In April 1863, he explained the transition:

> There has been a great change for the better, in the minds of the men of the regiment during the last few months respecting the war, and no doubt the whole army are improved in the same way. A while ago it was no uncommon thing to hear men answer to their names "Here, but it is the last time," and often they made their true statement. Officers as well as men spoke frequently of their determination to desert, and not help carry on an "abolition war." It is very materially changed now. Good discipline is effectively restored. Confidence in the Government, and respect for it, is reestablished. Many a time have I heard boys, with more perverseness than good sense, remark that they would never carry a gun against the enemy again. There is but little of this disposition manifested now, and it is becoming decidedly unpopular. As soldiers see more fully the depths of principle involved in this controversy, and the wisdom of the policy the Government is adopting to bring it to an issue that God must forever approve, the more determined and anxious are they to carry the war out successfully.[114]

The despair that had hung over the Army of the Potomac all winter was lifting.

5th Street Presbyterian Church, Washington, D.C., ca. 1890s. This photo shows the church as it would have appeared around the time Francis Grimké served as its minister.

Charlotte Forten, ca. 1870s.

Abraham and Tad Lincoln, 1865.

Willie and Tad Lincoln with their cousin Lockwood Todd in 1861.

Willie Lincoln, ca. 1861.

ary Todd Lincoln in 1861.

Lieutenant General Ulysses S. Grant, ca. 1864.

Ulysses S. Grant photographed with his family after the war.

fferson Davis and Varina Howell
avis the year they married, 1845.

Winnie Davis, the daughter of
Jefferson and Varina Davis, born
during the war.

Jefferson Davis's inauguration as Confederate president on February 18, 1861 in Montgomery, Alabama.

Opposite: Leaders of both the Union and the Confederacy drew on conventional images of women at the heart of the family. Loyalty to kin and community, it was hoped, would ensure that most women endured their losses with patient martyrdom.

OUR HEARTS
ARE WITH OUR BROTHERS
IN THE FIELD.

Family in camp with the 31st Pennsylvania Infantry Regiment, ca 1861–1865. Two poses. Civil War families often hoped to visit their soldiers, while others would come to stay with their men during the long winter encampments. It is not clear from this photo if the soldier's family is just visiting or staying, but hints of domestic home life abound, right down to the little boy's puppy.

Dead in front of Dunker Church, The Battle of Antietam, Sharpsburg, Maryland, September 1862.

onfederate dead behind the Stone Wall at the Battle of Fredericksburg, rginia, December 1862.

Above: Unidentified Union girl in mourning dress. Man in photo is identified as her father, a Union cavalryman.

Right: The reverse of "The Children of the Battlefield" image shown below.

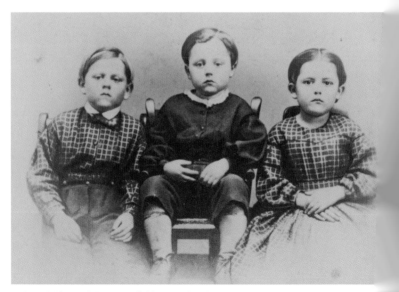

"The Children of the Battlefield." Frank, Alice, and Freddie Humiston, ca. 1860. This was one of the reprinted images of the Humiston children that was sold raise funds for the Orphanage at Gettysburg.

James Madison Bowler and Elizabeth Bowler, 1862.

James Rodgers Loughridge, ca. 1861–1865.

Mary Felicia Martin Loughridge, ca. 1880s–1890s?

Andrew Nelson Erskine in 1853.

Sarah Katherine "Kate" Stone Hudson, date unknown.

William T. Shepherd, ca. 1860.

James Rodgers Loughridge, ca. 1861–1865. This wartime photo of Loughridge shows him without the polish of a studio photo and uniform, and more realistically captures how he and other Confederate officers looked during the war.

Taylor Battery Monument, Rosehill Cemetery, Chicago, Illinois. The inscription at the base reads, "I die for liberty, boys: go back and man the gun," the famous dying words of Taylor Battery member Oscar E. Beckers at the battle for Fort Donelson, February 1862.

Example of the "kiss" symbols J.R. Loughridge always drew in his wartime letters home to his wife, Felicia, and daughters, Mary and Ella. Taken from July 25, 1863 letter.

Mary and Ella Loughridge, ca. 1860s–1870s.

Wilbur Fisk, ca. 1861–1865.

Wilbur Fisk, ca. 1890s.

U.S. Senator and Colonel Edward D. Baker, killed at the Battle of Ball's Bluff, October 16, 1861.

Lieutenant General Ulysses S. Grant
ca. 1864–1865.

General Robert E. Lee (center) and
Major General George Washington
Curtis Lee (left), his son, and Lieutenant
Colonel Walter Taylor.

n April 9, 1865, General Robert E. Lee surrendered the Confederate Army
Northern Virginia to Lieutenant General Ulysses S. Grant at the home of
lmer and Virginia McLean in the rural town of Appomattox Court House,
ginia.

President Abraham Lincoln with General George McClellan in a tent at the Antietam battlefield in October 1862.

Three young African-American boys huddle against a pillar amidst the ruins of Charleston, South Carolina, ca. 1861–65.

Commodore Franklin Buchanan, Confederate States Navy, ca. 1861–1865.

Unknown African American soldier, wife, and two daughters, ca. 1863–1865

fferson Davis's plantation home, Brierfield, after it was occupied by Union oops and Freedmen's Bureau workers.

Confederate dead lying behind the stone wall on Marye's Heights, Fredericksburg, Virginia, ca.1861–65.

Union defenses on Little Round Top at the Battle of Gettysburg, Pennsylvania, ca. 1863

he gate house cemetery at Gettysburg.

Above: General William Tecumseh Sherman photographed in 1865. Note the black armband he wears in honor of the late President Abraham Lincoln.

Opposite: General Ulysses S. Grant's forces at Young's Point north of Vicksburg, March 1863.

William Seward and his daughter, Fanny, ca. 1861–1865.

Frederick W. Seward, ca. 1860–1865.

William H. Seward, ca. 1865.

Nellie Nugent Somerville, ca. 1920s.

Weapons captured from Lincoln's assassins and an original poster offering a reward for any information.

An artist's impression of the moment John Wilkes Booth leaned forward to shoot President Abraham Lincoln as he watched a play at Ford's Theater, D.C., in 1865.

Annie Surratt, ca. 1860–1865.

Lewis Powell aka Lewis Payne during his trial, ca. 1865.

Lewis Powell aka Lewis Payne during his trial, ca. 1865.

Clara Harris, ca. 1860–1865

Major Henry Rathbone,
c. 1860–1865.

Mary Surratt, ca. 1865.

group of freed slaves who worked as laborers and servants for the 13th
Massachusetts Infantry Regiment during the Civil War.

An idealized depiction of life for slaves both before and after emancipation. The reality was much starker.

"THE DAWN OF FREEDOM"

Hundreds of miles to the south, a far more entrenched despair was lifting as well. It had hung over generations of blacks, free and enslaved, and the opportunity to destroy it, once and for all, had kept Charlotte Forten from sinking into the melancholy that plagued Tally Simpson and Wilbur Fisk that winter. Indeed, if there was one person who never questioned the purpose of this war and why it was necessary, it was Forten.

Raised in Quaker Philadelphia in a prominent free-black family, this had never been simply a war for Union for Forten and millions of other Africans and African Americans, both free and enslaved. Forten's family had been struggling for generations against slavery and the prejudice it bred. Her grandfather, born free in 1766, had served as a powder boy on a privateer during the American Revolution. Disgusted by the slavery that remained in a nation founded on freedom, James Forten traveled to England and worked with leading abolitionists before returning to the United States to continue their mission in his native land. He quickly rose to prominence in Philadelphia's free black community, and after a period of apprenticeship to a sail maker, Forten amassed a fortune when he invented and patented a device for handling sails.

While learning his trade and reaping his wealth, Forten never lost sight of the cause of abolition. When the American Colonization Society (ACS) and its plans to "return" free blacks to Africa became increasingly popular among whites, it was Forten who made a powerful case against it and highlighted the plan's hypocrisy. The Society's directors had asked him to be a spokesman for the movement, even offering him the leadership of the colony they planned to found, Liberia. But Forten scoffed at the idea of endorsing a movement that would ensure the enslavement of millions, and he stunned the ACS when he organized a countermovement to warn free blacks and whites against colonization. He reminded his audience that sending him "home" to Africa was impossible. America was his home, just as it was for the growing numbers of free blacks who read Forten's pamphlets and heard his speeches. Calmly but consistently, Forten made his case for racial equality at a time when even many abolitionists did not agree with him.

It's little wonder that his granddaughter, Charlotte Forten, inherited his determination. Raised in an affluent family with every physical comfort she needed, young Charlotte could not help but notice that when the Fortens traveled on trains, they sat in black compartments. They also ate in separate restaurants and attended separate theaters and lectures from whites. By the time she entered her teens, Forten was fluent in French, German, and Latin, and she had a better overall education and was better read than most white women of her age and economic background in Philadelphia and throughout the country. But she was still treated separately, and opportunities were withheld because of the color of her skin.

When the war began, it was, from the start, about much more than Union. And, ironically, as it dragged on and Northern and Southern whites stumbled in their faith in late 1862, Charlotte Forten's purpose was clarified. During that challenging winter, at the age of twenty-five, Forten saw a chance to continue her grandfather's work toward racial equality by becoming a teacher of freedmen in an experimental program on the Sea Islands off the South Carolina coast. The program had two key goals: to demonstrate that former slaves could become educated, self-sufficient, and free members of a democracy and to train former male slaves as soldiers of freedom in the North's changing war for the Union. Forten had already been a teacher for years in New England by this point in her life, but working toward freedmen's education was unlike anything she had ever considered, and her enthusiasm for the Sea Islands project was unsurpassed.

On New Year's Day 1863, as Union and Confederate soldiers sat in depressed reflection, Forten watch the first Dress Parade she had ever seen. As the newly trained men of the First South Carolina Volunteers marched past, she delighted in their success. "It seemed to me," she wrote, "nothing c'ld be more perfect ... [I]t was more than a grand triumph—that black regiment doing itself honor in the sight of the white officers, many of whom, doubtless, 'came to scoff.' It was typical of what the race, so long downtrodden and degraded will yet achieve on this continent." As the day came to a close, Forten struggled to capture in words just how rapidly life was changing. "Ah, what a grand, glorious day this has been

The dawn of freedom which it heralds may not break upon us at once; but it will surely come, and sooner, I believe, than we have ever dared hope before. My soul is glad ..." A new year approached, "a year of such freedom as we have never yet known in this boasted but hitherto wicked land." For Charlotte Forten, the bright future that spread before that Sea Island community cast away all previous doubts and filled her with a zealous optimism that few whites had shared that winter.[115]

"THE SWORD OF DAMOCLES ...
IS SUSPENDED OVER US"

If the moods of Northern whites were improving that spring, and the spirits of Northern blacks were fairly soaring, just the opposite was true for Southern whites in Mississippi and Louisiana. Kate Stone certainly didn't share Forten's optimism, or that of the men in Fighting Joe Hooker's camp. Stone was twenty years old when the Civil War began, the daughter of a wealthy Louisiana widow who owned more than 150 slaves. Had the war not come, Stone's immediate future as a child of one of the state's elite class would have revolved around one party after another, one suitor after another, thinking little about the labor system that provided her family's security and wealth and the looming conflict that would shatter it.

When the war began, Kate Stone complained more about not being able to join the fight than about missed cotillions. She was devoted to the Confederacy, and she despised the trick of fate that made her a woman who had to suffer through "the weary days of watching and waiting that stretch before us! We who stay behind may find it harder than they who go. They will have new scenes and constant excitement to buoy them up ..." Nearly a year later in 1862, Stone was still frustrated, writing from the family plantation in northern Louisiana, just across the Mississippi River from Vicksburg.

But by March 1863, the "new scenes and constant excitement" of war had come to Kate Stone's world and left the region "in a deplorable state." She couldn't decide if she were more scared of the Union troops or of the slaves all around her. "The sword of Damocles in a hundred forms is suspended over us, and there is no escape. The water hems us in. The Negroes on Mrs. Stevens', Mrs. Conley's, Mr. Catlin's, and Mrs. Evans' places ran off to camp and returned with squads of soldiers and wagons and moved off every portable thing—furniture, provisions, etc., etc. A great many of the Negroes camped at Lake Providence have been armed by the officers, and they are a dreadful menace to the few remaining citizens. The country seems possessed by demons, black and white."[116]

The previous December, in 1862, Union General Ulysses S. Grant had launched a two-pronged offensive against Vicksburg, Mississippi. Forces under his command invaded the Magnolia State from northern Tennessee while General William Tecumseh Sherman led another force down the Mississippi River to take Vicksburg. Neither operation succeeded, and Stone, just across the river in Louisiana, had celebrated Grant and Sherman's failures with glee. Southern families cheered when word arrived that Nathan Bedford Forrest and his Confederate cavalry had destroyed the Federal supply lines necessary for Grant's invasion. More celebrations followed when Confederate General Earl Van Dorn destroyed the Federal supply base at Holly Springs on December 20. Sherman faced a similar mess when his invasion force failed to get any closer to Vicksburg than Chickasaw Bayou, where Confederate gunners stopped the invaders and turned them back on December 29. Southern whites in Louisiana and Mississippi, who had witnessed the fall of New Orleans, Baton Rouge, and Corinth with horror that year, delighted in the Federal failures that had brought 1862 to a close.

What they didn't realize—few did at the time—was that there was something different about Ulysses S. Grant. Other commanders might have been deterred, but the numerous failures Grant had suffered in his prewar life had taught him perseverance. It also developed in him a keen ability to learn from his mistakes. During the next several months, Grant attempted to dig canals to get his force around Vicksburg's defenses. He failed. He tried to approach Vicksburg from Yazoo Pass and a number of other waterways around the river fortress. He failed, again.

But by the time Kate Stone was horrified by the "demons" all around her, Grant was proposing a plan for Admiral David Dixon Porter to run his gunboats past the heavy Confederate guns at Vicksburg while Grant led the infantry to the far bank of the Mississippi, where they would then march downstream and cross back over the river on Porter's recently arrived boats, and land south of Vicksburg. This plan might just work.

At least, Grant thought it would. His staff, however, declared the move too risky at best and impossible at worst, and raised the question of how he planned to supply the men once they did cross back into Mississippi. He would fail again, they said. There was no doubt. But Porter liked the plan, and he liked Grant, who was far more intelligent than many Americans recognized at the time. Porter agreed to race past the guns at Vicksburg, transport Grant's forces across the river, and once Grant and Sherman pushed into Mississippi, they would live off the land, obviating the need for the supply lines that proved so vulnerable to Confederate raiders on their previous attempts. As for the other risks, Grant thanked his staff for their opinions and launched the operation.

On April 16, Confederate gunners peered through the darkness and spotted a Union gunboat rounding De Soto Point. Men rushed to their positions, officers barked orders, and it seemed as though all fifty guns overlooking the river opened at once. For 30 miles in every direction, Kate Stone's family and neighbors clutched each other as the cannon roared for four long hours. As dawn approached, there was no sign of the boats as Grant watched from downstream. But then, a smoky, charred but floating barge appeared. Then another steamboat. And then a gunboat, followed by another and another. The Federals had lost only one of Porter's thirteen gunboats, the necessary transports survived their runs as well, and not a single sailor or soldier had died. It was, the Union commanders cheered, a success, though a few dozen miles to the west, Kate Stone declared it just the opposite.[117]

"ANOTHER REPULSE AND ANOTHER HOPELESS RETREAT"

Later that month in Virginia, Fighting Joe Hooker finalized his plans to slip between the rebels and their capital. Lincoln was not entirely convinced it would work, and he was not happy about Hooker's focus on Richmond rather than on the destruction of Lee's army. But Lee refused to cooperate with either of their plans and responded to Hooker's initial move with audacity at the Battle of Chancellorsville. Hooker was quickly outmaneuvered. Before he had a chance to recover the situation for the Federals on the following day, a Confederate shell hit the column he was leaning on, and Hooker collapsed to the ground unconscious. Staff officers rushed to his aid, but for thirty minutes the men looked on in horror as the commander of the Army of the Potomac, the man who, likable or not, had brought the army back to life, lay unresponsive. When he did regain consciousness, he still seemed in a daze.

Years later, rumors circulated that several of Hooker's corps commanders wished he had remained unconscious. Just days earlier they had had so much faith in their bold leader. Hooker sent most of his army across the Rappahannock on April 30, sweeping in behind Lee's position while the Confederate general had much of his army scattered around Virginia gathering food and supplies for the coming campaign. But Lee failed to blink. He didn't even stumble. Instead, he turned the forces he did have, which was only half those available to Hooker, and by the end of the day on May 1, Lee had maneuvered the Federals into a wooded region with thick underbrush that made their superior numbers useless.

That evening, Lee met with his famous corps commander, Major General Thomas J. "Stonewall" Jackson, and the two men devised a plan to divide their forces, violating the classic military maxim to always consolidate one's strengths when faced by a more numerous enemy. But Lee and Jackson gambled, and twenty-four hours later, Jackson was rolling up the Federal right and rear while Hooker watched in stunned silence. Once so aggressive and confident that he had advice for everyone, Hooker now could not settle on a plan. The one he had tried had led to such disaster that he seemed frozen in fear. Perhaps he lacked Grant's experience with failure, or perhaps he was simply overwhelmed. Whatever the cause, Hooker's men were either racing away from Jackson's flank attack or wringing their hands at a lost opportunity. By May 6, 1863, he knew he was defeated and he ordered the army back across the Rappahannock.

Five days later, Wilbur Fisk captured the army's mood for his readers at home in Vermont. The task of telling about the battle, he explained, "would be much more agreeable if it related to a glorious victory instead of another repulse and another hopeless retreat. We really think we ought to have one general victory after so much hard fighting, and so many times driving the enemy, but we will try and not be unreasonable."[118]

Lincoln spent the next several weeks trying to revive Hooker's self-confidence while tempering the man's recovered arrogance. The President felt like he was dealing with McClellan's twin, well versed in complaints and excuses, and the general was just as disgusted with his commander-in-chief, whom Hooker believed failed to understand the complexities of field command. By late June, it was clear that something had to be done. Lee and the Confederates had launched their second invasion of the North, and when Hooker offered his resignation in a moment of frustration, Lincoln jumped at the offer.

The good news was that the Federals were rid of yet another man who seemed incapable of commanding an army. The bad news was that the man who replaced Hooker, Major General George G. Meade, was nearly as unpleasant as his predecessor (though without quite so much arrogance), and he was taking command of an army that was already racing after Confederate forces that had just invaded the Union.

"BOTH SIDES WERE WHIPPED, AND ALL WERE FURIOUS ABOUT IT"

Marching with that Southern army was young Dugat Williams, who was in fine spirits in late June 1863. He and his fellow members of the Texas Brigade crossed the Potomac River at Williamsport on June 26, marched straight through Maryland, and pushed on to the rolling hills of south central Pennsylvania. Encamped at Greencastle that night, Williams worried a little about the Confederates besieged in Vicksburg, Mississippi, knowing the Texas Brigade would be completely cut off from their families at home if the city fell. Still, Williams and his compatriots felt better than they had for months.[119]

British Lieutenant Colonel Arthur J. L. Fremantle, an observer accompanying General Lee's Army, noticed this, too. He overheard two Louisiana officers boasting that the army had never been "so well equipped, so well clothed, so eager for a fight, or so confident of success."[120] Confederate General John Bell Hood's division, Fremantle mused, showed similar bravado. There was something different about this outfit, which included Hood's old command, the Texas Brigade. They were, Fremantle claimed, "a queer lot to look at. They carry less than any other troops; many of them have only got an old piece of carpet or rug as baggage; many have discarded their shoes in the mud; all are ragged and dirty, but full of good-humour and confidence in themselves and in their general, Hood."

Marching with that queer lot was Sergeant Major Mark Smither, who wrestled with his unfamiliar role of invader. "I wish I could describe to you my feelings," he told his mother. "At first it was a feeling of exultation and then looking on every side of me as far as the eye could reach and seeing nothing but unfriendly looks from the whitehaired sirs down to the child. I confess it made me feel very badly." Smither was fascinated to find that the Texans' and Arkansans' reputation had preceded them, noting "we passed a crowd of people who enquired of me what troops were passing and on receiving the answer of 'Texas Brigade' one turned around to the rest and remarked 'they are the ones that have killed so many of our soldiers'!"[121]

Smither and his compatriots followed their own sense of morality when it came to looting, and years later, the Texans and Arkansans told nearly every story of the invasion of Pennsylvania with a wink. Their favorite was of General Lee, smiling at his rebellious Lone Star sons as they marched along, well fed and happy, commenting, "General Hood, when your Texans come about, the chickens have to roost mighty high!"

Alcohol may have been at the root of some of their antics. Years later, Val Giles of the 4th Texas laughed over the effect of the whiskey issued to every man when the Confederates crossed the Potomac. "It was chain lightning," he recalled, and it knocked out many a valiant soldier, especially those who happily accepted the rations of their abstaining friends. As Giles recalled, "We ate breakfast in the State of Virginia, dinner in the State of Maryland, supper in the State of Pennsylvania, and slept in the State of Intoxication—four states in twenty-four hours."[122] The melancholy that had pervaded the men that winter had disappeared with the army's overwhelming victory at Chancellorsville and the renewed faith that maybe, just maybe, this would be the last year of the war.

With their bellies full and confidence high, the Texans and Arkansans made camp on June 30 at Greenwood, Pennsylvania, on the Chambersburg Pike, about 16 miles west of Gettysburg. James Hendrick of the 1st Texas spoke for the entire brigade when he promised his parents that "this is not like the Maryland trip. We are in the North and are going to stay in the North until this war is ended."[123]

On July 1, Confederate General James Longstreet ordered his First Corps, which included John Bell Hood's Division and the Texas Brigade, to the quiet Pennsylvania town of Gettysburg. Hood's Division spent most of that day, however, waiting for the remnants of General Richard Stoddert Ewell's Second Corps to proceed down the road in front of them. A line of march, after all, had to form and follow as ordered, or the wrong divisions would show up in the wrong places at the wrong times. Frustrated by the laws of war, Hood's boys finally fell into line behind Lafayette McLaws's division around 5:00 p.m. and marched down Chambersburg Pike. It was a terrible 12- to 13-mile march of starts and stops, not necessarily fast, but without any rest. At 1:00 a.m., Hood's division reached the fields on the western bank of Marsh Creek where McLaws's men had collapsed an hour earlier on its eastern bank. Hood's boys joined them, sleeping with their weapons, about 3.5 miles from Lee's headquarters on Seminary Ridge.[124]

Hood's division had only two hours rest before they were on the march again. They drank from Marsh Creek and made their way over rolling hills to the western edge of Herr Ridge. They arrived there around 8:00 a.m., stacked arms, and rested in the fields where McLaws's division joined them about an hour later. The 14,500 men had several hours to sleep, write letters, and try to relax despite the clear signs of the nearby battle. For Private A. C. Sims, however, it was hard to rest with "the bloody shirts, the men who had been wounded in the previous day's battle" walking past him, likely to the nearby Confederate field hospital.

Sims had joined the Texas Brigade just a few months earlier in April. His twin brother, Albert Hubert Sims, had volunteered for Confederate service in the 13th Texas Infantry Regiment the previous fall, even though both boys were underage at the time. A. C. had begged his brother to "wait until spring," promising that "I would go with him anywhere he might wish, but he would not consent." A. C. believed that if his brother entered the camps that winter, he would die of disease before he could be of any service to their country. Tragically, he was right. And so, in the spring of 1863, A. C. "was so crazed with grief for him who had ben my constant associate from infancy that I resolved to go to that then seeming far off land Virginia to fight the battle of my Country."

By July, Sims's journey to Virginia had taken him to the gentle hills of Pennsylvania, which now rumbled with cannon and musket fire. Most of the Texans and Arkansans around him were veterans of several bloody fights, and the young Sims observed with concern the "bloody shirts" walking through their lines. "What effect they had on the old soldiers, I know not," Sims recalled, "but to me, who had never seen the like, it was no pleasing sight to behold." [125]

At approximately 11:00 a.m., Lee, growing frustrated with Longstreet's delays, ordered the general to shift McLaws's and Hood's divisions into position for their attack on the Federal's left. Longstreet, unhappy with orders that did not seem prudent, asked for one further delay. He wanted to have Hood's division at full strength when it went into the fight. Lee agreed that they could wait for Evander Law's Alabama brigade, which was rushing in from New Guilford as the generals spoke. When Law arrived at noon, Longstreet ordered Hood and McLaws to their positions astride the Emmitsburg Road.

This was easier said than done. Part of the problem was tied to the fact that General Lee ordered Longstreet to be sure to conceal their movements and Lee gave direction of the march to Captain S. R. Johnston, who had, at least in theory, reconnoitered the march route that morning and declared it clear. It remains unknown if Johnston did a poor job scouting the area or if he was confused about which sections of the Union line he actually saw. What is known, though, is that there were Federals on the Round Tops on the far left of the Union line.

For his part, Johnston insisted that he did not know that he was to lead the entire force to their position opposite the Union left. As one Gettysburg historian remarked, what followed was a comedy of errors one would hardly expect from Lee's "War Horse" and veteran troops. It was shortly after noon when Longstreet ordered his two divisions southward from their resting spot on the western slope of Herr Ridge. Staying close to tributaries of Marsh Creek, they marched through low rolling fields to Black Horse Tavern Road, and then, at the intersection of Black Horse Tavern and Fairfield Roads, McLaws's division continued southward for another quarter mile until they reached a rise. It was here that Johnston, McLaws, and Longstreet worried they would reveal their position to Union signal stations. Hood's division likely came to a halt on the Black Horse Tavern Road well before the Fairfield Road intersection.

Longstreet, McLaws, and Johnston decided to reverse their route. They could have ordered a simple about-face of the entire command, but this would have placed Hood's division at the lead of the force, and Lee had ordered McLaws's to lead the attack. Instead, Hood's men waited, likely with the green troops frustrated while the veterans, more accustomed to military inefficiency, simply rested, until McLaws's division worked its way back to Black Horse Tavern. Both units then used farm lanes as they traveled eastward to the protection of Herr Ridge.

Once over the ridge, Hood's division marched southward in the protected valley of Willoughby Run. As they reached Pitzer School House, Sims, Smither, Williams, and their fellow Texans paused as McLaws's men, ahead of Hood's division, stopped with shock, discovering that there was no way they could follow Lee's original order to attack up Emmittsburg Road.

Dan Sickles, Mary Todd Lincoln's old Blue Room friend, commanded the Union 3rd Corps. Without permission, he decided to deploy his men in an advance position along the Emmitsburg Road angling back from the soon-to-be famous Peach Orchard, through the equally famous Wheat Field and ending in an ugly cluster of rocks called Devil's Den in front of Little Round Top. The situation differed greatly from that which existed when Lee first gave his orders, leading to further delays as Longstreet revised the plan of attack and ordered

Hood's division to extend McLaws's line to the south. Hood's men were now in position to strike the unsuspecting and, they hoped, undermanned Union forces at Devil's Den and Little Round Top.

That was how the men of John Bell Hood's Division found themselves standing on the western slope of Warfield Ridge in the hot, late-afternoon sun on July 2, 1863. In the Texas Brigade ranks, Colonel Van Manning's 3rd Arkansas, fondly known as the 3rd Texas by the rest of the unit, rested on the far left of their position about 200 yards west of the Emmitsburg Road. To their right, the 1st Texas shifted into line by the right flank on the crest of Warfield Ridge, where, as Texan Thomas McCarty remembered fondly more than thirty years later, they welcomed the protection the trees and rolling ground provided from Federal artillery fire.

The ground before them was littered with boulders, stone walls, and fence rails that rose to high, rocky hills swarming with Federal troops. Hood's men loved him for his boldness, but he was not a fool. He knew impossible ground when he saw it. Hood made several requests to approach the position from a different direction and took the time to send some Texans to find an alternate route, which involved swinging around Round Top and using the country lane his men had found. But Longstreet had tried alternatives with Lee, though not as well reconnoitered as what Hood proposed. Regardless, the Georgian denied Hood's request, explaining that "General Lee's orders are to attack up the Emmitsburg Road." When Hood challenged him once more, Longstreet cut Hood off: "We must obey the orders of General Lee." Frustrated, Hood returned to his command.

As Hood's old brigade waited along with the rest of his division, each man went through his quiet ritual to prepare for what would come. Some prayed, while others teased their favorite targets in the ranks to break the tension. To the Texans' right were Evander Law's exhausted, parched Alabamians, a number of whom had sent men to refill the units' canteens. They were still waiting for these when Hood rode up to order them forward.

It was around 4:00 p.m., and as Hood stopped before the 4th Texas, his old regiment, cheers rolled up and down the line. With a yell to advance, Hood led Dugat Williams, Mark Smither, A. C. Sims, and the rest of Hood's old brigade out through the tree line.

They had some support from Captain James Reilly's battery at the center of the brigade and from the rest of the Confederate First Corps guns under E. Porter Alexander, most of which were focused on the Federal 3rd Corps artillery in the Peach Orchard. Colonel Van Manning rushed his Arkansans forward as quickly as he dared, trying to get them across the open ground. As they were crossing the Emmittsburg Road, he realized that there was no way he could keep his left anchored there and keep his right tied to the 1st Texas, as he'd been ordered to do. Plus, they could not push up that road, rolling up the Federal line as Lee had originally intended. To do so would leave the Confederates' right flank completely exposed to the Federals swarming around the Round Tops. So Manning decided to untie, so to speak, from the road and keep his right flank connected with the rest of the brigade and focus the unit's full attention on removing the Union troops from the Round Tops; then they could focus on rolling up the rest of the Federal Line.

The trouble, though, was that the entire Confederate advance was breaking apart. The 3rd Arkansas and 1st Texas—receiving the majority of the fire from Federal artillery in the Peach Orchard as well as fire from the sharpshooters in front of them and more Union guns atop Devil's Den—were rushing for the cover of Rose's Woods in front of them. They rapidly outpaced the 4th and 5th Texas to their right, whose men had been pushed further away by a large knoll that helped to divide the brigade. For the rest of the day the Texas Brigade would fight as two units, the 3rd Arkansas and 1st Texas, focusing on Federal forces at Devil's Den, and the 4th and 5th Texas, linked with Law's Alabamians attacking Little Round Top.

On the brigade's left, the 3rd Arkansas and 1st Texas suffered casualties from Federal artillery fire as soon as they cleared the crest of Warfield Ridge and crossed the Emmittsburg Road. For the next 800 to 1,000 yards, Texan Thomas McCarty recalled a man going down "at every report" of the cannon, not to mention the impact of the Federal sharpshooters posted behind a stonewall at the edge of Rose's Woods. Manning and the Arkansans managed to push the riflemen back about

150 yards when they started receiving fire from Ward's Brigade on their left and rear.

Union General John Henry Hobart Ward had ordered his men—which included the 99th Pennsylvania, the 86th New York, the 124th New York, the 4th Maine, the 20th Indiana, and the 2nd U.S. Sharpshooters—"not to fire until they could plainly see the enemy."[126] Their late but effective volley tore through Manning's men. He tried ordering Company A to change their front to the rear "but the noise consequent upon the heavy firing then going on swallowed up my command." This fire likely came from the 20th Indiana and the 86th New York, which Ward had ordered forward to a slight rise and in advance of the 124th New York, which held the far left of the brigade. Manning decided to pull the entire left wing, which put sufficient pressure on Ward's men to drive them back and allow the 3rd Arkansas and 1st Texas to continue their progress, though the New Yorkers, Pennsylvanians, and Indianans continued to threaten their flanks.

While the Arkansans continued their advance through the woods, Union Colonel Regis de Trobriand ordered the 17th Maine forward to support Ward's defense. The Maine men marched to the edge of the woods and stopped along a stone wall, placing themselves directly on the 3rd Arkansas's flank. A Maine soldier, Frank Whittemore, heard "their fearful yell through the woods" as he and his regiment lay down behind the wall. Their colonel ordered some of his men forward as sharpshooters, who became part of the intermittent but consistent and troubling pressure on Manning's left. With help from Colonel Work and the 1st Texas, as well as some assistance from Colonel F. H. Little's 11th Georgia, which arrived in support on the Arkansans' left, the Confederates managed, "again [with] that furious yell to drive the Federals back to the stone wall." Whittemore and the 17th Maine waited until the sharpshooters cleared their line and the Confederates came within close range. The "we opened upon them so furiously that they began to skedaddle again but were finally rallied and turning round began to pour in to us a terrible fire."

The fight in Rose's Woods continued like this, back and forth, with the Confederates slowly but steadily pushing up the slope toward Devil's Den.

One of the most famous scenes of the fight included Private Wilson Barbee of the 1st Texas. He was a courier on General Hood's staff, but after Hood was wounded and carried away, Barbee lacked clear orders, so he rode his horse down the slope, joining the rest of the 1st Texas. When his horse was shot from under him, Barbee continued on foot, picking up a dropped musket and cartridge box. As several men later related, Barbee positioned himself on a large boulder, firing shot after shot at Ward's men until he was wounded in the right leg. He fell from the boulder, climbed back up, and began shooting again. Within two minutes, he was hit in the other leg and again knocked from the boulder, but he crawled up once more, laying prone on the rock, before being hit again, falling to the ground on his back, and crying for and cursing the men around him for failing to help him back up.

Despite a desperate charge down the hillside into the Texans, with bayonets fixed, Ward's men could not stop the Confederate assault. The men of the 1st Texas launched a counterattack and, with the help of the 20th Georgia and the 15th Georgia, who were sent in behind the Texans, they reached the high ground atop Devil's Den. The exhausted Confederates raced to seize the Federal guns, spun them around, and made ready to fire on any Federals who had moved into position behind them. The problem for the Texans, though, was that there was no ammunition left. Securing the ground and capturing prisoners, the Texans and the Georgians managed to hold Devil's Den and sleep there most of that night.

Meanwhile, the 4th and 5th Texas had continued their advance, which took them along the western slope of Big Round Top and up the southern and western side of Little Round Top. They were linked with Evander Law's Alabama Brigade, climbing through woods, over and around boulders in a nightmarish fight. Zack Landrum of Company H, 4th Texas called the ground a "Mountain," not "Little Round Top," and declared it covered with "rocks as large as a meeting house .... I had gone a considerable distance up the Mountain when one of the rascals put me to a stand still by means of a minnie ball through the thigh." The round cut through Landrum's left thigh, exited his leg, and continued, smacking his right thigh, but it lacked enough momentum to do more than severely bruise the leg.[127]

J. D. Cadell was fighting near Landrum and managed to get close to the Federal defenders before he, too, was hit in the leg and fell among the rocks. Opposite them was a Yankee named John Berry fighting in the Sixteenth Michigan. He and his fellow soldiers had barely gotten to their position on the crest of the hill when the Texans came at them, rushing again and again at their line. Just to his left was William Brown, one of the defenders in the 44th New York. Like Berry, Brown noted that they scurried into position and almost immediately "saw a line of Rebels advancing ... [I]n a few moments the battle raged fearfully." Again and again the Texans and Alabamians advanced up the hill, fell back, and then advanced again. But they could not break the Federal defenses.

Val Giles of the 4th Texas summarized best the brutal fighting on the Round Tops that day:

> There seemed to be a viciousness in the very air we breathed. Things had gone wrong all the day, and now pandemonium came with the darkness. Alexander Dumas says the devil gets in a man seven times a day ... At Gettysburg that night, it was about seven devils to each man. Officers were cross to the men, and the men were equally cross to the officers. It was the same way with our enemies. We could hear the Yankee officer on the crest of the ridge in front of us cursing the men by platoons, and the men telling him to go to a country not very far away from us just at that time. If that old Satanic dragon has ever been on earth since he offered our Saviour the world if He would serve him, he was certainly at Gettysburg that night ... White-winged peace didn't roost at Little Round Top that night! There was not a man there that cared a snap for the golden rule, or that could have remembered one line of the Lord's Prayer. Both sides were whipped, and all were furious about it.[128]

In the days that followed, the Texas Brigade tallied their losses with astonishment: 84 killed, 393 wounded, and 120 missing. A total of nearly 600 casualties in a fight they started with 1,100 men; 54.3 percent losses. Perhaps even more astonishing was the impact on the brigade's commanders. In addition to division commander Hood, who fell from his horse, in full view of most of the troops, with a devastating wound to his arm at the start of the advance, also wounded were brigade commander General Robertson, Colonel Van Manning (commander of 3rd Arkansas), J. C. G. Key (commander, 4th Texas), and R. M. Powell (commander, 5th Texas), as well as Lieutenant Colonel King Bryan (a huge favorite of the 5th Texas), and B. F. Carter (a favorite of the 4th Texas, mortally wounded).

"THIS MURDEROUS STORM"

For nearly a century, historians would argue that this bloody battle marked the turning point of the Civil War, the high-water mark of the Confederacy. American families, North and South, had some suspicions of the battle's greater meaning during the summer of 1863, but many could only fathom its immediate meaning to them. Women grasped for word from the front about their husbands and their sons. Reports came in newspapers almost every day in the weeks immediately following the battle, but women knew by now that the casualty lists were often filled with errors. And so they waited for a letter to make it past the Union lines or to come home with a wounded soldier. Or, in the case of Philinda Humiston, they waited for the news to come in the form of a story picked up by dozens of newspapers from Maryland to Maine.

Her husband, Amos Humiston, had not been one of the enthusiastic volunteers of 1861. At thirty-one, he was older than most privates, and the outside world held no temptation. Three years on a whaler in the early 1850s had inspired in Amos Humiston a deep appreciation for the sleepy towns of western New York. But when President Lincoln called for 300,000 volunteers in the summer of 1862, Humiston felt the pressure to respond. After securing the promise from the townspeople of Portville, New York, that they would care for his wife and three children if anything happened to him, he joined the 154th New York in late September. By the following summer, Humiston was a veteran of Burnside's debacle at Fredericksburg and his infamous "Mud March," and despite being in the thick of fighting at Chancellorsville, where the 154th New York suffered 40 percent casualties, Humiston somehow managed to survive.

Just days after that battle, a package arrived from his wife, Philinda, and Amos found enclosed a glass-plate photograph of their three children. The homesick soldier quickly wrote a response, telling Philinda that her gift "pleased me more than eney thing that you could have sent to me … How I want to se them and their mother is more than I can tell I hope that we may all live to see each other again if this war dose not last to long."[129] Weeks later, Humiston and the rest of the 154th New York marched into Pennsylvania as they chased after Dugat Williams, Mark Smither, and the rest of Lee's Army of Northern Virginia.

On the first of July, Humiston's unit was rushed into the early fighting on the northeast side of Gettysburg, and when Confederates surrounded the New Yorkers, nearly all of the men were captured. Only a handful, including Sergeant Humiston, managed to slip past the rebels, but they were spotted. Confederates chased after them, firing, and Humiston fell to the ground with a mortal wound. He managed to prop himself against a building, or perhaps a soldier helped him, and as Humiston's body grew weaker, he clutched the image of his three children in his hands.

In those overwhelming days following the battle of Gettysburg, the townspeople became numb to the tens of thousands of dead men and horses the armies had left in their wake. But one account stood out. A tale began to spread about how Benjamin Schriver's daughter had found the body of an unidentified Union soldier holding a photograph of three children. The story became a favorite in Schriver's tavern and quickly spread beyond their little town. A Philadelphia doctor, John Francis Bourns, moved by the tragic story of a dying Union soldier who determinedly shared his final moments with his children, started a newspaper campaign with a description of the "Orphans of Gettysburg."

Headlines asked "Whose Father Was He?" and offered detailed descriptions of the photograph that could not be reproduced with the newspaper technology of the day. The story was hauntingly familiar in nearly every town in the country, but it was not until the first week of November that a reader of the *American Presbyterian* shared his copy of the paper with a friend in Portville. As the issue made its way through the town, it eventually reached Philinda Humiston, who had not heard from her husband in three months and feared the worst. She asked the town's postmaster to write to Dr. Bourns, who promised readers that he would send them a *carte de visite* copy of the ambrotype if they believed they might know the identity of the children and their father. When the image arrived, the thirty-two-year-old mother realized that she was a widow and her three children, Franklin, Alice, and Frederick, ages eight, six, and four, were fatherless.

In the months that followed, Northerners continued to discuss the story, and by the end of the war, they had founded a home in Gettysburg for the children who lost their fathers in what was to remain the largest battle of the war. Philinda Humiston accepted the position as head mistress of the orphanage (the Federal government used the term "orphan" for children whose father was killed in the war, regardless of whether their mother survived). Her three children joined her there, but it never felt like home. Perhaps the beautiful town held too much sadness for them. Or maybe the family despised the spotlight of tragedy the nation kept on them. As the years passed, they all left Pennsylvania and, like the veterans who had seen too much, never spoke of their fame as the "Orphans of Gettysburg."

Thousands of miles to the South, another family also awaited news from Pennsylvania during the summer of 1863. Felicia Loughridge was trying to run a farm with the help of her brother-in-law, raise two daughters, manage the few slaves her husband owned, and somehow make decisions about selling stock and planting grain. She was hardly alone, though. In fact, she was actually one of the lucky wives who had had her husband home all winter, recovering from a wound he received while fighting at the Battle of Gaines's Mill. By May 1863, however, James Loughridge had returned to the Texas Brigade, and in a letter the following month, he expressed outrage at how Federal forces were mistreating Southern women and children. He prayed that God would arm the Confederacy with "superhuman strength to strike these witches from the earth." Since that letter, Felicia had heard nothing but rumors in the papers she knew not to trust, and as the weeks passed, she began to fear the worse.

And then came his letter. Dated July 26, Loughridge struggled to put the battle into words. He had ended the second day's fighting at

Gettysburg as commander in the 4th Texas Infantry because they lost so many officers, all for ground they gave up a day later. "Tis true we drove the enemy from a part of the high mountains that he occupied and retained the same for as long as we wished yet we finally had to fall back leaving the Yankees to take possession of our ground ..." The rage that he expressed in June had shifted into a dark depression. "How terrible is this war upon the people of our land," J. R. Loughridge confided to his wife. "[H]ad a Prophet arose 4 years ago & told of these horrors" to "the people North & South ... that in a short time they would butcher each other up in cold blood no one would have believed him." He could only pray that, "God Almighty, the God of Hosts the mighty God of Battle is at the helm. & at the proper time will speak peace to this murderous storm that now makes all eyes sick with horror!"[130]

Loughridge was hardly alone with his horror that summer. William Nugent dashed off letter after letter to his young wife in Union-held Washington County, Mississippi, encouraging her to survive the "depredation of the Yankees" as best she could. As word arrived in the 28th Mississippi's camp of Lee's invasion of Pennsylvania, Nugent insisted on believing and repeating every fantastic, hopeful rumor. He reported that the men had learned that Lee was

> driving everything before him and making every Dutchman, woman & child take the oath of allegiance to the Southern Confederacy. This is done, I suppose, for the purpose of exchanging them for our Southern men who have been forced to take the Lincoln oath, and is a very felicitous idea. Our Virginia Army is now feasting on crackers and cheese, coffee, bacon & everything else that heart could wish. This dash will open old Abe's eyes. He has left Washington and is removing the public records and archives. He will doubtless leave Washington to its fate and establish the capital at New York or Chicago....

Meanwhile, Nugent reported, Confederate General Braxton Bragg was on the verge of bringing Kentucky into the Confederacy. "I have greater hopes than ever," Nugent promised his wife, "of an early termination to this war and think I will be at home again before January for good."

Just over a week later, though, he wrote from Deer Creek, Mississippi, on July 8, 1863. Distraught over the Union victories at Vicksburg and Gettysburg, Nugent admitted that "One thing is sure the River must be surrendered to the Yankees and our country now belongs to them by right of conquest." Nellie's grief would have matched her husband's as she struggled to find a way to survive an increasingly dark future, a challenge made all the more difficult by the burdens of the last trimester of her pregnancy. Sensing this, Nugent quickly gathered himself and his mood. "When you can remove with safety to yourself you had all better go to Texas," he advised. "The war will soon be terminated one way or another this year, and we will either be defeated absolutely or some compromise made that will restore the old Union as it was. In any event wherever you go, if advised, I shall follow you & your & my fortunes shall be identical."[131]

William Nugent's letter, written four days after the fall of Vicksburg, showed the astonishing challenges that American families, North and South, faced that summer. For Northerners, the dual victories in Pennsylvania and Mississippi were tremendous morale boosters that would help sustain them in the long months to come. For Southerners, the melancholy winter of 1862–63 had hardened them for the long war they had not expected, and the chaos that ensued in Mississippi in 1863 tested them beyond anything they could have imagined.

Part of this was tied to the fact that enslaved families from across the western portion of the state were racing towards Grant's army as fast as they could. The first Union advances in 1862 had brought many slaves to Union lines, even before their freedom could be protected by the Emancipation Proclamation. White Southerners near the plantations of Joseph Davis, the Confederate president's brother, marveled that even the enslaved men and women of Davis Bend were among those who had left. Davis was known throughout the area for the "community of cooperation" he had supported on his lands, where those bonded to Davis managed daily discipline largely by themselves in slave courts, had access to his library, and benefited from living and health standards that exceeded those available to most poor white Mississippians of the day.[132]

By the summer of 1863, however, most of Davis's holdings had been destroyed and the countryside around Jackson and Vicksburg endured a similar fate. In nearby Madison County, Helen Johnstone and her widowed mother, Margaret, watched and waited for the worst. They tried to occupy themselves with reading and other distractions, but nothing could shut out the nearby "booming of the cannon," Helen complained. The Johnstone women had armed a Confederate company that took the name "The Helen Johnstone Guards" in the young belle's honor in the hopeful spring of 1861. Now she sat in their magnificent home, Annandale, with few men nearby to defend it, and could only listen with frustration and worry as the smell of destruction filled the air. In the weeks that followed, they discovered that Union forces had, indeed, devastated much of the surrounding area, including the city of Canton, where locomotives and rail cars lay in charred heaps near the burned-out skeletons of dozens of machine shops, railroad buildings, and warehouses, none of which could now support the Confederacy. Union forces had, as Colonel Cyrus Bussey reported proudly, destroyed "every dollar's worth of public property" they found in Canton, just as they had in many of the towns around Jackson and Vicksburg.[133]

Most of the Confederates in the area demonstrated an amazing ability to adapt. In the coming months in Mississippi, women like Amanda Cage, who barely reclaimed her stolen milk cow after its first kidnapping, boasted that she learned to keep the valuable bovine inside her home when Union troops came through the area. Similarly, I. N. Holliday saved her carriage by removing a wheel and rolling it into her pond. She smiled quietly to herself as Northern forces, as well as the Northern and Southern plunderers who followed in their wake, all passed by her "useless" buggy for more tempting items.

Such determination surfaced throughout the South that summer of 1863. It wasn't that people weren't troubled by their losses, but they could see no alternative but to continue their struggle for independence. And just as Mississippians on the home front adapted to their losses, J. R. Loughridge also recovered from the defeat at Gettysburg. Three weeks after grappling with the horrifying losses endured in Pennsylvania, he, too, had recovered his optimism. On August 30, 1863, Loughridge, now a captain, boasted to his wife that he had commanded Company I, 4th Texas Infantry in the fight, leading the men "through a shower of bullets & canister & grape shot." He told Felicia that she might have heard that the Confederates lost the battle of Gettysburg (indeed, he himself had told her that just weeks earlier), but the truth was quite different. "[I]t has gone forth to the world that Lee was defeated, [but] such I think was not the case, as we took twice as many prisoners as they did and also according to their own statement killed & wounded many thousands more of their men than they did of ours."

And so it was that the armies refused to quit that summer; that Northerners and Southerners refused to admit that either side had settled anything. There were two great battles left of the campaign season in Chickamauga, Georgia, and a few miles and a few months away at nearby Chattanooga, Tennessee. The fighting proved equally deadly there, but the year seemed to be leaning toward the Union. Federals emerged victorious in each battle, and it was at Chickamauga that a native-born Virginian named George Thomas, whose sisters had turned their "traitor brother's" portrait in their family home to face the wall, saved the Union line and the battle. In November, Federal soldiers continued their months of success at Chattanooga, placing their forces in superb position for the next season of war.

After the fighting, both sides settled into camp to lick their wounds. Loughridge was a hero of the Texans' determined assault at Chickamauga, and one report referred to him as the "Marshal Ney" of the battle, comparing Loughridge to one of Napoleon Bonaparte's greatest commanders. But when word arrived that winter that Loughridge's friends and neighbors had elected him to the state legislature, the lawyer turned soldier resigned his commission and went home. He had done his duty in uniform, and he would continue it in Austin.

In a Vermont regiment far to the North, Wilbur Fisk marveled at his ability to survive the destruction of 1863 and pledged his determination to see the war to its bitter end, with the Union restored and slavery destroyed. Charlotte Forten echoed Fisk's determination while she continued to teach on the Sea Islands off South Carolina, understanding in a way that Fisk never could just how important their mission was.

And not far from Forten, Tally Simpson's family gathered to read a letter from their friend and pastor, who served with Simpson in Kershaw's Brigade, which had fought so desperately against the men George Thomas, the "Rock of Chickamauga," had gathered to defend a rise called Snodgrass Hill.

"My dear brother Simpson," began the letter, "It is my mournful duty to communicate to you" the death of "your son and my dear friend." A Minié ball had torn through his chest while another round or perhaps solid shot broke his left arm. Either grape shot or canister, Reverend Carlisle was not sure, had finally crushed his skull, though by that point, the minister assured them, or perhaps himself, Simpson was already dead. "He was doing his duty and met his fate as a brave soldier," Carlisle comforted them, adding that Simpson, "fell with his face to the foe." Corporal Taliaferro N. Simpson—the boisterous, brave college boy of Spartansburg, South Carolina, so different from his quiet, bookish brother, the same Tally who had written dozens of letters home for the last two years, often cheerful, sometime delightful, and increasingly reflective—was gone.[134] Another season of war had come to a close, and the end of the conflict might be approaching, but no one dared count on that anymore. Peace could still be quite far off.

$$\approx 4 \ll$$

THE WAR'S DARKEST HOUR

In typical style, Ulysses S. Grant arrived in Washington in the spring of 1864 with no one there to greet him. He was in town to meet with President Lincoln, who was about to promote him to lieutenant general, a rank previously held only by George Washington. The White House planned to have a committee to meet Grant at the station, but that fell through, and when he stepped onto the platform along with his thirteen-year-old son, Fred, the quiet commander probably let out a sigh of relief that he would be able to avoid another speech demanded by another crowd of supporters.[135]

They made their way to the Willard Hotel, where Grant almost managed to remain incognito until the desk clerk read "Ulysses S. Grant and son, Galena, Illinois," on the registry. He cast aside the only room that he had claimed was available for the man in the crumpled linen duster and rushed to relieve Grant of his bag, taking him to the suite that Lincoln had occupied just before his inauguration. Word spread quickly of their arrival, and when the Grants came downstairs for a bite of supper, they could barely start their meal before the dining room's self-designated leader jumped up to lead the room in "three cheers for Lieutenant General Grant." Fred watched as his father stood awkwardly, fumbled with his napkin, and nodded his thanks. Despite Grant's best efforts to return to his meal, the stares and expectant grins from his fellow diners became unbearably awkward and the quiet commander from the West was forced to return to his room.

If Grant thought he had escaped the limelight, he was mistaken. His victories in Tennessee and Mississippi during the previous two years had cemented his fame. He had given Northerners hope when they seemed to face one failure after another in the East. Even George Meade's Union victory at Gettysburg the previous summer dimmed when he let Lee's army escape to Virginia to lick its wounds. In contrast, Westerners boasted, when Grant's forces finally defeated the Confederates at Vicksburg, they captured General John Pemberton's 30,000 officers and men, as well as all of their cannon and nearly 60,000 rifles and muskets. This was a man, Northerners proclaimed, who knew how to finish the job.

As Fred Grant followed his father back to their suite that evening, he must have marveled at how quickly their lives, like their sleeping quarters, had changed. Just a year earlier, Fred had joined General Grant in camp, resting his head on saddles or cane cots that sympathetic soldiers, likely missing their own sons, made for him. While the war was separating nearly every family, North and South, the Grants responded with an unusually determined approach to remain together. They weren't the first family to join a husband in camp during the winter, nor was Grant the first officer to have a son serving on his staff. But very few generals had a twelve-year-old boy tagging along in 1863.

It wasn't just the general who wanted Fred in camp; the boy's mother understood the necessity of surrounding her husband with family. Grant was a good man with a strong work ethic. He was also a homebody who was never entirely at peace unless he was surrounded by the wife he adored and the children he spoiled. The determined commander who brought Mississippi to its knees had a soft heart and a far more reflective soul than many of his contemporaries realized.

Ulysses S. Grant's father, Jesse, had sought to avoid his own father's reputation for drink and sloth, and Jesse was largely successful. His pride and joy was his son, Ulysses, who was raised to surpass all of his father's achievements. Where Jesse was largely self-educated, Ulysses was sent to day schools despite their fees and the time they took from work. When he was home, Ulysses kept up with his father's demanding pace, though he despised formal education and preferred the freedom of work on the farm.

Despite Jesse's faith in him, their small Georgetown, Ohio, community saw little promise in the boy. Some wondered if "Lyss" was a bit slow, while his classmates demonstrated the timeless gift for unwanted nicknames and christened him "Useless." Neighbors loved to share the story of Grant failing to negotiate with a neighbor when purchasing a horse for his father. They always grinned at the right part of the tale, waiting for the punch line where young Ulysses blurted out the maximum price he could offer before the negotiations had even begun. Years later, Grant enjoyed telling the story, too. By adulthood, though, it had become an example of his ability to outsmart people, for the horse, with Grant's natural abilities as a trainer, was eventually worth far more than his father had paid.

As a young man, Grant smarted under his image as too slow to keep up with the rapid pace and raw wit of antebellum America. In the years leading to the Civil War, Grant was still struggling to keep up. He survived his education at West Point, though he had never wanted to go and only succeeded there to avoid disappointing Jesse. Similarly, Ulysses served in the Mexican War because he felt it his duty to go where ordered, despite his opposition to what he saw as an indefensible expansion of territory and slavery. By the 1850s, Grant had married Julia Dent, the sister of his West Point roommate. Stationed at forts too far from home, and desperately missing his wife and children, Grant could barely function in his misery. "You don't know," he confided to Julia, "how forsaken I feel here."

For years, Julia moved from one fort to another with Grant, sensing from the start that her husband needed her nearby. And it was true. The moment Julia traveled home to give birth or whenever she remained with her family in St. Louis when Grant's orders took him to forts too remote for her to safely join him, Ulys, as Julia came to call him, would slowly unravel. By 1852, he admitted to Julia that he was "almost crazy sometimes to see Fred," his young son, and declared, "I cannot be separated from him and his Ma for a long time." Rumors surfaced that Grant was drinking excessively, and then a brutally unfair and malicious commanding officer charged Grant with being drunk on duty. Rather than take the time to clear his name, Grant grasped at the fastest exit from the army and resigned in disgust.

It's never been proven that he actually drank to excess, and Grant was hardly the only American man consuming alcohol in the nineteenth-century. The accounts of abuse, modern biographers theorize, were likely tied to Grant's tendency to appear intoxicated after just a few drinks. It's far more likely that stories of his occasional drinks, consumed to self-medicate against debilitating migraines or loneliness, resulted in public intoxication and embarrassment. It was these moments, during which he failed to handle his liquor as a nineteenth-century man was expected to, that his enemies pounced upon him with such success that the stories have now become legendary. History will never truly know the details of Grant's battle with the bottle, but it is clear that he and Julia understood his inability to either handle or process alcohol, and, consequently, they strictly limited its consumption. They also made sure that Grant always had with him the one thing he needed to succeed: his family.

That was how twelve-year-old Fred Grant wound up on the banks of the Mississippi River in the spring of 1863 and in the dining room of the Willard Hotel the following year. When the war began, Ulysses had told his wife that he needed her to "be cheerful and try to encourage me," insisting that this was key to his success. That same year, he complained about a hasty letter she had mailed to him in camp, noting "this is my forty second birth day. Getting old am I not?—I received a very short letter from you this evening scratched off in a very great hurry as if you had something much more pleasing if not more important to do than to write to me." Clearly, his melancholy was setting in, and Julia struggled to find ways for her and the children to be with him. When she realized that visits would not suffice, that a member of the family needed to be his ever-present rock, she sent their oldest son, Fred, to join Ulysses as he trained his Illinois volunteers in 1861. As she explained years later, especially to those who raised a brow at sending such a young boy to camp, "I think it was a tender thought for my beloved husband that prompted" the idea to send her son, "as well as a desire to gratify the importunings and pleadings [of] our boy Fred."

Grant seems to have enjoyed having his son with him in camp, but as the possibility of battle approached, he ordered Fred home. "We may have some fighting to do," Grant explained, "and he is too young to have the exposure of camp life." But Julia insisted, sensing that as the pressures of war increased, her husband would need his family more than ever. She had three other children at home to care for; Fred should stay with Grant despite his wife's concerns about his safety: "Alexander was not older when he accompanied Philip. Do keep him with you." But Ulysses refused to listen and sent the boy home.

"I'VE BEEN KILLED"

By the spring of 1863, however, Grant had changed his mind. Perhaps the setbacks of the previous year shook the general. Modern readers look back at his wartime career and see a steady trajectory that carried Grant from Illinois to the White House. But in the spring of 1863, things were not so clear. Shiloh had brought a Union victory at tremendous human cost, and rumors circulated that Grant was to blame for this. Some said he'd been needlessly reckless, while others insisted he was drunk. Still others cited both reasons as they christened Ulysses "The Butcher." As if this wasn't worrisome enough, when Grant had sent Sherman to break General Pemberton and his Confederates at Vicksburg at the end of 1862, his dear friend had returned in defeat.

As a fresh campaign season approached, Grant may have sensed that he needed the rock that his family always proved to be—at least his immediate family. His father-in-law continued to voice praise for the Confederacy and was known to walk the streets of St. Louis proclaiming his right to retain his slave property. Meanwhile, his wife's brothers donned gray uniforms to defend their family's beliefs. But Grant's wife and children were constants, his foundation. When they had left after a visit to his headquarters at Corinth, Mississippi, in August 1862, barely missing an engagement with Confederate forces, Grant complained that he and his entire staff missed Julia and the children, observing that "without Jess to stauk through the office it seems as if something is missing." And so, in the spring of 1863, he wrote to Julia and asked if she would send Fred to join him at the front. The boy, they both knew, brought with him a child's optimism and love, pure and uncomplicated, and his parents knew it would sustain Ulysses in the dark days that loomed ahead.

Of course, there was the challenge of having a small boy in headquarters with no tutor or staff officer assigned to protect him. Nor did Julia send any of her slaves; her beloved house servant, Jule, seemed to be Julia's rock when Ulysses was gone, and she could not bear to part with her. Julia never mentioned the irony of owning slaves while her husband was fighting to liberate them. It's possible that, having grown up surrounded by the peculiar institution, Julia never bothered to question the situation, but it's difficult to imagine that the entire family failed to see that irony. Indeed, when Julia did travel to camp later that summer of 1863, Jule traveled with her and seized the opportunity to run away. Julia was frustrated, but Ulysses was relieved. He'd never entirely approved of his wife's "property," and he refused to allow anyone to chase after Jule.[136]

In his attempt to convince Julia to allow Fred to return to camp, Grant promised her that their boy would continue to "read and study his arithmetic." From Julia's own complaints about their boys' campaign against their studies, it's likely that she doubted Ulysses's promise, but he needn't have made it. He failed to realize that her primary mission was to provide him with whatever he needed to win the war. From the start of the conflict, she focused all of her energies on her family. As Julia explained years later, she couldn't sew to save her life and had to confess as much when a local ladies auxiliary had called on her to support soldiers at the front. Instead, she argued, "As my husband had already offered his sword and his services to his country, I felt it to be my duty to give all my care to his little ones, which I faithfully did."[137]

Julia had been her husband's greatest champion from the day they married. Every setback had been not doom but a challenge on the journey to their bright future. He was her light, she was his, and together they would sustain each other through this dreadful war. It was that simple. They had survived a secret engagement while he served in

Mexico, they had weathered the storm of his departure from the Old Army, and they endured one economic failure after another. Death and destruction came knocking in peace and in war, at home and at the front. If the years had taught them anything, it was that they could not avoid tragedy and that they fared better in every scenario when they stood together. Julia helped Fred pack and sent him to Ulys.

Fred arrived in camp at the end of March 1863, "happy as can be," his father reported. "His age," Ulysses observed, "enabled him to take in all he saw, and to retain a recollection of it that would not be possible in more mature years." Having young Fred there throughout the campaign and siege "caused no anxiety either to me or to his mother, who was at home. He looked out for himself and was in every battle of the campaign."

Indeed, their time together often sounded like a grand adventure as Grant wrote to Julia, boasting that they had just returned "from a trip of fifteen miles up the river where we had quite a horseback ride. He enjoys himself finely and I doubt not will receive as much perminant advantage by being with me for a few months as if at school." Weeks later he told her that Fred "has heard balls whistle and is not moved in the slightest by it." If such reports made her anxious, Julia did not admit to it. After all, the home front wasn't much safer. A few weeks before Fred rejoined his father, Julia Grant's sister, Emma Dent Casey, had been stopped by two Confederates near her home in Caseyville, Kentucky, and asked for a moment with her nephew Fred, who was visiting the Caseys. She managed to evade their questions and then sent word for Grant's son to be placed aboard the next boat heading down the river to safety. "There is no doubt," she admitted, "that they were looking for Fred, and had they found him they would certainly have dealt his father a hard blow."[138]

In April 1863, Fred was with his father as Grant and Admiral Porter discussed their plans to run the Union gunboats past the Confederate defenders at Vicksburg. Fred had been horrified by the damage already done to Porter's crew in an earlier fight, and he admitted to being "sickened at the scene before me. The deck was covered with blood and pieces of flesh; several dead men, torn and lacerated, lay about us. Some of the gunners, with still bleeding wounds, were standing firmly by their guns." As the men landed at Bruinsburg, Mississippi, young Fred snuck ashore with them, where again he was horrified by the bloody carnage of battle.

During the campaign that followed, Fred watched as the U.S. colors were raised over Jackson, was nearly killed when, alone again, he stumbled upon a house full of wounded Confederates, and, near Vicksburg, was nearly wounded when Confederate infantry men began shooting at him from across the Big Black River. When a round hit Fred in the leg, he went white with pain. Colonel Clark B. Laglow, a staff officer, rushed to Fred's aid and blanched when the terrified boy announced that he'd "been killed." Laglow checked the wound and then exhaled with relief. It's "all right," he smiled, "you're not dead."[139]

"NOT MINE, OH, LORD, BUT THINE"

At about the same time that Ulysses and Fred Grant entered the Willard Hotel in early 1864, Varina Davis's faith in Confederate victory, if she had ever had any, was collapsing. Even worse, she felt like her whole family was collapsing with it. That spring, the newspapers ran rumors of her husband, Jefferson, fathering children with women in Mississippi and Wisconsin, and some editors even insisted that his son born by a Mississippi slave was now serving in the Union Navy. Then, if anyone continued to doubt the ability of the Emancipation Proclamation to encourage slaves to flee to the freedom offered by the nearby Union lines, the stories of Varina Davis's slaves escaping the Confederate White House convinced them. They included Varina's personal maid, Betsey, who took with her $80 in gold and more than $2,000 in Confederate bills, along with stories of the CSA First Lady's vicious and violent temper. Years later, Varina would insist that Betsey had confided in her that she was leaving and deny all the rumors, but her response at the time indicated only the shocked disappointment that echoed throughout the South as other Confederates discovered similar escapes.

And then, in March, she learned that a prewar acquaintance had tried to assassinate her husband. It was Colonel Ulric Dahlgren. His plan, likely drafted with U.S. Secretary of War Stanton, had been to launch a surprise attack on Richmond that would free Union prisoners from the jails, burn the city, and murder President Davis and his cabinet. Word of Dahlgren's raid leaked before he reached the Confederate Capital, and when he discovered this, he raced back toward Washington. Before he could cross into Union territory, Confederate soldiers caught up to him and killed Dahlgren. In fact, they mutilated the man who had planned to wreak such destruction on Richmond and the Southern government, and then they displayed his body in public as a warning to others. Varina was devastated. Ulric had been the fair-haired son of Admiral John Dahlgren, with whom the Davises had enjoyed many evenings before the war. It was the destruction of one more old friendship. Worse, Varina would argue, it was a violent betrayal.

Shaken from the particularly chaotic spring of 1864, Varina climbed into a carriage in the early afternoon of April 30 to bring lunch to her husband at the Custom House. While they chatted, a messenger dashed in, breathlessly reporting that there had been an accident at the White House. The Davis's five-year-old son, Joseph, had fallen from the balcony. As his parents arrived home, they found that their boy's breathing had slowed and far too much blood had spilled on the pavement where he lay. Doctors were called and prayers were said, but in less than an hour of reaching his side, Joseph was gone.

The past three years had brought one death after another, but this one came closest to breaking both of the Davises. That night, friends heard the President pace the floor, back and forth. Earlier that day, as Joseph faded away, they had heard him moan, "Not mine, oh, Lord, but thine," and all night he seemed to be willing himself to accept the death of his young son while in another room Varina continued to weep in inconsolable grief.[140]

In the days that followed, Jefferson Davis occupied his mind with his work, touring the Confederate positions around the city as he and General Lee focused on the war that continued stubbornly. In a tangle of trees and underbrush so thick that the locals had named the spot "The Wilderness," Union and Confederate soldiers opened another campaign season one week after Davis had watched, tortured, as his son died in his arms. The armies fought there for three days, and then continued on to

Spotsylvania Court House, where battles raged sporadically for two weeks. After a brief break, the men rushed to kill each other again along the North Anna River and then again at a place called Cold Harbor.

While Varina mourned her son, tens of thousands of mothers discovered that they, too, had lost their boys, but on distant lands where mothers could not offer their arms or their prayers before their sons were gone. It created a scenario that horrified a generation that believed that a good death required a person to be at peace with God and with their life as they passed from this world. The Confederate First Lady seemed to embody the confused, grief-stricken nation as visitors found her "utterly depressed," and "grey and forlorn" as summer approached. Eventually, melancholy evolved into chronic exhaustion and the desire to shut out the world. By the end of May, Varina admitted to her mother that her only solace came in finding a quiet room in the house where she could sit alone.

And then, on June 27, 1864, the anniversary of the battle that had saved the Confederate capital two years earlier at Gaines's Mill, little Varina Anne Davis arrived. The baby did not erase her mother's doubts about the Confederacy's future, but she did save the First Lady from the depths and forced her attention to shift to the needs of the present. "Nicknamed "Winnie"—Jefferson Davis's pet name for his wife—the child pulled Varina from what she later called the "war's darkest hour."" [141]

"YOU PROMISED YOU WOULD COME"

A thousand miles to the north, Lizzie Bowler's faith in the war was also wavering. She had fallen in love with James Madison Bowler around the age of twenty, when he was her schoolteacher in a small Minnesota town. He boarded with her aunt and uncle, and they had been courting for several years when the war began. While he was away visiting family in the spring of 1861, Madison tried to explain to Lizzie why he had enlisted in the 3rd Minnesota Infantry. He believed that "somebody must go; and who can go better than young men like myself without business and with[out] family to demand my attention." Lizzie wasn' entirely convinced, responding only that Madison should "go if you think it your duty."[142]

By the winter of 1862, Madison was still trying to defend his decision, arguing "Lizzie, you know that I love you; but sinner as I am, I believe that next to my duty to God comes my duty to my country and its sufferings." They had married just months before, and Lizzie was already pregnant. But Madison had had to rush back to war, leaving Lizzie behind to face the daily struggles that defined frontier life in peace and in war, which had recently included the Sioux uprising that Madison's unit helped suppress months earlier. When their daughter Victoria was born, Lizzie felt little relief. Pregnancy had constrained her ability to travel, and a young child restricted her further. Madison hoped that they could visit him in camp, but Lizzie explained that travel with an infant was impossible.

For Lizzie, home was no longer the happy place it had once been. Lizzie's sister Kate had slowly withered and died of tuberculosis the same year Victoria arrived. Colicky, the baby wore Lizzie's nerves raw, as did the loneliness of missing her sister and husband on top of the demands of running their farm and managing their budgets by herself. By the spring of 1864, much like Varina Davis, Lizzie Bowler was done.

"You still speak as though you wished me [to] come to Little Rock," she told Madison on June 2, "but under the present [cir]cumstances I do not [think] it best." He responded with claims of patient understanding, but fired back repeated complaints. "I judge from the tenor of your letter, that you will not come to Little Rock. I have a nice place engaged for our board …. But I shall not look for your coming any more—though you promised that you would come when I sent for you. I should not complain, however; and I do not wish you to do an act against your own judgment and inclinations, just for my sake. I could not think of having you come here unless it should perfectly accord with your own wish and will. But Lizzie, you must pardon me for my petulance …"

In his next letter, Madison succumbed to his lonely frustration and asked why on earth Lizzie had weaned their daughter if she did not plan to come to visit him in camp. He had suggested she do so in order to simplify travel and allow them more time together, but Lizzie decided against traveling. Madison's frustration grew, and it came out in hi letters to her. Lizzie was just as irritated and fired back, "I think whe you wrote you felt rather sarcastic …. I think you had better try & fin some of those southern girls that wouldn't be so willful."

For the next several weeks, Madison complained that sh misunderstood him, and she responded with the same. Miserable each tried to reassure the other, but both remained stubbornl disappointed that their spouse would not budge. Madison was bus trying to recruit fresh troops and to train newly enliste African-American soldiers, and Lizzie worried about his fate shoul he be captured, knowing that Confederates had expressed thei outrage at the Union's decision to arm free blacks. By the middle o August, her frustrations turned to the men at home, whose civilia freedoms seemed to require her husband's absence. "Sometimes almost envy some of the girls when I see them going about with thei husbands & think that they might take a turn while you come hom after spending three long years in the army. I know that I ought to b thankful that things ar[e] as well as they are while thousands hav been cut down by sickness & sword, that you are still spared an unharmed. But my lonely [heart] will rebel sometimes."[143]

But then came word that Madison would not promise to retur home the following winter, at the end of his enlistment. Lizzie wa shocked. "You cannot imagine how it makes me feel to know that yo are down there dying by inches with the ague & ruining your constitutio forever & yet say that you are going to remain in the army as long as th war lasts," she fairly shouted.

You cannot know what my feelings were when I read your letter, for I thought that you would certainly come home some time during the fall or winter, & I do not see any more prospect of the war ending for the next three years than I did three years ago, nor half so much. My prayer to God is that you will never be permitted to lead that Regt of negrows into battle, for I feel well assured what your fate will be if you should. I have always said that I would never try to hinder you from doing what you think is your duty, but … I want you to really think the matter over whether it is your duty to spend all the best of your life away from those who love you best and sighs for your presence ever[y] moment of her life time or to come home & get a good little house & live happy as we should while others who have had the comforts of home take their turn in the battle field.

Back and forth they went all summer, worn out by worry and loneliness. Madison admitted that he felt guilty about his absence from Lizzie, Victoria, and their home. But, he reminded her, she had given her consent up to this point and advised him to do as he saw fit. He was desperate to see them, he promised, but he was torn between two obligations of equal importance. "I can hardly express how greatly I desire" to "see you and be with you," Madison explained. "But ... it has been my intention all along to remain in the army until the end of this war. I cannot disregard your expressed wish in a matter of so much right and reason on your part; yet I do not wish to be compelled to leave the army until I can see fully and clearly that we have a country in which we can live in peace and security—an undivided country and a good government. Without these I would not live in the country ...," he wrote, making it clear without directly saying it where his priorities lay. "If the copperhead ticket should be successful, the country ... would be ruined. If the Union ticket shall succeed, and Abraham Lincoln, or any other good union man shall be elected president, the rebels will then see no hope." He offered some general news once again, and, as always, asked after Lizzie's and Victoria's health and happiness, but then closed with brutal honesty. "Please make up your mind to let me stay in the army until I take a notion to go home ...."[144]

Lizzie's frustrations represented the loneliness of hundreds of thousands of women across the country. "Why do you talk ... so about my patriotism?" she asked. "I have been willing to make almost any sacrifice to have the north gain her part in this awful contest. For three years you know I have waited patiently, have always tried to look on the bright side .... As long as your health remains good, I did not feel as I now do. But now you are ruining your constitution by staying there .... You cannot expect me to love this country as you do, nor feel willing to sacrifice that that I would not be willing to sacrifice for my own country."[145]

And there was the rub. Lizzie's immediate family had arrived in Minnesota from Canada in 1856, and they had long prided themselves on their loyalism during the American Revolution. Years later, Madison's and Lizzie's daughter Victoria would recall that her mother's marriage to her father "was the first mixture of this family with Yankee blood."[146] Lizzie rarely referenced Canada in her letters, and the majority of her extended family had all settled on farms in Nettinger, Minnesota, or in nearby townships. It does not appear that she felt any mixed loyalties between her roots in Canada and her new life in the United States. Rather, her loyalty, like many people across the country, was to her family. In her eyes, her husband had done enough for the war effort, and it was time for him to focus on his family to whom, in her eyes, his first loyalty should be. In four years of war, they shared a total of twelve weeks together, a mere eighty-four days. Despite Madison's powerful arguments for reenlisting, she remained unconvinced. He had done enough. Let someone else go to the front. It was time for her husband to come home.

"THE SACRIFICES I HAVE MADE"

Far to the south, Gertrude Thomas agreed. She had been the daughter of an Augusta, Georgia, planter and had married and settled on a plantation not far from her father's home before the war. In 1861, Thomas had been a strong supporter of the Confederacy, but years of want, so different from the life she had known, had broken her down. By 1864, as she pondered her husband's fate in the army that summer, her faith in the war withered away. "Am I willing to give my husband to gain Atlanta for the Confederacy?" she asked rhetorically. "No, No, No, a thousand times No!"

Months earlier, in February, a Virginian named Mary Chichester had proposed an escape from service to her son held in a Northern prison. "I hope when you do get exchanged," she confided to him, "you will think the time past has sufficed for *public* service, & that your own family requires your protection & help—as others are deciding."[147] By October

North Carolinian Sally Mabry was asking her husband a similar question: "What do you think of going back into the Union[?] dont you think it would be better than to have all our men killed[?] ... I often think if I could make peace how soon I would have you and all my loved ones with me."[148]

Later generations would romanticize Civil War families' sacrifices and speak of women's stalwart determination to save the Union or the Confederacy, but in many homes in 1864, regardless of their location above or below the Mason–Dixon line, wives were demanding that their men come home. This was especially true in the South, where Confederate families faced rapid inflation and limited food supplies. Farmers were successfully changing crop and livestock production to ensure that they produced enough to feed Southern armies. But much of their harvest went straight to the front, and shipping costs increased the price of what goods remained at home. By the spring of 1863, Confederates on the home front were barely able to purchase or produce enough food to feed their families.

In the spring of that year, women across the South took action. In the early morning hours of March 18, 1863, nearly two dozen women entered a shop in Atlanta and asked about the price of bacon. When the merchant informed them it was $1.10 a pound, the tallest member of the group retorted that it was an "impossibility" of impoverished women to pay such prices, especially those who had already given so much by sending their husbands and sons to the front. When he refused to lower the price, the woman, who seemed the leader of the group, pulled a Navy revolver from her shirt, leveled it at the man, and told the women to take what they needed. As the group left, they took a moment to tell the stunned people watching them that they "had been deprived of anything to eat ... save a small portion of corn bread."[149]

What could have been an isolated incident in Georgia spread quickly across the South. On March 19, one day after the incident in Atlanta, a group of forty to fifty women, now backed by a mob of men, went store to store in Salisbury, North Carolina, demanding the food that they believed they were owed as "respectable poor women ... all Solders' wives or Mothers." As one of them, Mary Moore, explained in a letter she later sent to Governor Zebulon Vance, they were simply seizing the food that they had been promised. "Our Husbands and Sons are now separated from us by the cruel war not only to defend their humbly homes but the homes and property of the rich man," she argued.

About two weeks later in Richmond, Virginia, a mob of an estimated three hundred women followed by a crowd numbering close to a thousand demonstrated just how well organized these women were. Mary Jackson, a farmer's wife and a soldier's mother who sold meat in Richmond's Second Market, led them. For weeks she had been appealing to the War Department for her son's discharge to come aid her on the farm. When that approach failed, she decided to use her sales networks to call area women to a meeting to discuss how they would protest the exorbitant food prices that had left many of their families on the brink of starvation. The object, according to one woman, was to "demand goods of the merchants at government prices and if they were not given the stores were to be broken open and the goods taken by force." Mary Jackson made sure the women understood her. They were not "to go along the streets like a parcel of heathens ... but to go quietly to the stores and demand goods at government prices." Jackson told the women that if their requests were not met, they should "break open the stores and take the goods." As she closed their April 1 meeting, Jackson told the women to leave their children at home and arrive the following morning at 9:00 am fully armed. The next day, Jackson and the women launched the largest riot in Confederate history as they marched from store to store, shouting "Bread or Blood," and making their demands just as they had planned.

At first, shocked Southerners had insisted that the riots were all the work of Yankee saboteurs, attacking Confederate society from within. But as the government began to investigate, they found that the women had acted on their own, despite nineteenth-century social mores that traditionally restricted such action to men. More importantly, the public began to sympathize with the women. They were, after all, people who were making daily sacrifices for the Confederacy. Many of their husbands and sons had, indeed, been promised by state and Federal recruiters that the community or the government would ensure that their families were provided for in the men's absence. And everyone knew that the women's complaints were justified. As Confederate families watched food prices rise each month, the Bread Riots, as they became known, sparked both sympathy and action on the part of city, state, and, though to a lesser degree, the Confederate federal government from Virginia to the Gulf Coast.

One week after the Richmond riots, a city committee raised $20,000 "for the relief of the families of soldiers." Later that year in North Carolina, the legislature passed the Act for the Relief of the Wives and Families of Soldiers in the Army, which told millers that government subsidized corn was to be delivered "first to soldiers' wives" and only after they had all been provided for would the impoverished members of the community receive their portion. Georgia's government offered similar reforms as well.

The trouble, however, was the enormity of the problem. By the fall of 1863, John B. Jones, a government clerk in Richmond, confided to his diary on November 20 that a soldier had written to the secretary of war that his mother was "in danger of starving—as she failed to get flour in Richmond, at $100 per barrel." The soldier warned that if the Confederate government continued to fail to address their families' needs, "he and his comrades will throw down their arms and fly to some other country with their families, where a subsistence may be obtained." On the very next line, unable to leave the subject just yet, Jones added, "Every night robberies of poultry, salt meats, and even of cows and hogs are occurring. Many are desperate."[150]

By 1864, most Southern politicians had realized that "the fact is undeniable, that the great question in this revolution is now a question of bread." After a second wave of riots occurred in Savannah, Georgia, newspaper editors criticized the state and Confederate governments' failure to "come up to the full measure of their duty" to soldiers' wives and children.[151] Others, though, insisted that the complaints at home had to be silenced if the South hoped to win the war. Confederate Captain B. M. Edney had little sympathy for the women and suggested censorship of the mails, telling Secretary of War James Seddon in 1863, "the source of all the present evils of Toryism & desertion in our country is letter writing ... to the army."

While some historians have used the riots and letters like those by Edney as evidence that Southern defeat was, in part, caused by the loss of will on the home front, others have rightly argued that the women were making demands astonishingly similar to those of their husbands and sons in the army. They were not all insisting on quitting the war. They were, however, arguing that promises made by county, state, and federal governments to entice their husbands to enlist must be kept.

As South Carolinian Margaret Easterling explained in a letter to Jefferson Davis, she had sent two sons to the army. "I need not tell you of my devotion to my country, of the sacrifices I have made, and of the many more I am willing to make .... But I want my oldest boy at home."[152] She did not demand the end of the war; she did not insist that the boys had fulfilled their duties to their nation and that it was now time to return to their duties to their families. Instead, she asked for one son to be sent home, the oldest, who could fulfill both boys' responsibilities to her while the other fulfilled the family's responsibilities to the nation.

Arguments like Easterling's, which highlighted the fact that promises had been made by governments to their citizens and that these promises were not being kept, echoed Revolutionary-era lessons of republican social contracts between the government and the governed. Confederate leaders knew that when citizens believed that this contract had been broken, they would insist they had the right to rebel. It was, after all, one of the arguments Southern leaders had made to support secession in 1861, and it was the same argument that spread across the Confederate home front in 1863 and 1864. Knowing what lay ahead, state governors continued to work to respond to Southern families' needs throughout late 1863 and 1864.

Under Governor Joseph Brown, Georgia provided so much support through free salt, free corn, and tax exemptions that their budget for soldiers' families nearly matched the state's military funding. This made sense, he argued, because the families' needs on the home front were military necessities. This was the only way, he had come to realize, to keep soldiers on the front lines.

As early as 1863, even after Union forces had overrun his capital at Jackson, Mississippi Governor John Pettus had insisted that more be done to provide for soldiers' wives and families. Pettus argued that they were the "one class of our citizens whose claims upon the state [are] as imperative and as sacred as any claim the State can have upon the soldiers in this perilous hour." When Pettus's term in office expired in the fall of 1863, he went off to serve in the Confederate Army while his successor, Charles Clark, continued Pettus's emphasis on the needs of soldiers' families. Any failure to meet this issue, Clark insisted in his first legislative address, would lead to the failure to muster sufficient troops to wage the war.[153]

"IT IS NOT … MY DUTY TO REENLIST"

And so it was that the concerns of the summer of 1864 had come to match those of the previous year. While governments North and South worked to address these issues with an ingenuity and a dedication that has been largely forgotten, the question was whether their efforts would be enough to win. Plus, one key problem remained. For some men, it wasn't simply concerns about their families that drove them home. Some had seen too much, while others believed that they had done enough—and that it was time for someone else to make the soldier's sacrifice.

By the spring of 1864, Willie Shepherd was among those who believed it was time for someone else to step up. He did not have a wife calling him home, nor do any of his letters indicate that his family suffered financially by his absence. But as far as he was concerned, he had done his part. In the summer of 1862, the army had overcome its tradition of assigning recruits to tasks entirely unsuited to their skills when they realized that Shepherd, formerly a Chicago clerk, might fill clerical duties brilliantly at headquarters. Since then, Shepherd had seen little combat, with his last significant exposure to the "butcher's bill" having occurred at Shiloh. Since then, he had largely observed Union forces conquering and occupying of Mississippi, including the fall of Vicksburg in the summer of 1863, and he spent much of the winter of 1863–64 in Memphis, Tennessee, and Huntsville, Alabama.

Working in the 15th Army Corps, which served in what became Sherman's Army of the Tennessee with Grant's departure for the East, Shepherd enjoyed a far safer, more privileged existence than most of his fellow enlisted men. He attended church in both Memphis and Huntsville, where the locals did not offer a particularly warm welcome. There were exceptions, though, and Shepherd took comfort in his visits with the mistress of the boardinghouse where he stayed. Still, the signs of war were everywhere, and he could not help but observe the young women at the local college who mourned the loss of brothers or beaus. And, despite his distance from the fighting, Shiloh continued to haunt him.

In 1863, he met a boy in Memphis, standing at the gate to his home as Shepherd passed. When the boy stopped him, asking his name, they struck up a conversation and Shepherd inquired about where his father was. "He's dead," the boy answered, "killed, the soldiers killed him at Shiloh." The beautiful Sunday afternoon disappeared that second, and Shepherd was back along the Tennessee, in "those two fearful days." He couldn't help but wonder "if it was our Battery that killed the little boy's father—or if he was among those we gathered into the grave at one of our camps. Perhaps he was! The little fellow's face and the shade of decay and desolation about the house,"—which moments earlier Shepherd had seen as "fine" with "pleasant grounds" and "pretty fence"—gave him "proof of the sad reality of our War."[154]

But joy has a way of interfering with misery, and throughout the winter and spring of 1864, Shepherd developed close friendships with the locals in Huntsville, Alabama. He spent much of his free time socializing with a Mrs. Wilson, who had about forty ladies under her care at the Huntsville Female College while her husband was being held prisoner at Camp Morton, Indiana. Despite their clear sympathy for the Confederate cause, she and her students often entertained Shepherd on his visits. Shepherd attended church with Mrs. Wilson and spoke well of her students, in particular "Miss Ada Morris of Tenn. and Miss Lizzie Coffey of Miss, both finely educated, pleasant, agreable, and musical." Their friendship grew to the point where, when reports surfaced in January 1864 that "Rebels were coming ... to attack and capture our whole force here," Mrs. Wilson insisted that if the rumors were true,

Shepherd "must come right to the College and *she* would take care of me, and save me from being taken or harmed in the least by the Confederates."[155]

Despite the threats, Shepherd's winter remained quiet. This did not, however, convince him to stay in the army. As March approached, he admitted to his sister that his "situation is indeed a pleasant one compared with being with the Battery" in which he had served in the first two years of the war. But "I shall not be with the Battery any more while in the Army, and shall take good care not to get shot elsewhere. Two years and a half, I've survived the trials & dangers & hardships of a soldier's life, and I feel confident that I am able to stand five months more." Beyond that, though, Shepherd's thinking was more in line with Lizzie Bowler's than her husband's. Shepherd had volunteered for three years, and he had fulfilled that commitment. "I little thought when I first came into service," he mused, "that it would be necessary to serve the full term … but it has been *quite* necessary." It had not been all bad, he reassured his sister. "My health is greatly improved, my knowledge of men and the world more perfect, and my morals, I hope, as good as ever." Despite the fact that many of his friends and, indeed, "thousands are reenlisting for 3 years," Shepherd insisted, "*I* shall not." In the end, it was simple: "I have done my duty to the Country, I hope faithfully, and as there are so many—*many* thousands that have not served, & who *can*, just as well as I, it is not, in my mind, my duty to reenlist."[156]

Shepherd was shocked, then, when he learned in May 1864 that one of those thousands at home who stepped up to take his place was his own brother, Freddy. "I regret it very much," Willie confided to their father. "One soldier at a time from our family is enough!"[157] By June, he took some comfort in the idea that Freddy had enlisted only for a hundred days, though Willie had hoped his brother could serve in an artillery unit as he had. "It would have been much preferable, but as they may have little or no fighting to, excuse me, I should say *marching* to do, it will not make so much difference. I hope too they may have no *fighting*! I think it quite improbably, as they are intended only for a rear guard."[158]

On June 19, 1864, Willie passed through Huntsville, Alabama, again on his way home. He had only a few days, but he made time to attend service in his favorite church and made plans to visit "my lady friends."

He was saying goodbye to the family he had created, those who had sustained him, even though they were technically enemies, while he was away from his own family. A month later, Shepherd made time for one last visit with his old unit, Battery B of the 1st Illinois Light Artillery, and "all the Kenosha Boys." Then he went home.

Willie Shepherd did not see this war as Madison Bowler did. Shepherd enlisted in the summer of 1861 to do "something to rescue my Native land from destruction and ruin." Three years later, with memories of the fight at Shiloh still haunting him, Shepherd was content in the knowledge that he had done his part to save the Union. He saw no reason, as Bowler did, to reenlist in order to see the war out to the end.

"GOD NEVER INTENDED FOR MAN TO STEAL HIS OWN FLESH AND BLOOD"

Outside Atlanta, boys in blue and in gray continued their fight. Private Laforest Dunham of the 129th Illinois Infantry Regiment was among them, and he explained that many of the men had found ways to ease the bloodshed, at least a little, by 1864. "We maid a bargain with the rebs," he explained, "not to shoot at one another heare on the scourmish line unless one side or the other went to advance, so it makes it mutch pleasanter."[159]

Confederates, though, seemed less inclined to find pleasant solutions to their situations. During the spring of 1864, G. W. Waggoner of the 20th Tennessee declared, "I am fond of that [skirmish] duty. I fired several rounds at the sons of bitches if I should say such a word. I cant tell whether I hit one or not but I tried like the devil." Similarly, Samuel Watson, fighting with Hood's Texas Brigade in defense of Petersburg, Virginia, in the fall of 1864, was determined to kill every last Yankee he could find, especially the black soldiers who symbolized his world turned upside down. In October, he told his family that, "them Blooddy Niggers of Grant made a charge on us and a charge it was. They came rite up till you could See the White of thare Eyes, the boys litterley coverd the ground with Dead nigs, dont think I am braging for it is so."[160]

A few months earlier, G. H. Freeman had been one of those African-American soldiers opposite the Confederate lines at Petersburg. On August 19, 1864, it was his difficult duty to tell the mother of his best friend that her son had been lost in battle. Rebecca Guy had heard rumors that Billy was gone, but it wasn't until Freeman's letter arrived that she knew "thear is no dobt of his Death." Freeman tried to offer her some comfort in the knowledge that her son, "Died A Brave Death in Trying to Save the Colors of Rige[*ment*] in that Dreadful Battil," but he could only apologize for his failure to send Billy's personal belongings home. "In the bustil of the Battil every thing was Lost," Freeman explained.[161]

For African-American families in this war, particularly for the enslaved, there were no governors to write to with complaints. The people in power had little interest in addressing slaves' needs, as Richard and Martha Glover discovered in Missouri. When Lincoln announced emancipation, his decision to limit its reach to "Confederate held territory" meant that it did not touch a slave state that had remained in the Union like Missouri. In 1863, Richard decided to steal his freedom by running away, possibly in the belief that if the Union could win the war, in part with the help of black military service, slavery would die with the Confederacy. This plan, however, did not involve bringing his wife and children with him, and in December 1863, Martha Glover begged him to come home, writing,

> I have had nothing but trouble since you left. You recollect what I told you how they would do after you was gone. They abuse me because you went & say they will not take care of our children & do nothing but quarrel with me all the time and beat me scandalously the day before yesterday— Oh I never thought you would give me so much trouble as I have got to bear now. You ought not to left me in the fix I am in & all these little helpless children to take care of …. Remember all I told you about how they would do me after you left–for they do worse than they ever did & I do not know what will become of me & my poor little children. Oh I wish you had staid with me & not gone till I could go with you for I do nothing but grieve all the time about you. write & tell me when you are coming.[162]

Richard was not the only newly freed black soldier who had left a family behind. Nearly a year after Martha wrote to her husband, Spotswood Rice lay on a hospital bed in Benton Barracks, Missouri. Just days earlier, Atlanta had fallen to Union forces, sending a wave of optimism through Union ranks in every theater of the war. Taking pen in hand, Rice began a letter to his young daughters, who were still enslaved in Glasgow, Missouri. "Be assured," he promised them, "that I will have you if it cost me my life." An army of 800 white and 800 black soldiers was heading to Glasgow at the end of September, he pledged, and "when they Come I expect to be with them and expect to get you both in return. Dont be uneasy my children I expect to have you."[163]

Rice wrote a separate letter to his former owner, Kitty Diggs, criticizing her for calling herself a Christian while willingly owning other Christians and chastising Rice for wanting to "steal" his children from her. "God never intended for man to steal his own flesh and blood .... If I ever had any Confidence in her I have none now and never expect to have And I want her to remember if she meets me with ten thousand soldiers she [will] meet her enemy." As for the bonds that once kept him under Diggs's control, Rice admitted that he "once ... had some respect" for her, but that was gone. "And as for her cristiananty, I expect the Devil has Such in hell. You tell her from me that She is the first Christian that I ever hard say that a man could Steal his own child especially out of human bondage."[164]

Some African-American soldiers insisted on bringing their wives and children with them, fearing that they would suffer as the Rice and Glover families had if the men left their enslaved families behind. Proximity, however, did not guarantee security, as Joseph Miller discovered the day before Thanksgiving in 1864. A year before, President Lincoln had declared that the fourth Thursday of November would be, from that point forward, a nationally recognized day for offering prayers and thanks for the blessings, though sometimes hard to see, that the nation enjoyed. Across the North in November 1864, Americans prepared to focus on their blessings once more, offering thanks to their all-powerful God, and strengthening themselves for the struggles ahead. In Kentucky, white Union soldiers decided that they could better enjoy these blessings in the quarters that were currently occupied by the families of the runaway slaves turned soldiers in their camp. Among these families were Joseph Miller's wife and children.

In the frigid evening hours of November 22, soldiers appeared before Isabella Miller's tent and informed her that she and her four children had to leave the camp by dawn the following morning. Her husband, Joseph, had enlisted in Company I of the U.S. 24th Colored Infantry with the promise that his wife and children would have shelter in the "contraband" section—where runaway slaves lived, free from slavery but lacking any real legal status or protection in the North—of the Union lines at Camp Nelson, Kentucky.

The eviction order puzzled Isabella Miller because she knew it contradicted the promise her husband had been made one month earlier when he had enlisted in the Union Army. Busy nursing her ill seven-year-old son, not to mention caring for her other children aged ten, nine, and four, and having neither the money nor the means of going elsewhere, Miller decided that she and her children would remain where they were.

Early the next morning, much to her astonishment, a mounted guard appeared and evicted Isabella Miller and her four children, placing them in a wagon along with hundreds of other contraband families from the camp. Joseph Miller rushed to his family's aid. "I told the man in charge of the guard," Miller explained later, "that it would be the death of my boy I told him that my wife and children had no place to go and I told him that I was a soldier of the United States. He told me that it did not make any difference." The soldier explained that he was following orders, and then, turning to Isabella, he warned that if they "did not get up into the wagon … he would shoot the last one of them." Terrified, freezing in the wind that cut through the threadbare clothing they had been wearing since they escaped slavery, Isabella and her children disappeared down the road as Joseph Miller looked on with horror, following them to the edge of the camp, not knowing where his family was being taken.

Later that night, he went searching and found his wife and children 6 miles away at Nicholsville in an African-American meetinghouse. Despite this shelter, his children and Isabella were still freezing, and they had not eaten all day. There was only one fire to heat the entire room, and although a number of freedmen had been placed there, their body heat offered insufficient comfort against the cold. As he looked at Isabella, holding their youngest son in her arms, he realized that their boy was dead.

Under orders to return to camp that night, Private Miller had to leave his family in the frigid building until he could walk back the next morning, another 12-mile round trip, to dig "a grave myself and bur[y] my own child." He died, Miller insisted, "directly after getting down from the wagon. I Know he was Killed by exposure to the inclement weather." During the next several weeks, Joseph Miller watched Isabella and their three remaining children die of disease. And in January 1865, he, too, succumbed to disease amid the tragedy of war. No one in the Miller family ever saw the official end of slavery.[165]

"MAKE A THERMOPYLAE OF TEXAS, TO WIN OR DIE"

The same month Joseph Miller died at Camp Nelson, Kentucky, Texans and Arkansans in the Texas Brigade gathered in a Confederate camp near Richmond to pledge their determination to fight to the bitter end. They weren't alone. Soldiers from other elite units throughout Lee's Army took similar oaths that month. They were disgusted by the news from home that claimed that civilians were too busy with parties to gather packages to send to the front, and that their neighbors were willingly cooperating with Union occupiers. As cold winds whipped through their camp, the men pledged their

> determination to maintain, at all hazards, and to the last extremity, the rights and liberties which a merciful God has been pleased to bestow upon us, and even to contend for the perpetual separation from the hated and despised foe, who have murdered our grey-haired fathers, insulted our women and children, and turned out thousands of helpless families to starve—after robbing them and burning their houses—leaving them destitute of all except their honor ....[166]

The men sent their proclamations to Congress, where they were then forwarded to newspapers across the Confederacy. Hopefully, the soldiers wrote, this would inspire the men and women at home with similar determination and reenergize the war effort.

Some civilians responded to their pleas, but for others, the exhaustion of worry, terror, and death gave way to an instinctive, almost survivalist, demand for frivolity. Such behavior horrified Augusta Jane Evans of Mobile, Alabama, who chastised her peers, asking, "Are Southern women so completely oblivious of the claims of patriotism and humanity, that in this season of direst extremity, they tread the airy mazes of the dance, while the matchless champions of freedom are shivering in bloody trenches or lying stark on frozen fields of glory?"

Evans was the oldest of eight children born to parents who had been raised among the South's planter elite. She had known every comfort that life provided until her father lost much of their fortune in the economic panic of 1837. It may have been this early brush with poverty that toughened her for the hardships that came with the war and left her little patience for the easy airs of the belles and their soirees. Her family had recovered much of their wealth by the time Alabama seceded, and Evans would make her own fortune as one of the best-known Southern women writers of the nineteenth century, but she never lost her impatience with the frivolity she came to associate with the old planter class.[167]

One woman who would have earned Evans's wrath was Martha Pierce Stannard, a scion of Richmond society who spent more than $30,000 entertaining guests during the winter of 1864–65 while Confederate soldiers suffered from cold and malnourishment in camps not far from the Stannard's parties. Ironically, the Stannard house was one of those burned nearly to the ground when Richmond fell in April 1865.[168]

In Texas, soldiers themselves took care of the problem of inappropriate frivolity. When the ladies of Galveston tried to host revelries in 1864 for the Confederate officers defending the port, enraged enlisted men threatened to attack the party. Lacking sufficient food, pay, and basic care, the men were furious that the civilians they were protecting could even propose such waste, and only for the wealthy men in the ranks, when poor Southern soldiers and their families suffered at home. The Confederate officers were as out of touch as the women of Galveston, it seemed, for their solution to rumors of this threatened raid was to order a cavalry unit to stand guard over the party. The troopers refused, however, and the party was cancelled. But clearly such gatherings continued to be proposed, if not hosted. As late as April 8, 1865, one day before Robert E. Lee surrendered his Army at Appomattox Court House, Virginia, Presbyterian elders in Alabama felt obligated to declare their abhorrence of "the presence, and we fear, the growing prevalence, of a spirit of gaiety, especially among the female members of some of our congregations."[169]

Several hundred miles to the west, in Tyler, Texas, Kate Stone frowned at a similarly gay mood. She had lost two brothers in the Confederate service by the final year of the war. She, her mother, younger siblings, some slaves, and her extended family had fled their Louisiana plantation in a terrifying journey through swamps, chased by Union soldiers, to live in relative poverty as refugees in what she saw as a wasteland. "We have not seen a good-looking or educated person since we entered the state," Kate declared with disgust in 1864.[170] When the family deigned to attend a barbecue hosted by some locals, Kate and her mother refused to eat, declaring the food unclean and such occasions as opportunities to "see the animals feed."[171]

A year in Texas settled Kate's airs, and her introduction to strained finances forced a young woman raised on one of the wealthiest sugar plantations in Louisiana to face the realities of life and grow up. By 1865, she was replacing her family's tattered clothes with the used castoffs of her more affluent, if less refined, neighbors. It was odd, she mused, "to be wearing other people's half-worn clothing," she admitted, and she worried that in the postwar period, her hard years in Texas would actually prove to be some of her best.

When parties ran late into the night in Tyler as they did in Richmond and Mobile, Kate was disgusted by the feverish revelries of a dying nation. She had little patience for such behavior, though she did understand that, "people do not mourn their dead as they used to. Everyone seems to live only in the present—just from day to day— otherwise I fancy many would go crazy."[172] But the festivities "shocked and repelled" her, leaving her appalled that Southerners could "rejoic[e] and delight at the close of the war."

Throughout the final months of the conflict, Kate Stone hung on with grim determination. She had believed in the Confederacy from the beginning, regretting only that she was unable to serve as a soldier like the men in her family did. And even after losing two brothers, their home, their fortune, and in most cases, their health, Kate Stone reassured herself as late as March 1865 in the faith that "the darkest hour is just before dawning."[173]

But then came word of Lee and the Army of Northern Virginia's surrender at Appomattox Court House on April 9, 1865. Stunned by the wave of inconsolable depression that crashed over her, Kate wept for her brothers, for her family, for "the best and the bravest of the South sacrificed—for nothing." Her neighbors in Texas, many of them refugees like the Stones, reminded her of aristocrats in the final days of the French Revolution. "It was distressing," she admitted, "to see the gloom on every face ... all seemed in the depth of despair, could think and talk of nothing but defeat and disaster."[174]

Some Confederates hoped to rally forces in Texas, and for a brief time, Kate thought it might be possible. Maude Jeannie Young, the mother of Private S. O. Young of the Texas Brigade, was one of them. A widow since the late 1840s, Young had made the battle flag for the 5th Texas in 1862 and accepted it when the Texans returned it to her two years later for safe keeping. It was so torn and tattered that it could no longer be flown.

For several years, Maude Young had been publishing editorials in Houston newspapers signed "A Confederate Woman," imploring those at home to make every possible sacrifice for the war effort and their men at the front. On May 16, 1865, just days before Confederate General E. Kirby Smith officially surrendered his forces in Galveston, Young, a widow who had sent her only son to war, insisted that the Confederacy's last chance now lay with those at home. Hood's Texans, she warned, were returning, "a little handful of wearied, battle-scarred, maimed men, but with hearts bold as lions, and with scorn for cowards burning in their tyrant-bating eyes that will consume you as they gaze upon you if you are not also brave and true and determined and resistful." While they "excused you ... for not coming to help defend Virginia," she claimed, "they will curse you with the curse of outraged patriots if they find you faltering in defending your alters and fire sides, your own land, your own mothers and sisters." She challenged, "What if you do go down in battle, and do not return, if your country and children are free?" Cries like Young's echoed in Texas papers that month, but to little avail. The state failed to embrace Young's call to make "a Thermopylae of Texas, to win or die."[175]

Eventually, Maude Young, Kate Stone, and their compatriots in rebel gray could no longer resist the burden of defeat. "*Conquered, Submission, Subjugation* are words that burn into my heart," Kate Stone wrote, "and yet I feel that we are doomed to know them in all their bitterness …. And Nature smiles down on all this wretchedness."

Far to the North, Lizzie Bowler had an entirely different reaction, which is hardly surprising. She was happy the North had won, certainly. But she was happier still that her beloved Madison was coming home. For well over a year, she had begged, cajoled, teased, and then insisted that he recognize that his primary duty was to his family. Month after month, Madison had matched her complaints with letters that ranged from pleading to sullen to bitter explanations of his more important duty to his nation. But by June 1865, it still was not clear that her husband would return, and Lizzie worried that Madison was going to remain in the Army for good. Madison wrote frequently, explaining that he could not return home until he was mustered out, and in the end, it was Lizzie and Victoria who finally went to Madison, who served as an agent of the Freedmen's Bureau through early 1866.

"GREASE AND SLIDE BACK INTO THE UNION"

When William Fletcher looked back on the war in the autumn of his life, one event stood out to him as the darkest period of the conflict. Fletcher had volunteered for service in the 5th Texas Infantry Regiment, which had him fighting with Hood's Texas Brigade from Gaines's Mill to Second Manassas, where he was wounded, and then again at Fredericksburg and Gettysburg. Wounded in the foot at Chickamauga in September 1863,

Fletcher had knocked over the surgeon who tried to amputate the limb. Furious, the doctor abandoned him in disgust to the care of the Sisters of Charity in a makeshift hospital in Augusta, Georgia. The wound healed, but not enough to return to infantry service, so Fletcher transferred to the 8th Texas Cavalry in the spring of 1864. That year, he was captured, though he escaped and managed to link up with Joseph E. Johnston's army in North Carolina. He surrendered with them near Bentonville in 1865, and it was this period of surrender—not his two wounds, not any of the battles—that Fletcher remembered as his darkest hours. "The thought of returning home, defeated," he recalled, "seemed to be depicted on each face, and for a few days I don't think I saw a smile." That period was, he insisted, "the blankest part of my existence."

As the Confederate veterans, now surrendered civilians, made the journey home, Fletcher recalled Southern cavalry and infantry men passing along a sunken country road one night, the infantrymen leaning against the road bank, letting the horse soldiers pass. After a brief exchange between the forces, a North Carolinian called out, "Boys, have you got any bacon?" The cavalrymen answered that they did, and Fletcher remembered the advice of the North Carolina man who responded, then "Grease and slide back into the Union."[176]

This was the challenge of the late spring of 1865. How effectively could these men "slide back into" their old lives, and how willing would they be to accept the Union's terms of peace? How would the final, deadly struggle of the war influence their fates? It came in a theater on Good Friday eve, a day of peace and a night of hope, when two assassins would destroy four more families.

∌ 5 ∈

THE FINAL ACT

anny Seward watched her father's eyelids sag as he drifted off to sleep. His breathing slowed, and she closed the copy of *Legends of Charlemagne* that she had been reading aloud and then turned down the light. Hopefully tonight would bring the peaceful rest her father needed. Earlier that week, doctors had given him valerian to help him sleep, but instead it inspired nightmares. Now, finally, his body seemed to relax and continue to heal from the most terrifying experience of her life.[177]

It had been a week earlier, Wednesday, April 5, 1865, when Fanny and her friend, Mary Titus, called on Fanny's father, Secretary of State William Seward. He and her brother, Fred, the assistant secretary of state, often broke for an afternoon ride with Fanny, and the day's weather promised a delightful respite from their work. The mood in Washington was grand. Rockets, fireworks, and torches had the capital ablaze as Northerners celebrated the fall of Richmond and checked the news hourly for reports that the war was finally over. The Sewards and Miss Titus bundled into their carriage and had barely started their regular afternoon ride when Secretary Seward noticed that the door was ajar and called to the coachman to stop and latch it properly. Henry Key leapt to the ground and had just closed the door when something startled the horses. Their ears twitched, their muscles tightened, and then, with a bolt, they took off.

Fanny watched with horror as Key, who held the reins as long as he could, was dragged along the street beside the carriage until he lost his grip. Fred Seward decided their best chance was for him to leap from the door and hope that he could grasp the reins and bring the team under control. But the carriage was moving too quickly when Fred landed, and he was thrown to the ground. Secretary Seward concluded that he had to make a similar attempt, despite the fact that he would be celebrating his sixty-fourth birthday in less than a month. Fanny begged him not to, but her father insisted and pushed himself out the door. As he came down, the heel of his boot caught on the curb, and Seward crashed face first into the pavement, breaking his jaw, severely dislocating his shoulder, and collapsing into an unconscious heap as the carriage raced on.

Fanny sat facing the horses and did not see her father fall, but she knew something was wrong when the team continued their wild race and the reins whipped like snakes beside the open door just beyond her grasp. The whole scene struck her as surreal with "the houses & the sidewalk lit with peaceful sunshine while we seemed to be whirling on to certain destruction." A nearby alley caught the frightened animals' attention, and as they made the tight turn, the carriage banged against a tree. A brick house loomed before them, and Fanny was positive they were about to perish when one of the horses tripped and fell. Realizing as the carriage came to a stop that their terrifying ordeal was over, Mary and Fanny released their deathlike grips on the sides of the carriage and rose to greet the gloriously motionless ground. Before they could, though, the horse regained its footing and the girls were knocked back into their seats. Just as panic set in, a passing soldier managed to catch the team before it could get up speed. Their afternoon ride was finally over.

Fanny was barely out of the carriage when she realized that neither her father nor Fred was hurrying toward her. Surprised, she rushed back around the corner and discovered a crowd of men carrying the Secretary's limp body. Fred assured her that their father was still alive, though badly hurt, and hurried her home to prepare a bed. The family tried to shelter Fanny, as they often did, and they sent her to wait patiently in the library, turning to the books that had always proved "a great help in distracting attention and changing the mind's current," as she had once observed.[178]

Fanny could hear her father cry out in pain as doctors set his arm and tried to bandage his jaw. When she was finally allowed in his room, the Secretary was "so disfigured by bruises, his face so swollen, that he had scarcely a trace of resemblance to himself." When Seward realized that it was Fanny standing by his bed, he managed to murmur, "And you were not hurt? ... And Mary was not hurt?" to which Fanny assured him they were both fine.[179]

Throughout the next week, family and close friends nursed Secretary Seward in shifts. This included Secretary of War Edwin Stanton, who, although known for his terrifying temper, visited Seward on the day of the accident, wiping blood from his lips and nose while he "spoke gently" to his longtime friend. Old Mars was "like a woman in the sickroom," Fanny mused as she watched Stanton, and far more efficient than she, who knew little of nursing such a battered body.[180] Stanton returned throughout the following week despite the demands of his office, where he waited to hear if Confederate General Robert E. Lee would surrender his Army of Northern Virginia. On Palm Sunday, Stanton called three times. As he sat close by the bed, clasping Seward's hand, Fanny watched as her father tried to express his thanks, whispering, "God bless you, Stanton—I can never tell you half ..." before tears choked his voice and Stanton, whose voice broke, too, hushed his old friend. Later that day, President Lincoln visited Seward as well, and the two old lawyers spoke quietly on the bed, with Lincoln sprawled across the mattress at the foot of his one-time rival and now trusted advisor. When Fanny entered the room, Lincoln grasped her hand in greeting. She was struck by the president's kindness, watching as he looked back at Seward, smiled, and expressed his relief that his wounds were not mortal, as Stanton had first feared. When Stanton came for one more visit, it was to bring word that Lee had, indeed, surrendered. The horrible war was almost over.

Day and night, Fanny tended to her beloved father. Seward was known for his absences from their home in Auburn, New York, a habit that endured throughout her youth and strained his marriage. Frances Seward had been a superb match for the future Secretary when they wed in 1824. Witty, intelligent, and a Quaker-educated free thinker, she was also the daughter of Seward's then employer, Judge Elijah Miller. But years of difficult pregnancies and an increasing horror of the crowds and demands of her husband's political world kept Frances from his side. She enjoyed the quiet functions that allowed her to host society's elite in New York and Washington, but she had no patience for the middling classes that her husband would insist on entertaining from time to time. After all, he would remind her, they did vote.

Also complicating their relationship was the fact that Frances's father had insisted that the couple live in his house. This created a marriage in which Seward was never master of his own home, which a nineteenth-century man expected and was expected to be, as well as one in which Frances failed to fully separate herself from her girlhood world. By the 1860s, she was more often ill than well, citing debilitating headaches and showing signs of what many have theorized was depression and migraines, spending most days confined to her room in their Auburn home.

Fanny was a combination of her parents. She lacked her mother's grace, beauty, and wit, but she inherited Frances's passion for reading—Fanny's personal library numbered more than three hundred volumes by 1865—as well as her belief that a life should be dedicated to the improvement of society. She also developed her mother's sickly ways; although Frances's condition was likely tied to migraines and depression, both women suffered bouts of consumption, and Fanny never seemed to fully recover.

When it came to her father, Fanny was, as her mother once observed, his "shadow—she cannot bear to have him leave the house." By the Civil War, she shadowed him nearly everywhere. In her early twenties, she became her father's political confidant as Seward shared his worries about the political battles that defined his life. She also conquered her shyness and accompanied her father on the campaign trail in 1860, and by 1865, she was the hostess of his Washington home.

On April 7, two days after the accident, Fanny's mother arrived from Auburn, New York. She hurried to her wounded husband, but within a short time took to her own bed, racked with fear that he would never recover. It was Fanny, her brothers, Fred's wife, Anna, and a hired nurse who tended to Seward day and night. As she sat by her father, Fanny read aloud, shared news from the capital, and did anything she could think of to distract them all from memories of the carriage ride that had nearly destroyed their world.

During Easter Week, Fanny took heart in the celebrations that raged day and night in the capital. On occasion, Frances joined Fanny and Anna as they watched marching bands and cheering crowds tramp past their home. They smiled when they saw a sign at the State Department building that Secretary Seward had optimistically designed years ago, proclaiming: "The Union saved by fidelity to the Constitution, Faith in the People, & Trust in God."[181]

Fred kept his father apprised of events at their office, but for the most part, Seward spent that week enduring a painful recovery. Fanny was pleased, though, that the doctors' decision to wire the Secretary's jaw together had been less painful than they feared, though she worried about the gout that had developed in her father's right foot.

On the evening of Friday, April 14, 1865, Fanny and her brothers discussed which shifts each of them would take. It had been a good day. Their father had slept well the previous night, and he managed to eat an egg, milk toast, and shad and to drink some coffee that morning. In the afternoon, they celebrated the news that soldiers had raised the American flag over Fort Sumter, which the Union had grudgingly left in Confederate hands four years ago that day. Marveling at how much their father had improved in a week, Fanny's brother Gus went to bed early so he would be ready to take the 11:00 p.m. shift, and Fanny went upstairs to start her watch.

That was how Fanny came to be closing *Legends of Charlemagne* and turning down the light at about 10:00 p.m that night. Sitting nearby was Sergeant George Robinson, a Union soldier who was recovering from a battlefield wound. He had been assigned to assist with the night shifts when the attending physicians fired the civilian nurse who was discovered drunk on duty several days earlier. Robinson was a thirty-two-year-old from Maine who found himself in the Seward house largely because he was available, he was sufficiently healed to manage light duty, and he abstained from alcohol consumption. He had not planned to be in the room until 2:00 a.m., but Mrs. Seward was worried about her husband, and that evening she requested that Robinson take the earlier shift, perhaps to be on hand to assist Fanny.[182]

Shortly after she noticed her father drifting off, Fanny and Robinson observed her brother, Fred, open the door, peer inside, and then close it firmly behind him. Concerned that Fred needed to discuss a matter of business with her father, Fanny walked to the door to assure him that the Secretary was available. But the moment she saw Fred's face, Fanny sensed that "I had better not have opened the door." Standing beside him was a large, handsome man, she recalled, wearing an expensive, light hat and a long coat. He seemed "impatient" to Fanny and spoke to her "in a tone that struck me at once as much more harsh & full of determination than such a simple question justified." He had asked, "Is the Secretary asleep?" to which Fanny responded, after glancing back at her father, "Almost." At that, Fred quickly closed the door and Fanny walked back to her seat, puzzled.

The trouble Fanny had sensed was real. In the hall beside Fred stood Lewis Thornton Powell, also known as Lewis Payne. The six-foot-four Floridian was the son of a Baptist minister and a veteran of Robert E. Lee's Army of Northern Virginia. He had been wounded and captured at the Battle of Gettysburg, but he escaped while recovering in Maryland and had met the famous actor John Wilkes Booth through their mutual friend, John Surratt, Jr. Originally, Powell was the muscle Booth recruited to help them secret President Lincoln out of Washington after they were to have kidnapped him and demanded as ransom the release of all Confederate prisoners. But on the previous Sunday, when Lee had surrendered along with Powell's fellow Confederates in the Army of Northern Virginia, Booth had been forced to revise his plan. The new strategy called for the murder of the top leadership of the United States government: President Lincoln, Vice President Andrew Johnson, and Secretary of State William Seward. The idea was to sink the North into chaos while inspiring the South to renew its fight for independence.

Powell had forced his way into the Seward home by insisting that he had to personally deliver medicine to Secretary Seward from a nearby pharmacy. A family servant, William H. Bell, had tried to stop him at the door, but Powell's confident determination convinced the former slave to step aside, and Powell made his way up the stairs. Fred observed him approaching his father's room and stopped Powell, who again claimed that he had to deliver the medicine in person. It was then that Fred peered into his father's room, closed the door, and frowned when Fanny reopened it to announce that their father was awake. Closing the door once more, Fred forcefully insisted that the Secretary could not be disturbed, and Powell turned angrily back down the stairs.[183]

Just when Fred thought the puzzling man might be leaving, Powell spun around, drawing a pistol from his coat. Fred froze as Powell pressed the muzzle against his forehead. Fred heard a "click." The gun had misfired. Before Seward could move, Powell raised the pistol over Fred's head and brought it down with a force that brought blood pouring down his face.

Beyond the closed door, Fanny and George Robinson sat listening to what seemed to be soft thuds just beyond them in the hall. Robinson later reported that he sensed a fight had ensued, and he rushed to the door to aid Fred Seward. But Fanny recalled things differently. She insisted that her memories of that night were "very vivid in my own mind—but I cannot describe all that took place, because in many instances I cannot remember to have seen some who were in the room ...." She recalled, though, that she was entirely oblivious to the brutality Powell had unleashed just outside the door. It sounded, she said, like they were "chasing a rat in the hall," and she flashed to a memory of just such an encounter that had once occurred. When the thuds continued, though, she asked Sergeant Robinson, "What can be the matter? Do go and see," and then she moved quickly after him toward the door.

As Robinson turned the knob and swung the door back, Fanny recognized Powell again. She watched as he and Fred walked in, with Fred closest to her. She puzzled at the sight of him, with the "side of his face covered with blood, the rest very pale, his eyes full of intense expression," and when she asked him what was the matter, Fred "could not answer me." Then, just beyond her brother, Fanny saw Powell with his arms stretched out before him. In one hand he had a knife and in the other, the misfired pistol. As he rushed toward Seward's bed, Fanny raced after him, crying, "Don't kill him!"

Seward heard the word "kill" as Fanny tried to protect him. Wakening, he looked up into Powell's eyes and watched his arm come down, stabbing him in the face. The Secretary felt only drops of blood as Powell drew his arm back and a flap of skin fell from where Seward's cheek had been. As it all was happening, Powell's sleeve caught his eye and all Seward could think in that surreal moment was what "handsome fabric" covered his killer. Powell plunged the knife toward Seward again and again, grunting in frustration when he accidentally struck the headboard and then struggling to turn Seward's face to be sure the jugular was exposed.

Fanny screamed at the sight of Powell kneeling over her father, bracing his left hand, still holding the pistol, against Seward's chest. Hearing her, Sergeant Robinson managed to pick himself up off the floor, where a blow from Powell had sent him crashing as the assailant pushed through the door. Robinson saw Powell's arm rise up again and the soldier realized with horror that he had no weapon with which to stop him. "My only chance," Robinson realized, "was to destroy the stroke ... catching his arm from behind as I stood over him. This I did, and he succeeded in only slightly cutting the neck on the side next to him .... As I was dragging him off from Mr. Seward and the bed, he struck over his shoulder at me, cutting my right shoulder to the bone in two places, only missing the large artery, by less than half an inch."[184]

In the moment when Sergeant Robinson jumped on Powell and distracted him, Secretary Seward managed to drag himself off the bed and out of Powell's reach. At about that time, Gus Seward, awakened by Fanny's screams, came racing into the room and helped Robinson pin Powell to the floor. When Gus ran to get a pistol, though, Powell managed to escape Robinson, who had been weakened by the gash Powell cut into his neck and shoulder. Before Gus could return, Powell dashed out of the room, confident that he had succeeded in his task. As he raced down the stairs, Gus heard him muttering "I'm mad! I'm mad!" and then, as if to prove the point, he struck one final blow with his knife deep into the back of a State Department messenger named Emerick Hansell who was at the home when the attack began and was now running for help. Powell leapt onto his horse and tried to race off, but then the events of the night seemed to pause. The beast would not move faster than a walk. When someone ran out of the Seward house screaming murder, three soldiers outside next door looked down the street and saw Powell whipping the horse with the reins, his calves smacking against the animal's sides. They nearly caught up with him when the stubborn horse suddenly responded and carried him off into the darkness.

Inside the Seward house, Fanny's eyes darted about, trying to make sense of what had just happened. She had been "pacing the room back & forth from end to end—screaming." Before Powell ran from the room, she'd managed to race out into the hall for help, summoning her mother and Anna. As they approached her, Fanny asked, "Is *that man* gone?" to which they responded, "What man?" It was only then that Fanny saw Gus, "his forehead covered with blood" and as Fred caught her eye, lying on the floor, and she noticed that "every man I met had blood on his face."

She then raced back into the room, desperate to find Secretary Seward and was shocked to discover that he was not in the bed. Instead she found, lying on the ground, "what I thought was a pile of bed clothes—then I knew that it was Father." Rushing to his side, her feet slipped in the blood that had soaked the rug, indeed, the entire room. Reaching for him, Fanny feared the worst. He "looked so ghastly I was sure he was dead, he was white & very thin with the blood that had drained from the gashes about his face & throat." Overwhelmed, she wailed, "O my God! Father's dead."

At that, George Robinson hurried over and listened for a heart beat. He managed to get the Secretary back onto the bed, assured Fanny that her father was still alive, and then directed her to staunch the blood as they both applied pressure to Seward's wounds despite Robinson's own injuries. Fanny was still certain her father was about to perish when she heard him reassure her, "I am not dead. Send for the police and a surgeon, and close the house."

While Robinson cared for the Secretary, the Seward women searched for another possible assassin. Frances and Anna checked the attic while Fanny descended to the parlor floor of the house and searched room by room alone. They could not call on the men for help; they were nearly all dead. Gus was barely conscious with gashes on his hand and forehead, and Sergeant Robinson suffered from multiple, deep wounds to his shoulder. Emerick Hansell lay moaning on yet another bloody bed, with a two-and-a-half-inch-deep knife wound in his back.

But it was the Secretary and Fred who worried the doctors the most. Fred lay in the hall at the top of the stairs. Powell's blow to Fred's head had fractured the skull in five places, exposed his brain, and left Fred unconscious for days. The Secretary had lost so much blood that the attending physician, Dr. T. S. Verdi, feared for his life. Everyone was stunned at first that Seward was alive at all, but then they realized that the painful metal contraption that doctors had placed around Seward's neck and jaw to heal the damage from the carriage accident had actually blocked most of Powell's blows. Despite the terrifying experience and tremendous loss of blood, as well as the nerve damage that would forever mar his face, it appeared that Secretary Seward would make a full recovery.

Indeed, it appeared that all of Powell's victims would survive. Oddly, though, it was the ones who showed no visible damage whom the assassin had mortally wounded. Frances Seward, weakened by years of headaches, heartache, and possibly depression was at first confused by the entire series of events. Fanny tried to help her mother understand, but Frances seemed to think, as Fanny recalled, "that the whole occurrence consisted in Father's being more than usually delirious, & that in that condition he had injured Fred. She had an indistinct view of Gus and Payne struggling at the door, & supposed it to be father with a knife." After leaving her mother to speak with the doctors, Fanny went back into her father's room, and she and George Robinson, still bleeding from his wounds, assessed the damage, recovering a hat that turned out to be Lewis Powell's while the wounded sergeant recovered the misfired pistol and looked for the missing primer that had saved Fred Seward's life. In the background, Fanny could hear her father groan as the doctor sewed his cheek, but Seward later comforted her, insisting that he remembered "no feeling of pain" throughout the entire ordeal, the shock of it all protecting him.

Fanny looked about the house and could only see blood. "It was a terrible sight," she marveled. "There was so much blood everywhere. The drugget [rug] on the stairs was sprinkled with it, all the way down to the floor below. On the inner side of the door of Father's room there was, in blood, the distinct impression of a hand, which seemed to have clenched it from without. While this was being wiped off I marked the door, to show where the place had been. When we found father there was such a pool of blood that our dresses were drabbled in it." As Fanny leaned against the wall, waiting for yet another doctor to finish examining her father, one of the surgeons came over and made an awkward attempt to comfort her while also continuing his work, commenting, "You have been a pretty brave little girl tonight, can't you get me a shirt for your father?" Fanny, far from a little girl, walked in a daze to Gus's room, retrieved some shirts, and then went to Fred's room, where doctors were increasingly worried about his condition.

Frances, however, worried Fanny almost as much as Fred did. Despite her reputation for a weak constitution and even hypochondria, Frances "bore up with the greatest fortitude," Fanny observed. Still, Frances was "ill in some way … perhaps with palpitation. She showed feeling & Anxiety that must have been anguish … as we spoke together she told me she was afraid Fred would not live."

No sooner had Frances said this than the women learned that Powell's accomplice, John Wilkes Booth, had shot Secretary Seward's old, dear friend. President Lincoln was lying in another bloodstained bed just a few blocks away, slowing fading with the night. The horror seemed endless, and it weighed heavily on Frances and Fanny. In the days that followed, Fanny kept thinking back to "those long dark hours" of that awful night. "The thoughts they brought," she insisted,

were almost overwhelming. The thought that such cruel & inhuman beings, as the man who had attacked my father & brothers, existed, made me wish myself dead, & out of such a world, anywhere seemed better. The anxiety of the condition of father & Fred was fearful. Although a guard sat in the entry, I could not reason away a feeling that the assassin who had wounded so many might return & finish his attempt. I had felt suspicious of every unknown face however friendly—I was too shocked to reason. "I have supped full on horrors"[185] rang over & over in my mind—and I retraced the dreadful scene—& remembered the moment when I felt almost beside myself, and Anna's hand laid on my arm, & her voice, "Fanny! Fanny!" recalled me, & I stopped screaming to answer her inquiries & to remember that I must be quiet & calm. Blood, blood, my thoughts seemed drenched in it—I seemed to breathe its sickening odor. My dress was stained with it—Mother's was drabbled with it—it was on everything. The bed had been covered with blood, the blankets & sheet chopped with several blows of the knife. Night wore away while we sat there—the gray light of morning came—"Risest thou thus gray dawn again"[186] repeated itself over & over in my mind—& that light should come, & the sun rise, & the birds sing & the green leaves rustle in the trees, seemed strange in such a world.[187]

Frances and Fanny Seward never did recover from the shock of that night. Within three months, as William, Frederick, and Augustus Seward regained their strength, Frances faded away. In June 1865, she died of a heart attack, but many suspected that the trauma of the April assault, on top of the coughs, headaches, moodiness, and sorrow that plagued her daily, simply wore her down.

Heartbroken over the loss of her beloved mother, Fanny developed an obsessive attachment to her father. Writing to him in August, Fanny reiterated her desire to return to Washington from Auburn, despite the fears that plagued her ever since that April night. "We are waiting to hear if I may yet be allowed to return," she told the Secretary, "to my place, with you, my dear Father, where I should comfort my self in trying to be of some little comfort to you." But within eight weeks of begging to see him, Fanny, too, succumbed to consumption and faded from William Seward's life. She was not quite twenty-two years old.[188] Lewis Powell may not have killed Secretary Seward that night, but his actions nearly destroyed that family.

"THE NEST THAT HATCHED THE EGG"

Three days after the attack on William Seward and just down H Street from his house, a woman stood in the entryway of her home. It was

11:00 p.m. on the night of April 17, and she turned to a Union officer and asked to pray. Major H. W. Smith saw little harm in the notion and granted the widow's request. Gathering her skirts, Mary Jenkins Surratt knelt on the floor of her home and began the rhythmic recitations that brought her comfort and salvation. She would need them. Union officers suspected her son of the attempted murder of Secretary of State William Seward, and they had reports that much of the planning for both Seward's attack and Booth's murder of President Lincoln had occurred at her home. Just minutes before, a search had uncovered a carte de visite bearing the words "Sic Semper Tyrannis," the Virginia state motto. That was the same phrase Booth had shouted when he leapt to the stage after shooting Lincoln at Ford's Theater. That, combined with the numerous other images around Surratt's room of Confederate generals and a Confederate flag, raised suspicions. But it was the photo of John Wilkes Booth that a young police lieutenant found, and especially the fact that someone had taken the time to hide it inside a framed print, which had the men convinced that the Surratts were somehow involved.[189]

As Mary prayed, the police stood nearby, watching her, her daughter, Anna, and the servants near the door of the Surratt boarding house, waiting for a carriage that would take the women to army headquarters for questioning. It was a good time to pray. Anna tried to stay calm as her mother had advised, but she was terrified by their arrest. With her eyes tearing, she looked to her mother for strength.

As the group waited, they heard the sound of footsteps as someone ascended the front steps and rang the bell. On edge, Smith reached for his revolver while two of his men stood beside the door. They opened it to reveal a large man, well over six feet tall. He carried a pickaxe on his shoulder and wore cloth tied on his head where a hat should have been. His eyes darted from one uniformed man to the next and he said, "I guess I have mistaken the house."

"No," Major Smith assured him, "you have not." One of Smith's men asked which home the man sought, and when he replied, "Mrs. Surratt's," Smith returned his hand to his pistol, insisting, "This is the house. Come in at once." As the stranger took a few hesitant steps forward, Smith's men closed the door behind him.

Standing in better light, they could see and smell the man's filth. His boots were coated in mud. Indeed, mud reached all the way to his knees. And the missing hat struck Smith as odd, too. Something was not right.

"What do you want here?" Smith asked.

"I have come to dig a gutter for Mrs. Surratt," came the reply. Smith raised his brow, noting that it was a strange hour to be digging. Powell hesitated, but then explained, "I came to get directions from Mrs. Surratt about digging a gutter tomorrow morning," and he hoped she would let him spend the night in her basement so he could get an early start on his work. The man would not have troubled her, he added, except he noticed that the house was well lit and he suspected he would not be disturbing her sleep. He had done work for her before, the man explained, so he knew his presence would not alarm her.

Major Smith turned to Mrs. Surratt, who had risen to her feet, and asked if she knew the man. No, she answered. The devout woman swore she had never seen him. Smith's men searched the stranger and found a certificate in his pocket that identified him as "L. Paine," but the name meant nothing to them. Something was clearly off, though, and Smith glared at the man, "I think you are a spy. Your story does not hang together." He pointed to a chair and had the man sit to await a second carriage. Everyone was under arrest and coming in for questioning.

When they arrived at the headquarters of General Christopher C. Augur, Union commander of the Department of Washington, Colonel Henry H. Wells, one of the special commissioners assigned to investigate the assassination by Secretary of War Stanton, handled Mary's questioning. Well, he tried to at least, but he could get nowhere when he pushed for the location of her son. Frustrated, he moved to the odd man who came to her door that night. Did she ask him to come, as the man stated, to do work at her home? "No sir," Mary insisted. "The ruffian that was in my door when I came away? He was a tremendous hard fellow with a skullcap on and my daughter commenced crying, and said these gentlemen came to save our lives. I hope they arrested him …. I believe he would have murdered us, ever one, I assure you."

As Mary spoke, the strange, filthy man waited in a separate room with a group of suspects the investigators planned to question. They also wanted William Bell, the servant who had opened the door at the Seward home to an assassin three days earlier, to take a look at the group and see if he recognized anyone. Police still believed that Seward's attacker was John Surratt, Jr., but they had had so many reports from soldiers, civilians, and even psychics during the past seventy-two hours that they watched Bell carefully as he scanned the room. Bell studied each face carefully, scrutinizing each man before moving on to the next, when suddenly he stopped. The digger from the Surratt house caught his eye. He did not flinch or look away, but held Bell's horrified gaze even as Bell's hand came up and he extended a finger, wordlessly identifying the man who had nearly killed Secretary Seward, his two sons, a state department clerk, and Sergeant Robison. Powell just stood there, offered no protest, and instead broke into a wide, teeth-baring grin.

Once police realized that it was Powell, not John Surratt, Jr., who had terrorized the Seward home the previous Friday evening, they tried to understand the Surratt family's role in the entire plan. Investigators, thanks to the testimony of one of Mary's boarders, Louis Weichmann, knew that John Wilkes Booth had met frequently with John Surratt, Jr., with Lewis Powell, and even privately with Mary. The question was how such a respectable widow came to be involved in such a despicable plot.

Mary Surratt was born Mary Elizabeth Jenkins in 1823 to a middling-income family in Prince George's County, Maryland. Raised on a small plantation with her two siblings, Mary's first few years were fairly stable until her father suddenly died when she was two. Faced with the management of the family farm, slaves, and three children under the age of four, including a newborn, neighbors assumed that the young widow, Elizabeth Jenkins, would remarry quickly so that someone could manage her husband's holdings. But Mary's mother refused that option and instead applied her mind and talents to handling those matters herself. She managed the work so successfully that by the time Mary was twelve, Elizabeth enrolled her at a nearby Catholic boarding school. The family was Anglican, but nuns at the Academy for Young Ladies would be trusted to educate Mary in the languages, literature, and arts that were expected in the wealthy young belles of Maryland.

Despite her wealth and talents, Elizabeth could not control Mary's independent spirit. The first sign of this came when she converted to Catholicism and remained devoted to the faith even when the school closed and she had to return home. The second sign came when Mary became involved with John Surratt, who had already fathered a child with a local woman. He never married Caroline Sanderson and, despite the scandal, John Surratt captured Mary's attention. The two were married in the late summer of 1840.

John was the adopted son of a wealthy couple named Richard and Sarah Neale, who had no children of their own. When they died, John inherited sizable land holdings, but his gambling habits forced him to sell off his inheritance bit by bit. He did display some sense for land investments, but he exhibited a greater gift for abusing alcohol and his wife. John despised Mary's Catholic faith, but on this she would not budge. Indeed, as many problems as it created at home, the church sustained Mary, especially her local priest, Father Finotti. Gossips whispered that their relationship was anything but pure. When Finotti was quickly transferred to New England in 1852, the locals nodded and smirked, especially those who agreed with the anti-Catholic novels that were all the rage at the time, which warned Protestant America of scandalous behavior by nuns, priests, and the Catholic hierarchy who threatened the nation's traditions.

But Mary remained true to her faith, and when John purchased some land in 1852 about twelve miles south of Washington City, she helped him manage the property. They gradually built a tavern and an inn, as well as a blacksmith shop. Mary liked that the land was near her mother's planation, as well as the farms of her two brothers, but she did not approve of the range of people to which tavern life exposed her three children. With their properties bringing in a fairly sizable income, Mary managed to convince John to send Isaac, Anna, and John, Jr., to Catholic boarding schools in Baltimore and Washington. They also marveled at how busy they were as more people opened businesses and built homes around the crossroads tavern. The area became known as Surrattsville, and the profits from that, as well as John's other holdings, allowed them to purchase a boarding house on H Street in Washington.

By the time the Civil War began in 1861, the Surrattsville crossroads had grown significantly. The Maryland legislature recognized it as a polling place and post office, and John Surratt became the area postmaster. The property's close proximity to Washington on roads that led to the nearby Confederate border, and the family's strong Southern sympathies, allowed the Surratts to make a lucrative living supporting smugglers and spies on top of their legal trade. The only trouble was that John Surratt was drinking more heavily than ever before, and too many of their profits were being consumed by his addiction to the bottle and cards.

When John Surratt died suddenly in 1862, Mary found herself in a position that echoed her mother's situation nearly thirty years earlier. And just as Elizabeth had, Mary realized that as John's increasing alcoholism had forced her to manage more and more of their business, he had unknowingly helped her to develop the skills that would secure her independence. John left behind sizable debts, the payment of which cost so much that Mary could no longer keep her children in boarding schools, but she had enough to hold onto the tavern and the boarding house.

John, Jr., came home and assumed his father's role as postmaster, while his brother Isaac served in the Confederate Army. Young Anna learned to assist her mother, but Mary did not like having the young girl in the tavern world of Surrattsville. But their work, Mary came to believe, was important. She and her children, especially seventeen-year-old John, Jr., became increasingly devoted Confederate sympathizers and John, in particular, used his position as postmaster to become a major player in the Southern spy network. As he later explained, by the fall of 1862 at eighteen years of age, he was

engaged in sending information regarding movements of the United States Army stationed in Washington and elsewhere, and carrying dispatches to the Confederate boats on the Potomac. We had a regular established line from Washington to the Potomac and I being the only unmarried man on the route, I had most of the hard riding to do .... I devised various ways to carry the dispatches—sometimes in the heel of my boots, sometimes between the planks of the buggy. I confess that never in my life did I come across a more stupid set of detectives than those generally employed by the U.S. government. They seemed to have no idea whatever how to search the men.

With Mary's tavern serving as a safe house along John's route, and Mary's proven ability in running the properties in Surrattsville, most scholars are convinced that there is no reasonable possibility that she was unaware of John's actions.

More damning, though, were Mary's own movements during the final year of the war. The Union government had removed John as postmaster, suspecting the tavern for the Confederate base that it was, and Mary had relocated to the boardinghouse in Washington. The move also allowed Mary to escape the increasingly watchful eye of Federal investigators and to move her daughter away from the unsavory world of taverns and their guests.

She secured reputable boarders for her home on H Street, including an old school friend of John's, Louis Weichmann. The young man was a clerk in the War Department, and he did not share Mary's or John's open Confederate sympathies. But the room was close to his job, it came at a reasonable rate, and Louis had appreciated Mary's warm, welcoming role as a host when John first introduced him to Mary several years earlier. Moving into the boarding house in late 1864, Louis enjoyed his time with the Surratts, though their friends puzzled him on occasion.

Particularly curious was their relationship with the famous actor John Wilkes Booth. The thespian would spend time at the home entertaining the boarders and enjoying convivial evenings in the parlor. But more often than not, he wanted to meet privately with John Surratt on business matters or, even more oddly, privately with Mrs. Surratt.

Most puzzling, though, were the unsavory characters that frequented the boarding house by the spring of 1865. These included a scruffy German-American named George Atzerodt (who would be assigned by Booth to kill Vice President Andrew Johnson, though in the end Atzerodt refused to do so), an odd pharmacy clerk named David Herold, and a tall, quiet, beast of a man who introduced himself as James Wood, but weeks later came to stay at the boarding house under the name of Lewis Payne, claiming to be a Baptist minister.

Other tenants in the house became suspicious, too. Eliza Holohan observed Powell's fine suits and expensive shirts and commented to Anna Surratt that he did not strike her as the type who "would convert many souls." Mary, however, disagreed. The confusions over the name of Wood and Payne seemed not to bother her, nor did his odd private meetings with John, Booth, and Atzerodt. Wood/Payne/Powell, Mary declared firmly enough to end the conversation, "was a great looking Baptist preacher."

After word spread of Booth's attack on Lincoln and the President's death, Louis Weichmann began to realize what he might have been observing in Mary Surratt's boarding house that winter. He went to the authorities, and this is how they came to arrest Mary and Anna on the night of April 17, and, ironically, Lewis Powell when he showed up at her door with astonishingly poor timing.

At first Mary stumped the investigators who tried to prove that she was involved with the assassination plot. She defended her acquaintanceship with Booth and claimed that her son was in Canada, but would offer little beyond that. Authorities did not need much more from her, however, to seal Mary's fate. Within weeks they had testimony from Weichmann and Mary's tavern tenant that proved particularly damning.

It appeared that on April 10, 1865, Mary asked Weichmann to escort her to Surrattsville. She sent him to Booth to see if they could borrow his buggy and horses. Booth said that he'd sold them, but he gave Weichmann $10 to cover the expense of renting their transportation. Along the route, Mary saw John Lloyd, the man who leased her tavern at Surrattsville, approaching them from the opposite direction. She ordered Weichmann to stop their carriage, and Lloyd hurried to Mary's side of the road to speak with her privately.

The topic of conversation was so private that Lloyd himself could barely understand what Mary whispered. Made cautious by Weichmann's proximity on the seat next to her, Mary continued until Lloyd finally insisted that she speak more clearly. That was when he heard her ask about the "shooting irons," which were hidden at the tavern. He replied that he had "forgotten about their being here" and added that they "were hid away far back, and that [he] was afraid the house might be searched." What he wanted to do,

Lloyd told Mary, was bury the guns; if Federal authorities found them and Lloyd was suspected of treason, he could be arrested or worse. But Mary insisted that they would be wanted soon. They must be available.

On Good Friday morning, April 14, Weichmann escorted Mary to mass, and then returned home to enjoy a day off from work. That afternoon, she insisted that she needed Weichmann to accompany her to Surrattsville again. She had some debts to settle and it had to be done immediately. Before they left, John Wilkes Booth appeared and asked to speak with Mary privately in the parlor. By 3:00 p.m., Mary was ready to leave and climbed into the carriage with a small package that Booth had left with her to take to Surrattsville. It was about six inches square, and she placed it gently on the floor of the carriage, declaring that it was made of glass, but she did not want it to get wet. After arriving at the tavern and waiting for Lloyd to return, she rushed out to see him as soon as he pulled up in a wagon to personally deliver the package.

Lloyd later testified, despite his fear that Booth's backers would kill him for the betrayal, that Mary walked up to him and declared, "Well, Mr. Lloyd, I want you to have those shooting irons ready; there will be parties here tonight who will call for them." She then handed him the package, which held a pair of field glasses, and told Lloyd to have two bottles of whiskey on hand as well. As Weichmann and Mary Surratt returned home, she observed the same festivities in Washington that Fanny Seward was watching from their home at Lafayette Square. "I am afraid all this rejoicing will be turned into mourning, and all this glory into sadness," she mused. Moments later, Weichmann heard her add, "after sunshine there was always a storm" and that the revelers were "too proud and licentious, and that God would punish them."

Within three days of that carriage ride, President Lincoln was dead, John Wilkes Booth was on the run, John Surratt, Jr., was nowhere to be found, and Mary and Anna Surratt and Lewis Thornton Powell were arrested at the H Street boarding house. Powell never tried to claim innocence, and Mary stood little chance once Weichmann and Lloyd testified against her. The one man who might have been able to clear her name was her own son, John Surratt, Jr., but he chose to stay in hiding in Canada.

On a blistering July day in Washington, Mary Surratt stumbled as she climbed the new, wooden steps in the Washington Navy Yard. She had spent the morning in her cell, wearing the same black dress and heavy veil that shielded her throughout the trial. Anna had tried repeatedly to meet with President Andrew Johnson to ask him to commute Mary's sentence, as had several others. But Johnson refused, insisting that Mary had "kept the nest that hatched the egg."

Mary heard men testing the ropes all morning, and by noon the doors that would drop beneath the conspirators' feet were snapping open with uniform consistency. It was time for the ugly business of execution to begin.

Soldiers stood on each side of Mary, helping her to her spot on the gallows. Additional men carried umbrellas to shield Mary, Lewis Powell, David Herold, and George Atzerodt from the sun's heat. The rope cut into Mary's wrists when the hangman bound her, and then he hesitated with the line for her legs. He had spent the morning positive that the president would commute her sentence at the final hour. Now he pondered the etiquette of binding the first woman he had ever executed, but then he shrugged, bent down, and proceeded to wrap the rope around her skirts, tightening it against her legs. Still feeling a bit awkward about the entire business of hanging a woman, the man stepped back and examined the others.

In her final moment, Mary cried out to the crowd, "I am innocent, but God's holy will be done." Herold, who had raced off with Booth after he killed Lincoln, was shaking too badly to say anything. Atzerodt admonished the crowd to "take warning," adding, "Good-by gentlemen who are before me, may we all meet in the other world." Lewis Thornton Powell said nothing and simply stepped forward to his proper spot. At 1:22 p.m. on July 7, 1865, Captain Christian Rath gave the signal. Four doors dropped and four bodies fell with a "heavy slam." Surratt, Herold, and Atzerodt died instantly when their necks snapped. Powell's monstrous body proved as resistant as Rath feared it would. Despite his precautions, he grimaced as Powell swung for a minute, then another, and another before life left his body. Then men cut the bodies down and Rath personally untied the ropes around Mary's legs and wrists and carried her to her coffin, "not being willing that any hand should desecrate her." Another family had been destroyed by the war.

"I REALLY CANNOT FIX MY MIND ON ANYTHING ELSE"

Clara Harris struggled to erase the events of April 14, 1865, from her mind. She was the daughter of New York Senator Ira Harris, the man who replaced William Seward when he became Secretary of State.[190] Senator Harris was a former New York Supreme Court justice who lacked Seward's political skills, but he made up for that with persistence. Indeed, he was so often at the White House pestering the President about one bill or another that Lincoln joked that he always checked under his bed at night to be sure Harris wasn't there waiting to ambush him.

Clara Harris lived in her father's home at 15th and H Streets, a block away from the Seward home at Lafayette Square, which was just across the street from the White House and about a dozen blocks from Mary Surratt's boarding house. Clara's mother had died when she was young, and so she was raised primarily by her stepmother, Pauline Rathbone, a widow who married Judge Harris in 1848. Pauline and Ira came from the old families of Albany, and their children were raised among the state capital's social elites. Pauline brought two sons to the marriage, and they were raised closely with Ira's son and three daughters. By the time the Harris family arrived in Washington, Clara was thirty-years old and quite close to her stepbrother, Henry Rathbone.

Henry was three years younger than Clara, the son of Albany's former major, and a very wealthy young man in 1860s Washington. When the Civil War began, he joined the 12th U.S. Infantry Regiment and fought on the Peninsula in 1862, at Antietam later that fall, and finally at the debacle at Fredericksburg that winter. Most of his service was in staff positions, but his years in uniform were still difficult. It appears that he was not entirely healthy from the start, but the disease and exposure that defined army life plagued him. He spent portions of 1862 and 1863 battling malaria-like symptoms, but he felt compelled to stay in the army, returning to the front in 1864 against his physician's orders. Warnings from doctors, however, that "these repeated attacks of a wasting and debilitating disease were likely to permanently injure your constitution," finally convinced Rathbone to accept a desk assignment in the capital during the final year of the war.

By that point, Clara, one of the great beauties of Washington, was a close confidant of the First Lady. She and Mary Todd Lincoln frequently enjoyed each other's company at the theater and on afternoon carriage rides, despite Mrs. Lincoln's distaste for Senator Harris. He had had the nerve one day in the late fall of 1863 to question whether Mary Todd Lincoln was sacrificing enough for the Union. Demonstrating unusual self-control, Mary bit her lip and reined her temper. Her half sister, Emilie, whose husband, Confederate General Benjamin Hardin Helm, had been killed at the battle of Chickamauga in September, sat beside Mary radiating cold fury. Opposite her, matching Harris's hostility, was Union General and an old Blue Room ex-favorite of Mary's, General Daniel Sickles.

Harris had actually warmed up by attacking Emilie first, staring at the recent widow as he declared, "Well, we have whipped the rebels at Chattanooga and I hear, madam, that the scoundrels ran like scared rabbits." Twenty-six-year-old Emilie had spent the past several weeks trying to get back to Kentucky with her three young children. She was already mourning the loss of too many family members when word arrived that her husband was gone, and the President had personally reached out to help his favorite Todd in her hour of need. Emilie's angry eyes snapped as she retorted, "It was the example, Senator Harris, that you set them at Bull Run and Manassas."

Having sufficiently highlighted Emilie's disloyalty, it was then that he decided to question Mary's as well. "Why isn't Robert in the army?" he asked. "He is old enough to serve his country. He should have gone to the front some time ago." Mary responded, "Robert is making preparations now to enter the Army, Senator Harris ... he is not a shirker as you seem to imply for he has been anxious to go for a long time." And then, taking a breath, the real Mary emerged. "If fault there be, it is mine. I have insisted," she fairly hissed, "that he should stay in college a little longer as I think an educated man can serve his country with more intelligent purpose than an ignoramus."

Undaunted, Harris shot back, "I have only one son and he is fighting for his country," forgetting his stepson, who was also serving, as well as his tact that day. And, because he had already said far too much, Harris felt compelled to direct one more thrust toward Emilie, adding, "And Madam, if I had twenty sons they should all be fighting the rebels." With only outrage to sustain her, Emilie fired back, mocking the patriot's own lack of military service. "And if I had twenty sons, General Harris, they should all be opposing yours."

Emilie could barely contain her tears as she stormed out of the room, and General Sickles didn't try to contain his rage. He thundered through the halls to find President Lincoln. Sickles stumbled a bit as he went, still awkward with the crutches required by the loss of his leg at the battle of Gettysburg the previous July. Sickles reported the entirety of the conversation, but highlighted Emilie's disloyalty in particular. Lincoln chuckled, "The child has a tongue like the rest of the Todds," but that only fanned Sickles's anger. "You should not let that rebel in your house," he shouted. Lincoln turned to the General, and in a tone that matched the Todd women's, though perhaps a bit softer, he said, "My wife and I are in the habit of choosing our own guests. We do not heed from our friends either advice or assistance in the matter. Besides," Lincoln added, "the little 'rebel' came because I ordered her to come, it was not of her own volition."[191]

Despite her lingering disapproval of Senator Harris, Mary Todd Lincoln remained fond of his daughter. And that was how, on the night of April 14, 1865, she and the President arrived outside the Harris home to pick up their guests for the evening, Clara and her stepbrother, now fiancé, Major Henry Rathbone.

The Lincolns had been in fine spirits that day, more light-hearted than they had felt in years. As they approached the theater, though, Lincoln's mind returned to the demands of war. Richmond had fallen and Lee had surrendered, but other Confederate armies remained in the field. And when the war ended, what then? Could he convince the radicals in Congress, not to mention the radicals in the South, to accept his plan for reconciliation?

The foursome arrived at Ford's Theater after the play, My American Cousin, had already begun. The orchestra broke into "Hail to the Chief" while the Lincolns and their guests made their way to the presidential box. Mary enjoyed seating everyone: her husband taking the rocker that Harry Ford, the theater owner's brother, had placed there for the president's comfort, while she and Clara took the chairs to his right, and Rathbone sat on the couch on the far side of the box. Mary tried to engage her husband in the play, but he had fallen into one of his dark broods, though he smiled softly as Mary grasped his hand and happily wondered if Clara would be shocked by their affection. It was not long after that when Mary heard a loud bang, felt her husband squeeze her hand, and then saw him slump forward in the smoky haze that hung over them.[192]

Rathbone looked over with shock at John Wilkes Booth, who still stood behind Lincoln. He heard Booth shout "Freedom!" or something to that effect as Rathbone leapt toward the killer. Booth twisted away from Rathbone, and when the Major came at him again, he slashed at Rathbone with a knife. "I parried the blow by striking it up," Rathbone recalled, but the blade still caught his left arm, slicing a deep gash from his armpit to his elbow. As Booth climbed atop the box rail, Rathbone lunged for him, throwing the famous actor off balance as he leapt to the stage.

Rathbone yelled, "Stop that man!" but the audience seemed mesmerized by the famous actor and the odd interruption of the play. Then Mary's piercing screams filled the air, and Clara shouted, "The President's been shot!" Doctors from the audience rushed to the box while Rathbone struggled to open the door that Booth had wedged shut.

When they decided to move Lincoln to a nearby house, Rathbone insisted on assisting them. It wasn't until the President was laid down in the back bedroom that Rathbone collapsed. With all attention focused on Lincoln, no one but Clara realized just how serious her fiancé's wounds were. Booth's blade had cut a major artery near Rathbone's elbow, and the loss of blood was slowly rendering him unconscious. Finally doctors realized the gravity of his injury and took him home, but Clara stayed to be a comfort to her dear friend Mary.

The problem, though, was that Clara was the perfect representation of their nightmare. Her face and hands were covered with blood, her eyes were bloodshot and swollen from crying, and her gown was soaked to a deep crimson. As she approached Mary, Clara recalled, the First Lady would "look at me with horror & scream, oh! my husband's blood, my dear husband's blood ...." It was Rathbone's blood, not Lincoln's, but Clara could not seem to get any rational thought through Mary's head. Always teetering on the edge of stability, Mary Todd Lincoln seemed to have finally toppled into the abyss.

Clara eventually went home and cleaned herself up. There she found Henry lying on a bed, deathly pale, and reliving the assassination in a delirium. "God in heaven," he cried, again and again, "save him!" Quietly composed, Clara assisted the army surgeon who treated Rathbone's wound and stitched him up. Despite all the water and bandages, though, Clara could not seem to cleanse the brutal images from either of their minds. Like Willie Shepherd after the battle of Shiloh, and Fanny Seward who had endured a similar nightmare that same night, Harris could think of little else. In the days that followed, she confided to a friend, "I [cannot] settle myself quietly .... When I [sit] down to write, I [do] not intend alluding to these fearful events at all, but I really cannot fix my mind on anything else—though I try my best to think of them as little as possible, I cannot sleep, & really feel wretchedly."[193]

Clara Harris managed to get through the weeks and months that followed with the same calm discipline that she displayed that dreadful night. The surgeon who treated Rathbone had marveled at her "remarkable courage" and "presence of mind," and it seemed that Clara would need to return to that well again and again to sustain both herself and Rathbone.

The trouble, though, was that Rathbone seemed unable to find that "presence of mind" despite both their efforts. He and Clara married two years after the assassination, and there may have been some happy times in their home on Lafayette Square, but by 1869, Rathbone was seeing doctors to treat "attacks of neuralgia of the head and face and in the region of the heart attended by palpitations and at times difficulty breathing." No one seemed to know how to help him. The problems became severe enough that in 1870, the year their first son was born—on Abraham Lincoln's birthday, no less—Rathbone suddenly retired from the army. Both he and Clara had enough family money that he did not need to work, and his increasing mental instability made work impossible even if they had needed the funds. But as the years went by, his nervous disorder amplified into what seemed to be paranoia. Friends reported that Rathbone was obsessed with the idea that someone was trying to hurt him, Clara, or their three children and that he would be unable to save them, just as he had failed to save President Lincoln.

By the early 1880s, Henry's ailments had evolved to include dyspepsia, a painful stomach disorder, and his paranoia inspired a habit of carrying a gun to keep his family safe, a habit Mary Todd Lincoln would develop as well. And, just as Fanny Seward clung to her father and Mary could not seem to keep Tad close enough, Henry Rathbone could barely let Clara from his sight. In the fall of 1882, Rathbone decided the family needed a relaxing vacation to Europe, and in November they set sail on the Werra heading to Germany. Traveling with Henry and Clara were their children Harry, 13, Gerald, 12, and Pauline, 10, as well as Clara's sister, Louise.

Years later, rumors spread that Clara had insisted that she would not go if Louise did not travel with them. Even after they settled in Hanover, the trip seemed to offer no peace to Henry. Stories spread that he would not let Clara leave the house without him and that he would not even let her sit near a window. Clara began to fear for her safety and that of their children. But what could she do? If anyone understood the guilt and trauma that plagued Henry Rathbone, it was the woman who had sat beside him that terrible night. She did everything she could to help Henry, but he continued to lose weight, appearing sickly and pale to the few people he allowed near him.

In the early morning hours of Christmas Eve 1883, Clara watched as Henry seemed to struggle through yet another hallucination. When he headed toward the children's room, she became terrified, yet displayed the same "presence of mind" that had kept her steady the night Lincoln died. She stopped Henry and somehow convinced him to come with her to their room, and one of them locked the door. A short time later, gunfire was heard. Then another shot. And another.

When the police arrived, Henry was distraught. Someone had shot his wife, stabbed her, and then sliced Rathbone's arm just as Booth had nearly two decades earlier. Rathbone was beside himself for failing his wife, just as he had failed his commander-in-chief and failed his nation. For the rest of his life, Henry Rathbone preferred this version of the story. As painful as it was, it was far better than the truth. And the truth was that Henry Rathbone had killed Clara and then turned the knife on himself.

Rathbone was "hopelessly insane," U.S. Consul William Fox reported after he visited the American. Everyone knew, after all, that it was Rathbone who had fought with the famous John Wilkes Booth. "He is suffering from the worst form of Melancholia and imagines that everyone is conspiring against him. He realizes fully what he has done" but this was a questionable conclusion since Rathbone also insisted, "that it is the result of a conspiracy."

As word spread to the United States, reporters asked anyone who was close to the Rathbones to try to explain why on earth Henry would kill his wife and then attempt to take his own life. His lawyer blamed the lingering trauma of the Lincoln assassination. "The scene always haunted his mind," he explained. Rathbone's doctor, G. W. Pope, agreed, arguing that Henry "never was thoroughly himself after that night ... I have no hesitation in affirming that the dreaded tragedy, which preyed upon his nervous and impressionable temperament for many years, laid the seeds of [this] homicidal mania."

"LOVE ONE ANOTHER"

In the winter of 1865, William Seward announced that the family was going on a trip to the Caribbean. His wounds had healed. Well, they had healed as much as they ever would. Gus, too, had made a full recovery, and the warm sun would nurse Frederick back to full vigor, the Secretary insisted. Anna and Fanny were stunned. Anna was exhausted from caring for Frances, Fanny, Fred, and Gus, not to mention the Secretary himself, and she dreaded the seasickness that the trip would bring. Fanny was tired, too, but she quickly acquiesced if the journey was the only way she could be with her father.

What the Secretary of State did not announce was his other agenda for the trip. They were headed for Santo Domingo, where he would explore his long-held interest in a U.S. naval base in the area. They set sail in January 1866, and while in the Dominican Republic, he met with William and Jane Cazneau, an American couple who had been promoting the idea of a U.S. presence in the region since the 1850s. Word of the trip and Seward's ties to the Cazneaus leaked out, as well as Seward's suggestion that President Johnson make William Cazneau America's commissioner and consul general in Santo Domingo. Seward's fellow Republicans were outraged. The Cazneaus represented the old Slave Power from prewar days. How on earth could Seward meet with them just months after Appomattox (which he had done) and again now? The Slave Power had just been defeated eight months earlier, his enemies cried.[194]

Cazneau did not receive the appointment, nor did Seward's family particularly enjoy the trip. But William Seward did. The jaunt to the Caribbean and his political work there symbolized an ability to heal that few of those directly affected by the events of April 14, 1865, could muster. That night broke Frances and Fanny Seward, as well as Henry Rathbone and Mary Surratt. Mary Todd Lincoln clung desperately to young Tad in the years that followed, just as Anna Surratt's wails, upon realizing that her mother really would be executed and leave her forever, haunted the prison guards who escorted Mary to her death.

But William Seward, who suffered the worst of the attacks except for the President himself, healed inside and out. He forgave political enemies and renewed prewar friendships. The politics and diplomacy of his country were his life, and he had not struggled for four long years of war and survived the attack of a brutal assassin to collapse now. The Union had been saved, but there was still work to be done.

After Seward retired from public life, he brought his family with him as he traveled to Alaska—his personal addition to America's empire— California, Mexico, and then across the Mediterranean, the Middle East, and Asia. He didn't cling to them, but the war years had taught him an important lesson about enjoying life, enjoying his family, and focusing on the work of his nation. In 1872, he looked at his children and grandchildren gathered around his bed as he took his final breaths. They asked if he had any parting advice for them. "Love one another," Seward answered as he slipped away.

❧ CONCLUSION ❧

As winter approached in 1900, an aging woman in Tallulah, Louisiana, reflected on years gone by. She was approaching her sixtieth birthday, young enough to be astonished that six decades had already passed and old enough to deeply ponder the hope, carnage, and dreams that had filled her days. It was the war years of 1861 to 1865 that dominated her memory, and as she greeted the new century, she reflected over all the war had taken. But she also recognized that the suffering had cleansed some sins.

"I was born and raised in the South (and to this day I have never been North of Mason and Dixon's line)," she wrote, "as were all of my relations before me as far back as we can recall them …. Yet with this unmixed Southern blood from generation after generation of slaveholders, my first recollection is of pity for the Negroes and a desire to help them." As she continued writing, it became clear that the pity she felt was equally, if not more so, for herself and for her family. It disturbed her to be tied to a slave's life, which she described as "even under the best owners … a hard, hard life … absolutely under the control of someone until the last breath was drawn; to win but the bare necessaries of life, no hope of more, no matter how hard the work, how long the toil; and to know that nothing could change your lot. Obedience, revolt, submission, prayers—all were in vain."

It was also the belief that she and her relations bore a responsibility for this suffering. "Waking sometimes in the night," she confessed, "as I grew older and thinking it all over, I would grow sick with the misery of

215

it all." Despite the pride she took in the fact that their slaves were "protected from cruelty," the woman knew, even as a girl, that "there were abuses impossible to prevent. And constantly there were tales circulated of cruelties on neighboring plantations, tales that would make one's blood run cold." She was also tortured by the idea of owning another human being. "Always I felt the moral guilt of it, felt how impossible it must be for an owner of slaves to win his way into Heaven. Born and raised as we were, what would be our measure of responsibility?" she wondered.

The woman, who had greeted 1861 in the lap of luxury, insisted that the war may have "swept from us everything and life since '65 has been a long struggle for the necessaries of life," but "I have never regretted the freeing of the Negroes. The great load of accountability was lifted, and we could save our souls alive. God would not require the souls of the Negroes at our hands. Everyone would give account of himself to God."[195]

That woman was Kate Stone Holmes, the spoiled nineteen-year-old belle who watched the war unfold from her family's grand Louisiana plantation with great excitement. She had revealed far more frustration with the family slaves during the war, and with their insubordination as freedmen afterward, than her later reflections would indicate. Perhaps the continuing years had softened her on the issue of slavery. She never spoke well of the North, or of President Lincoln, whose assassination she bitterly praised in 1865 as just retribution for the tyranny she believed he had unleashed on the South. And she remained a devoted Confederate for the rest of her life.

It is significant, though, how much her views on slavery changed in the years after the war. It's unknown if those enslaved to her family would agree that "the great load of accountability" was truly "lifted," but Stone's admission of guilt was unusual among Southern elites in 1900. Like most Northern and Southern whites of the day, she was not going so far as to embrace the idea of racial equality, but Kate Stone felt sufficiently troubled by the institution to take the time to discuss the costly salvation, as she saw it, that emancipation had secured for her family. And she reflected on this in the introduction to her diary, which she recopied into manuscript form in 1900, ensuring that it would be handed down among the other wartime lessons for her children, grandchildren, and future generations.

Indeed, emancipation and reunion exacted a costly toll from all involved. Even though the war technically ended with the last Confederate surrender in the summer of 1865, in truth, wars never really end. They simply transition to the struggle of peace, which can be as challenging as open conflict.

The most obvious toll of America's Civil War involves those who were lost forever. Modern scholars estimate that the nation—North and South, black and white, rich and poor—lost an astonishing 750,000 people between 1861 and 1865.[196] Then there were those who survived, changed forever by their experiences. This does not mean they were all haunted by the kind of nightmares that slowly destroyed Henry Rathbone. Indeed, some, like William Fletcher, did "slide back into the Union" with astonishing ease. Despite the heartache, Ann Erskine determined to face the world, a fatherless widow of six children under the age of thirteen, and she built a future for them on her own. Others, like William Seward, made an astonishing recovery from a nightmare only to watch his beloved wife and daughter fade away.

And then there were the thousands upon thousands of veterans with missing or damaged limbs that kept them from providing for their families as they once had. In Mississippi alone, 20 percent of the state budget in 1866 went to providing prosthetics for Magnolia State veterans.[197] Across the Confederacy, an estimated 300,000 men died of disease, battlefield wounds, and other maladies between 1861 and 1865. In more precise terms, that means that anywhere from one in every five to one in every three men from Virginia to Texas had been killed in four short years.[198]

The North was not far behind the South when it came to the brutal cost of war. By late 1865, Union families were expressing concern about the care of their sons' graves in what was just recently "enemy" soil. During the next six years, the Federal government paid for the exhumation and reburial of more than 300,000 Union men, including 30,000 black soldiers, in 74 new national cemeteries, at a cost of more than $4 million American (Northern and Southern) tax dollars.[199]

But it was over, at least officially, and Civil War families embraced the peace and struggled, as all wartime families have, to accept that they would never understand why some warriors come home and some never do, why those who do return are not the same people who left, why some causes triumph and others fail, and why the good must suffer before evil can be destroyed.

We seek lessons in their experiences, as we always do from history, "lest we are doomed to repeat it." In truth, though, history offers no clear lessons. It offers parables masked in legends cloaked in lies. But that's also the beauty of it. The lessons of life are buried in those twisted, contorted stories, and their familiarity offers comfort and, if we're lucky, hints of insight into the fate that, as Hector advised, is "born with us the day that we are born."[200]

"LET US BE WORTHY"

Our story would not be complete without a glimpse into the future, or the past as it were, of the families who made repeat appearances in our tale.

Jefferson and Varina Davis

The President and First Lady of the Confederacy never recovered their losses from the war. Jefferson Davis was arrested and held in prison from 1865 to 1867 facing possible charges of treason, which the Federal government eventually dropped rather than risk a failure to convict. Varina spent those years as she always had, balancing her effort to submit to her husband's wishes while having strong opinions of her own on how to best provide for her Howell and Davis families. Jefferson tried his hand at several business ventures in the 1870s and 1880s, but he struggled for the rest of his days to sufficiently provide for his family and was forced to depend on the support of friends and Varina's skills as a seamstress.

In the late 1870s, Jefferson moved to a Mississippi Gulf Coast home named "Beauvoir," provided for his use by an old friend and supporter, Sarah Ellis Dorsey. Varina and daughter Winnie followed him there later, in part, rumors swirled, because Varina wasn't pleased with just how supportive Dorsey might be to her husband. There Jefferson wrote his astonishingly dry history of The Rise and Fall of the Confederate Government—Davis himself called it "cumbrous"—and enjoyed moments of pleasure with grandchildren, who brought some comfort despite the losses of the 1870s that included the death of their two remaining sons, one to diphtheria and one to yellow fever, as well as Jefferson's favorite sister and his old wartime advisor and chieftain, Robert E. Lee.

After Jefferson's death in 1889, Varina shocked her peers by moving to Manhattan, New York, with Winnie, where she earned a modest income publishing articles and short stories. She also wrote a two-volume reverential memoir of Jefferson Davis that bore little resemblance to their life together, revealing that even after his death, Varina struggled to find the balance between her own desires and what was expected of her. Echoing her antebellum days in Washington City, Varina developed a diverse group of friends in New York that included Julia Dent Grant, the wife of the man credited for defeating the Confederacy. When Varina Davis died in 1906, it was Julia's son, Frederick Dent Grant—the boy who watched his father's armies conquer Varina's native Mississippi—who organized a memorial service for her in New York.[201]

William and "Nellie" Nugent

When Nellie Nugent Somerville was a girl, her grandmother told her the story of her father's return from the war. William Nugent arrived in Greenville, Mississippi, to discover the once vibrant community destroyed. Arriving at Oakwood Plantation, the grand antebellum home of his in-laws, Abram and Myra Cox Smith, William was told he could find his wife in a nearby field. Confused, Nugent rode on until he saw Nellie, and their young daughter, also named Nellie, in the distance. There stood his wife, the child of one of Greenville's most elite families, clearing weeds from a field. No scene so perfectly captured all the war had cost him.[202] Stunned by the sight, Nellie's grandmother recounted, William Nugent sank to the ground and wept.

The war had, indeed, taken its toll on the Smith and Nugent families. William's father-in-law, Abram Smith, was killed by fire from a Union gunboat in January 1863, and Union forces destroyed his plantation home at Oakwood later that year. By May 1863, the entire town of Greenville had been put to the torch as an early example of the hard war strategy that Ulysses S. Grant and William T. Sherman would perfect the following year in Virginia, Georgia, and the Carolinas.

The arrival of baby Nellie had been the Nugents' only bit of joy in 1863, and she continued to be a beacon of hope during the troublesome postwar era. Nellie Nugent, whom William addressed as "Dear Nellie" in dozens of wartime letters, died on the first day of January 1866, most likely from consumption, though young Nellie argued that "privation, malnutrition, and grief" had also killed her mother. Adding to their grief, Nugent and his mother-in-law, Myra Cox Smith, could only watch in stunned disbelief several months later as what remained of Oakwood Plantation fell into foreclosure.

But they persevered. Nugent formed a successful law practice in rebuilt Greenville with prominent Mississippian William Yerger. Their firm grew with each year, and by the 1880s, Nugent was the president of the state bar association. Myra Cox Smith, his indomitable mother-in-law, managed to care for her remaining children, including a veteran son permanently disabled by a war wound, and helped raise young Nellie while building a successful catering business. By the time Myra died in 1887, she bequeathed a sizable estate built upon the hard-won earnings that her mind and determination made possible.

And young Nellie? She took up the mantle of her father's efforts within the state's prohibition movement and inherited her grandmother's independent spirit. As Mississippi ushered in the twentieth century, Nellie Nugent Somerville was a married mother of four and founder of the state's Women's Suffrage Association; she eventually became the vice-president of the National Women's Suffrage Association. And in 1923, the daughter of William and Nellie Nugent, born amid war, became the first woman elected to the Mississippi State Legislature. Her daughter, Lucy Somerville Howarth, a practicing attorney and later judge in the 1920s, followed her mother into the state legislature in the 1930s and launched a life-long fight for the civil rights of women and minorities that she would continue through the Roosevelt and Kennedy administrations.[203]

Tally and Dick Simpson

Two weeks after Tally Simpson was killed in the Battle of Chickamauga in September 1863, his family laid him to rest in the Simpson family cemetery, which lies on the highest point of what was once a vast plantation. Tally's brother, Dick, went on to become a successful lawyer, and he served in the South Carolina state legislature during the 1870s. One of his most famous clients was Thomas G. Clemson, for whom Dick created the will that, upon Clemson's death, established the university named in his honor. When Dick died in 1912, he was buried near Tally in the family cemetery, which still lies on that beautiful hilltop near Pendleton, South Carolina.[204]

Abraham and Mary Todd Lincoln

Mary Todd Lincoln never really recovered from the trauma of her husband's assassination. Her obsessive mourning for Willie frustrated contemporaries in 1862, but with the loss of her husband, who squeezed her hand with shock as John Wilkes Booth's bullet entered his skull, the public became a little more sympathetic. But no one knew quite knew what to make of her repeated attempts to communicate with her lost loved ones through mediums and the spirit world. Then, in 1875, when she began carrying a gun to protect herself from unknown and unseen assailants, Mary's eldest son, Robert, had her involuntarily committed to an asylum. She was later released, and most scholars agree that although Mary suffered from acute narcissism, she most likely was not insane. Mary Todd Lincoln had simply lived an astonishingly tragic life that finally ended in 1882.[205]

James Rodgers and Mary Felicia Loughridge

In 1959, a boy exploring his grandparents' property in Athens, Texas, looked under their raised home and spotted an old trunk. He dragged it out, pried open the lid, and puzzled through the pile of envelopes filled with time-worn letters. Young David Loughridge had just discovered the misplaced record of James Rodgers, Felicia, Mary, and Ella Loughridge and their journey through the Civil War. David then remained their caretaker, just as his great-uncle Jackson had, for the rest of his days.

James Rodgers Loughridge had returned home to Texas when he learned in the fall of 1863 that his friends and neighbors had elected him to a seat he had not sought in the state legislature. Compelled by duty, he served in Austin through the end of the war, when he returned to Corsicana, resumed his law practice, and opened a thriving cotton warehouse on the Trinity River, the last stop for steamboats from Galveston. He reunited with his fellow veterans in Hood's Texas Brigade Association in the years after the war, and tried without success, as many of the men did, to lure their old commander, John Bell Hood, "home" to Texas.

Little is known of Felicia Loughridge's postwar life beyond the fact that she bore two more sons, Samuel Lycurgas, in 1864, and Jackson B. Loughridge, in 1871. Jackson saved their lengthy correspondence, which he left upon his death in 1942 to his brother, Samuel. His preservation efforts, along with his great-nephew David's, allowed modern readers a rare, detailed glimpse into the concerns and hopes of a wartime family, revealing not only the soldier's thoughts, but also those of his family at home in Felicia's carefully preserved letters to James Rodgers. The collection in that old trunk revealed that Felicia remained interested in military matters later in life, a habit formed during the war when she repeatedly requested more news and maps of the Texas Brigade's battles. There in the trunk lay a poem that she wrote mourning the fall of Charles George "Chinese" Gordon at Khartoum in 1885:

Dear friends of my native land
The days are long, so, long
The nights, are full of anxious thought.
For our devoted land
Not long, can we, Khartoum hold
Unaided, by your arms
Then why so silent all the while?
We hopeful, wait your aid
England's proud and noble name
Her soldiers, brave and true
All all demand, that Khartoum stand
Then why so slow so slow

Can you see the foe surround?
And hear our earnest call?
And not respond, by word or deed?
To cheer your soldiers on?

On the bottom of the page lies a careful notation by Jackson Loughridge, the family archivist: "Written by my mother."[206]

Ulysses S., Julia, and Frederick Grant

Ulysses S. Grant emerged from the Civil War as the North's greatest hero, and he was courted by both parties for the presidency as the election of 1868 approached. Having been a fan of the Lincolns, and having increasingly little in common with President Andrew Johnson, Grant accepted the Republicans' nomination and handily won the White House.

Julia Dent Grant, despite her quiet ways, thrived in her role as First Lady. Her only regret was that when they left Washington at the end of Ulysses's second term, it was amid an economic recession and scandals that, while not of his making, marred his political reputation. After leaving the highest office in America, the Grants enjoyed continued fame as they embarked on a grand tour that allowed them to dine with most of the world's leaders and realize how far Grant's fame had spread.

But the business failures that had defined their early years resurfaced in 1884 as much of the money Ulysses had invested with his son, Buck, was lost when Buck's business partner, Ferdinand Ward, ran off with their fortune as well as with the investments of many of their friends, family, and other leading New Yorkers. Ulysses turned to the publishers who had been paying him to write articles about his wartime experiences to recoup his losses. Several people had advised him to publish his memoirs, and *Century Magazine* presented him with a contract for them in the fall of 1884.

When Grant's friend Mark Twain saw the deal, he told Grant that he should insist on far more money, and wound up offering it if Grant would publish with him. As the tale goes, Grant still could not bring himself to fully accept the generous terms Twain offered, but in the end, he wound up with a sufficiently lucrative contract to provide for his family when he was gone. And that time was looming close. As Ulysses worked almost daily on his memoirs, a malignant tumor in his throat matched his fevered pace. Just days after he finished, Ulysses S. Grant died in July 1885. His memoir became an instant bestseller and allowed Julia to live a comfortable life in her favorite city, Washington, D.C., for the rest of her days. Her only complaint was the absence of her beloved Ulys.

William Shepherd

When Willie Shepherd returned home in 1864, he went right back to his old job as a bookkeeper at the print shop of Dunlop, Sewell, & Spaulding in Chicago. By the early 1870s, he had married Mary E. Bragdon, a connection that brought him into the area's elite social circles, and the couple soon celebrated the birth of their daughter, Rebecca, who became Willie's constant companion. That period also found him in a new business. Willie, or Will, as he became known, moved his family to suburban Evanston and opened his own florist shop, which thrived in the coming years. Like many soldiers, he became an active member of his veterans' group, Taylor's Battery Association, and took rightful pride in his service. There is no indication that the traumatic battlefield memories that haunted him during the war proved debilitating in the postwar period, but clearly he valued time with his old compatriots. In 1927, three years before his death, Will and fellow veteran Charles W. Pierce purchased on behalf of the Battery Association six lots in Chicago's Rosehill Cemetery and erected a memorial there in memory of the men of their unit. William Shepherd died in 1930 and was buried near his fellow Taylor's Battery veterans who, like few others, understood what he sacrificed in the days of 1861–64.[207]

Andrew and Ann Erskine

Ann Erskine never remarried. After that dreadful year of 1862, which took her father, father-in-law, brother, and husband, she somehow managed to keep the family properties running. Little is known about how she did this or how much help she received from her family, but census records of 1870 show her as the head of a household that included her six sons. She owned 70 acres of land and other property valued at more than $2,500, and, listed as a farmer, was one of the wealthiest in the area. Her eldest son, Blucher Haynes Erskine, was twenty-one years old by that point. Along with the Erskine brothers close to his age, he was likely crucial in her ability to manage all of the property. Still, tremendous credit is due to Ann, who refused, like so many other Civil War families, to give up in the face of tragedy. She died in January 1914 and was buried in Seguin, near the farm she started with her husband so many years before.[208]

Madison and Lizzie Bowler

Madison Bowler finally returned to Nininger, Minnesota, in the summer of 1866. He, Lizzie, and their growing daughter, Victoria, had spent the past year in Jacksonport, Arkansas, where Madison worked as a Freedmen's Bureau agent. During the next five years, Lizzie bore four more children, two of whom survived infancy. Then, in 1873, Madison felt compelled to move again, and the Bowlers carved out a new life for themselves in Bird Island, part of Renville County, Minnesota.

For Lizzie, it was literally starting over. "In 1856 my father and mother with their three daughters left the eastern home with all its comforts and immigrated to Minnesota where we built a new home on the raw prairie. That experience was helpful when ... I repeated it in Renville County where we had to endure so much inconvenience and hardship." But endure they did, and by 1878, Madison had emerged as a leader within their growing community. He served in the Minnesota State Legislature that year and continued his work in politics through the 1890s. Lizzie became the mother of five more children, the last of whom, Edna, was born in 1883, nearly twenty years after the birth of her elder sister Victoria had inspired the long, loving, and painful correspondence between their parents, one of whom, Lizzie, valued family—"those who love you best"—above everything, while the other, Madison, insisted that "next to my duty to God comes my duty to my country."[209]

Charlotte Forten

Charlotte Forten spent nearly two years in South Carolina educating former slaves to help them adjust to a life of freedom. In July 1863, she cheered for the soldiers of the 54th Massachusetts as they went off for their assault on Fort Wagner, which was key to the Union's hopes of capturing Morris Island and eventually Charleston, South Carolina. And she endured the terrible news later that month of the 54th's brutal defeat and the death of their abolitionist commander, Robert Gould Shaw. "I know it is a glorious death," she admitted, "But oh, it is hard, very hard for the young wife, so late a bride, for the invalid mother, whose only and most dearly loved son he was.... My heart bleeds for her." She reflected, too, on the fate of the African-American men who followed him, who had come from across the North to have a hand in the destruction of slavery. Forten "shudder[ed] at the thought of that place," Fort Wagner, and at the thought of Shaw and "his heroic men, some dead beneath the walls—some prisoners, doomed, doubtless, to a fate far, far worse than death." The difficulties of the war and the desperate struggle for freedom overwhelmed her that month. Why must it be, she wondered, "that the best and the noblest must be the earliest called away. Especially has it been so throughout this dreadful war."[210]

The debilitating headaches and respiratory problems that had troubled Forten for years returned in spring 1864, due in part, no doubt, to her exhausting schedule during the past two years. She returned to the North and spent the next decade in her native Philadelphia, teaching and publishing several accounts of her work in the South. Nearly a decade later, in the late 1870s, she met a student at Princeton Theological Seminary named Francis Grimké. He was the son of South Carolina planter Henry Grimké, who had had three boys by one of his slaves, Nancy Weston. Henry Grimké was also the brother of South Carolina abolitionists Sara and Angelina Grimké, whose outspoken and moving opposition of slavery had led to their relocation to the North before the war. When Henry Grimké died, he willed that his white son would free his three enslaved half-brothers, but this only happened for a brief period before Francis Grimké found himself enslaved once again. The end of the war and the end of slavery—thanks in part to the efforts of Charlotte Forten and the Grimké sisters, who did not know of Francis's existence until years later—freed Francis once more. He and his brother, Archibald, embarked on an education that eventually led to Archibald's graduation from Harvard Law School and his role as U.S. consul to

Santo Domingo from 1894 through 1898. Francis graduated from Princeton Theological Seminary in 1878, the same year he married Charlotte Forten. The two spent most of the remainder of their lives in Washington, D.C., where until 1928 Francis served as minister at the 15th Street Presbyterian Church, where he and Charlotte continued their work as educators and reformers.[211]

Wilbur and Angelina Fisk

Wilbur Fisk remained as deeply reflective on life after the war as he was during his time in uniform. By the time peace arrived in 1865, most of his Vermont family had emigrated to Kansas, and when Fisk mustered out of service, he and Angelina headed west to join them. He farmed their plot of family land for several years but felt an increasingly powerful call to the ministry. By 1874, he had received a license to preach from the Association of Congregational Churches of Kansas. The following year, Angelina's brother, Reverend Stephen Drew of Albert Lea, Minnesota, helped Fisk earn a position as minister to a church in Freeborn, Minnesota, where he and Angelina served the community for the next three decades.

In the 1880s and 1890s, Fisk became active in the Grand Army of the Republic, the leading Union veterans' organization of the day, and he spoke at several Memorial Day gatherings and other veterans' events. In his speeches during the summer of 1894, Fisk recounted humorous stories of their soldier days, accounts with which all the men could identify. But then he often paused to reflect on the larger meaning of the war, just as he so often had in his wartime articles for *The Green Mountain Freeman*. Thinking back on their time in uniform, Fisk encouraged his audience of veterans to "be worthy of all the good things that are said about us, be true men everywhere, just as true for the right everywhere as we were true to the old flag in the war." And with regard to the too many friends they had lost, the fathers, husbands, brothers, and sons the families had lost, Fisk wondered if the soldiers they gathered to remember were the fortunate ones. "Perhaps in the eternal ages of the future," he suggested, "it may be found that their lives served a better purpose than those of us who survived."[212]

And what of Hector and Andromache? In the final, and arguably the most powerful, book of *The Iliad*, we watch as an old man lifts his weary limbs into a chariot. Harnessed before him are grand horses that had been spared because of his power within his city; a city that the war had nearly destroyed and would soon finish. Behind him a wagon creaks under its weighty burden of finery and gold. With the crack of a whip, the man and his companion set off to pay a ransom to their enemy and retrieve the body of his beloved son and heir.

The aged man was Priam, king of Troy and father of Hector. Days earlier he had watched in horror from atop Troy's walls as the great Achilles killed Hector and then dragged his body around the walls for all of Troy to see. Hector, greatest defender of their city, the hero of their war against the Greeks, was dead, and as all of Troy realized their fate, their wails carried through the streets to Hector's wife, now widow, Andromache. Weaving in their home, she lifted her head and immediately knew that her prophecy had come true. Hector was gone to Hades, and she, their son, and all of Troy were at his enemies' mercy.

It was that mercy that Priam sought as he traveled, with the gods' help, to Achilles's headquarters. Without a word, the great Priam strode across the room, his once powerful body hunched with grief but strengthened by pride. Upon reaching the great warrior, Priam dropped to the floor, grasped Achilles's knees, and kissed his hands. Stunned by the king's humility, Achilles stared through a weary haze. He was weak with his own grief over the death of his best friend, Patroclus, whom Hector, son of the man who now knelt before him, had recently killed. "Think of your father, O Achilles like unto the gods," Priam begged,

who is such even as I am, on the sad threshold of old age. It may be that those who dwell near him harass him, and there is none to keep war and ruin from him. Yet when he hears of you being still alive, he is glad, and his days are full of hope that he shall see his dear son come home to him from Troy; but I, wretched man that I am, had the bravest in all Troy for my sons, and there is not one of them left .... The greater part of them has fierce Mars laid low, and Hector, him who was alone left, him who was the guardian of the city and ourselves, him have you lately slain .... Fear, O

Achilles, the wrath of heaven; think on your own father and have compassion upon me, who am the more pitiable, for I have steeled myself as no man yet has ever steeled himself before me, and have raised to my lips the hand of him who slew my son."

Achilles marveled at the bravery of the old man and, for the first time since Patrocles's death, the rage that filled Achilles's body began to fade. And together, the two warriors, one old and one young, discussed all the pain they had caused and all the pain they must now endure.

Hector's death all but guaranteed the fall of Troy and the fate that his beloved Andromache most feared. She was, as was common for the losers of wars for centuries before and after her time, sent into slavery. But because she was of a ruling household and the wife of the Greeks' greatest enemy, her fate was particularly brutal, at least in her eyes and in ours. She was forced to become the enslaved mistress of Neoptolemus, Achilles's son—the same Achilles who had killed her father, her brothers, and her husband.

Andromache found some comfort in the time she had left with her son, the beautiful baby Astyanax, who had laughed as Hector tossed him in the air not so long ago. But soon, as Andromache knew they would, her captors came for the child. They dared not let the son of such a powerful enemy live. Clutching him to her one last time, an act she knew too many mothers could not enjoy in times of war, she wept as she relinquished their son to be tossed from the walls of Troy, but buried if she promised not to resist their fates. And then, never again to return to her beloved city, her body rocked with the jars and jolts of the wagon as the Greeks carried Andromache to a life of slavery, a life, as Kate Stone knew, was "absolutely under the control of someone until the last breath was drawn .... Obedience, revolt, submission, prayers—all were in vain."[213]

Hector's and Andromache's fates were not the reality that most white Northerners and Southerners faced in 1865, regardless of which flag they followed. For the enslaved, however, Adromache's future was their present reality, as it had been since America's birth. This was one of the reasons why Charlotte Forten felt so called to serve in the Sea Islands and why so many slaves rushed to Union lines despite the hazards that awaited them along the way and even, as Joseph Miller's family discovered, once they were in camp.

For white Americans, however, defeat promised a figurative enslavement. That fear kept Tally Simpson and Wilbur Fisk in the ranks on opposite sides of the Rappahannock. It sustained the Loughridge and Nugent families far to the South, and the Shepherd and Bowler families in the distant North. For Union whites, it wasn't so much the fear that the Confederacy would replace their world, but rather the idea that the South would destroy their dearest traditions. For them, secession represented a dagger slicing through the dream of America. For white Southerners, it was an equally determined struggle for independence, but it became an increasingly desperate one as Confederates faced a future in a world they could not recognize, a world devoid of the traditions that defined them.

And so it was that nearly every American family came to see the Civil War as a struggle for their very survival. They fought, as Hector had, for a world where a son could be "a better man than his father" and "a joy to his mother's heart." For four long years, Americans North and South cut each other down to defend the freedoms they held dear and to literally or figuratively protect themselves and their families from Andromache's enslavement and Astyanax's murder. They waged America's *Iliad*, embracing the fate that "no one alive has ever escaped," with the hope that their children and their children's children could live lives of peaceful freedom on either side of Mason's and Dixon's line.[214]

≫ NOTES ≪

CHAPTER 1

1 Homer, *The Iliad*, trans. by Robert Fagles (New York: Penguin Books, 1990), 208–212. See also Homer, *The Iliad*, trans. by Samuel Butler (New York: Jonathan Cape, 1925), 55.

2 William K. Scarborough, "Not Quite Southern," *Prologue* 36 (2004): 20–29. See also Scarborough, *Masters of the Big House: Elite Slaveholders of the Mid-Nineteenth-Century South* (Baton Rouge, LA: Louisiana State University Press, 2006).

3 Clay Williams, "The Road to War (1846–1860)," *Mississippi History Now*, An Online Publication of the Mississippi Historical Society, http://mshistory.k12.ms.us/articles/206/the-road-to-war-1846-1860. Last accessed December 28, 2012.

4 James M. McPherson, *Ordeal by Fire: The Civil War and Reconstruction* (New York: Knopf, 1982), 141.

5 Michael Fellman, Daniel E. Sutherland, and Leslie J. Gordon, *This Terrible War: The Civil War and Its Aftermath* (New York: Longman, 2002), 78.

6 "Jefferson Davis' Farewell Address" in *The Papers of Jefferson Davis*, http://jeffersondavis.rice.edu/Content.aspx?id=87. Last accessed February 6, 2013. For details regarding the Senate that day, see http://www.senate.gov/artandhistory/history/minute/Jefferson_Davis_Farewell.htm . Last accessed December 28, 2012.

7 William C. Davis, *Jefferson Davis: The Man and His Hour* (Baton Rouge, LA: Louisiana State University Press, 1991), 296.

8 Hudson Strode, ed., *Jefferson Davis: Private Letters 1823–1889* (New York: Harcourt Brace Jovanovich, 1966), 580.

9 William J. Cooper, Jr., *Jefferson Davis, American* (New York: Knopf, 2000), 316–318.

10 Donald E. Reynolds, *Editors Make War: Newspaper Editors in the Secession*

Crisis (Carbondale, IL: Southern Illinois University Press), 137; original: New Bern Weekly Progress, September 25, 1860.

11 Reynolds op. cit., 166. Original: Nashville Republican Banner, January 20, 1861, and Little Rock Arkansas State Gazette, December 29, 1860.

12 James McPherson, Battle Cry of Freedom: The Civil War Era (New York: Oxford University Press, 1988), 252–254.

13 Harry V. Jaffa, Crisis of the House Divided: An Interpretation of the Issues in the Lincoln–Douglas Debates (Chicago: University of Chicago Press, 1999), 402.

14 Cooper op. cit., 315.

15 Cooper op. cit., 325–328.

16 Joan E. Cashin, First Lady of the Confederacy: Varina Davis's Civil War (Cambridge, MA: Belknap Press of Harvard University Press, 2006), 96, 103.

17 Guy R. Everson and Edward W. Simpson, eds., "Far, Far from Home:" The Wartime Letters of Dick and Tally Simpson, Third South Carolina Volunteers, 2nd ed. (New York: Oxford University Press, 1994), xv–xvii, 6.

18 Harold Holzer, "Give Peace a Chance," America's Civil War, 23 (January 2011): 45.

19 Holzer op. cit., 48–49.

20 Charles Francis Adams, An Autobiography (Boston: Houghton Mifflin, 1916), 75–77.

21 Roy P. Basler, ed., The Collected Works of Lincoln, IV, (New Brunswick, NJ: Rutgers University Press, 1953), 149, 171.

22 Basler op. cit., 159.

23 Basler op. cit., 270.

24 The Daily Dispatch, March 5, 1861.

25 New Orleans Delta, New Orleans Picayune, Oxford [Mississippi] Mercury quoted in Memphis [Tennessee] Daily Appeal, March 9, 1861. http://chroniclingamerica.loc.gov/lccn/sn83045160/1861-03-09/ed-1/seq-2/. Last accessed December 29, 2012.

26 "General Political Intelligence: More Southside Views," New York Times, March 12, 1861.

27 Albany Evening Journal, March 5, 1861.

28 New York Times, March 5, 1861.

29 "Reception of the Inaugural Address," New York Times, March 6, 1861.

30 William H. and Jane H. Pease, James Louis Petigru: Southern Conservative, Southern Dissenter (Columbia, SC: University of South Carolina Press, 2002), 156.

31 Theodore Talbot to Sister, November 20, 1860, Fort Moultrie, South Carolina. Collections "For Teachers," Civil War, Fort Sumter National Monument, South Carolina,

http://www.nps.gov/fosu/forteachers/upload/Sample-letters.pdf.
Last accessed December 29, 2012.

32 Theodore Talbot to Mother, January 3, 1861.
http://www.nps.gov/fosu/forteachers/upload/Sample-letters.pdf.
Last accessed December 29, 2012.

33 Reynolds op. cit., 198.

34 McPherson, *Ordeal by Fire*, 155.

35 Reynolds op. cit., 202.

36 "Abraham Lincoln and Delaware," Abraham Lincoln's Classroom, The Lincoln
Institute and the Lehrman Institute,
http://www.abrahamlincolnsclassroom.org/Library/newsletter
asp?ID=39&CRLI=119. Last accessed December 29, 2012.

37 "Abraham Lincoln and Maryland," Abraham Lincoln's Classroom, The Lincoln
Institute and the Lehrman Institute,
http://www.abrahamlincolnsclassroom.org/Library/newsletter.
asp?ID=108&CRLI=156. Last accessed December 29, 2012.

38 "Beriah Magoffin," Kentucky's Abraham Lincoln, The Kentucky
Historical Society,
http://www.lrc.ky.gov/record/Moments08RS/36_web_leg_moments.htm.
Last accessed December 29, 2012.

39 "Missouri State Journal," *Community & Conflict: The Impact of the Civil War in
the Ozarks*, http://www.ozarkscivilwar.org/archives/1363.
Last accessed December 29, 2012.

40 April 18, 1861, Diary of Kate S. Carney 1859–1876. Collection Number 00139-z,
Southern Historical Collection, Wilson Library, University of North Carolina at
Chapel Hill. Documenting the American South.
http://docsouth.unc.edu/imls/carney/carney.html.
Last accessed December 29, 2012.

41 William T. Shepherd, *To Rescue My Native Land: The Civil War Letters of
William T. Shepherd*, edited by Kurt H. Hackemer (Knoxville, TN: University of
Tennessee Press, 2006), 5. See also William T. Shepherd Civil War Pension File
C2485-519, National Archives, Washington, DC.

42 Braxton Bragg to Henry J. Hunt, April 21, 1861. "Battle Lines: Letters from
America's Wars." The Gilder Lehrman Institute of American History.
http://www.gilderlehrman.org/sites/default/files/swf/battlelines/chapter1_1a.htm
l. Last accessed December 29, 2012.

43 Henry J. Hunt to Braxton Bragg, April 23, 1861. "Battle Lines: Letters from
America's Wars." The Gilder Lehrman Institute of American History.
http://www.gilderlehrman.org/collection/battlelines/Hunt.pdf.
Last accessed December 29, 2012.

44 Carney diary op. cit., May 3, 1861.

45 Gary W. Gallagher, "The American Civil War," The Gilder Lehrman Institute of
American History,

http://www.gilderlehrman.org/teachers/module.php?module_id=281.
Last accessed December 29, 2012.

46 William M. Cash and Lucy Somerville Howorth, eds., *My Dear Nellie: The Civil War Letters of William L. Nugent to Eleanor Smith Nugent* (Jackson, MS: University Press of Mississippi, 1977), 42–43.

47 John Jay to unknown, Katonah, New York, July 24, 1861. John Jay Letter, Gilder Lehrman Collection #GLC02222,
http://www.gilderlehrman.org/collections/23550ab0-6e0d-469e-95da-183201342097?b ack=/mweb/search%3Fneedle%3DJay%252C%2520Jo hn%2520%25281817-1894%2529%2526fields %3D_t301000285.
Last accessed January 15, 2013.

48 David Hopkins to brother and sister, Philadelphia, Pennsylvania, August 18, 1861. David Hopkins (fl. 1861) Gilder Lehrman Collection #GLC03043, https://www.gilderlehrman.org/collections/5df62730-dd14-48c0-9198-346455693635?back=/mweb/search%3Fneedle%3DPatriotic%2520Postal%2520Cover%2526f ields%3D_t30100 1410.
Last accessed January 15, 2013.

49 Everson and Simpson op. cit., 23, 27, 32, 39–40.

50 Material on Ball's Bluff from James A. Morgan, III, "Ball's Bluff: 'A Very Nice Little Military Chance'," *America's Civil War* 18 (2005), 30–56; See also James A. Morgan, III, "Battle of Ball's Bluff: Then & Now," Civil War Trust, http://www.civilwar.org/battlefields/balls-bluff/balls-bluff-history/the-battle -of-balls-bluff.html. Last accessed December 29, 2012; See also U.S. Army Command and General Staff College "Staff Ride Guide to the Battle of Ball's Bluff," http://www.history.army.mil/StaffRide/ballsbluff/staff_ride_guide.htm.
Last accessed December 29, 2012.

51 General discussion of the Stone controversy and the Joint Committee on the Conduct of the War from Bruce Tap, *Over Lincoln's Shoulder: The Committee on the Conduct of the War* (Lawrence, KS: University Press of Kansas, 1998); Quotes are from Tap "Inevitability, Masculinity, and the American Military Tradition," *American Nineteenth Century History* 5 (2004): 19–46, and Tap, "Amateurs at War: Abraham Lincoln and the Committee on the Conduct of the War," *Journal of the Abraham Lincoln Association*, 23 (Summer 2002), http://www.historycooperative.org/journals/jala/23.2/tap.html.
Last accessed December 29, 2012.

CHAPTER 2

52 Mary Felicia Loughridge to J. R. Loughridge, Falls County, Texas, December 25, 1861. James Rodgers Loughridge Papers, Pre 1838–1972, Pearce Civil War Collection, Navarro College, Corsicana, Texas.

53 Nugent op. cit., 51–53.

54 This section on Mary Todd Lincoln and her family is sourced from Stephen Berry, *The House of Abraham: Lincoln and the Todds, A Family Divided by War* (New York: Houghton Mifflin, 2007); Jason Emerson, *The Madness of Mary Lincoln* (Carbondale, IL: Southern Illinois University Press, 2007); Carl Sandburg,

Abraham Lincoln: The Prairie Years and the War Years, Library of the Presidents Series (New York: Galahad, 2005); and *Washington During the Civil War: The Diary of Horatio Nelson Taft*, 1861–1865, Manuscript Division, Library of Congress,
http://memory.loc.gov/ammem/tafthtml/essay.html.
Last accessed December 29, 2012.

55 Jean H. Baker, *Mary Todd Lincoln: A Biography* (New York: W. W. Norton & Company, 1987), 25–28.

56 Berry op. cit., 100–102; Baker op. cit., 195–196.

57 Gertrude Woodruff Marlowe. "Keckley, Elizabeth Hobbs," *American National Biography Online*, http://www.anb.org/articles/20/20-00530.html.
Last accessed December 29, 2012.

58 Mary Felicia Loughridge to J. R. Loughridge, Falls County, Texas, February 13, 1862. James Rodgers Loughridge Papers, Pre 1838–1972, Pearce Civil War Collection, Navarro College, Corsicana, Texas.

59 Buchanan's story and that of the CSS *Virginia* is in Craig L. Symonds, *The Civil War at Sea* (New York: Praeger, 2009); See also James L. Nelson, *Reign of Iron: The Story of the First Battling Ironclads, the* Monitor *and the* Merrimack (New York: William Morrow, 2004).

60 Symonds op. cit., 21.

61 _____, "Henry Wagner Halleck (1815–1872)," *Encyclopedia of the American Civil War: A Political, Social, and Military History* (Santa Barbara, CA: ABC-CLIO, 2000). *Credo Reference*,
http://www.credoreference.com.logon.lynx.lib.usm.edu/entry/abcacw/halleck_henry _wager_1815_1872. Last accessed December 29, 2012.

62 _____, "William Tecumseh Sherman (1820–1891)," *Encyclopedia of the American Civil War: A Political, Social, and Military History* (Santa Barbara, CA: ABC-CLIO, 2000). *Credo Reference*,
http://www.credoreference.com.logon.lynx.lib.usm.edu/entry/abcacw/sherman_willi am_tecumseh_1820_1891. Last accessed December 29, 2012.

63 _____, "Albert Sidney Johnston (1803–1862)," *Encyclopedia of the American Civil War: A Political, Social, and Military History* (Santa Barbara, CA: ABC-CLIO, 2000). *Credo Reference*,
http://www.credoreference.com.logon.lynx.lib.usm.edu/entry/abcacw/johnston_albe rt_sidney_1803_1862. Last accessed December 29, 2012.

64 Shepherd op. cit., 93.

65 Shepherd op. cit., 93–94.

66 Shepherd op. cit., 101–102.

67 Ulysses S. Grant, *Personal Memoirs of Ulysses S. Grant* (New York: William S. Konecky Associates, 1999), 149; Shepherd op. cit., 107.

68 Shepherd op. cit., 165.

69 For the best analysis on Bierce's experience at Shiloh, see Bjorn Skaptason, "What I Saw of Shiloh: In the Footsteps of Ambrose Bierce," *The Ambrose Bierce*

Project Journal 3 (2007): 32. Some of this material is also from the walking tour notes Skaptson has gathered over the years and shared with the author. Special thanks to him for that.

70 Skaptason op. cit., 13.

71 Shepherd op. cit., 167–168.

72 For the experiences of Sam Todd at Shiloh, see Berry op. cit., 109–117.

73 Robert Campbell, *Lonestar Confederate*, 41.

74 The First Massachusetts Regiment op. cit., 132.

75 McPherson, *Ordeal by Fire*, 259.

76 Andrew N. Erskine, Monroe, Louisiana, to Ann Johnson Erskine, May 19, 1862. Unpublished family history and transcribed Andrew N. Erskine, "Civil War Commentary and Letters," 111–114. Hereinafter "Erskine Letters." Shared with the author by Erskine family descendants Melissa Lingwall and Melinda Kilian. Special thanks to them both for sharing the letters and other information on the Erskine family history.

77 Andrew M. Erskine, Gaines's Mill, Virginia to Ann Johnson Erskine, June 28, 1862. Erskine Letters, 138–140.

78 J. R. Loughridge Service Record. National Archives, Washington, DC.

79 Allen C. Guelzo, "The Emancipation Proclamation: Bill of Lading or Ticket to Freedom?" The Gilder Lehrman Institute of American History, http://www.gilderlehrman.org/history-by-era/african-americans-and-emancipation/ essays/emancipation-proclamation-bill-lading-or-ti. Last accessed December 29, 2012.

80 Abraham Lincoln Speech at Peoria, Kansas, October 16, 1854, in Lewis E. Lehrman, *Lincoln at Peoria: The Turning Point* (Mechanicsburg, PA: Stackpole Books, 2008), 56. See also Wilson Huhn, "Abraham Lincoln Was a Framer of the Constitution," *Washington University Law Review*, 89 (March 2009), http:// lawreview.wustl.edu/comments/abraham-lincoln-was-a-framer-of-the-constit ution/. Last accessed December 29, 2012.

81 Philip Sheldon Foner, *History of Black Americans: From the Compromise of 1850 to the End of the Civil War* (Westport, CT: Greenwood Press, 1983), 338. See also "Ending Slavery in the District of Columbia," http://emancipation.dc.gov/page/ending-slavery-district-columbia. Last accessed December 29, 2012.

82 "The District of Columbia Emancipation Act," Featured Documents, National Archives & Records Administration, Washington, DC, http://www.archives.gov/exhibits/featured_documents/dc_emancipation_act/. Last accessed December 29, 2012; see also C. R. Gibbs, "A Historical Overview of D. C. Emancipation," http://emancipation.dc.gov/node/105922. Last accessed December 29, 2012.

83 General Joseph Hooker, November 8, 1862. *The War of the Rebellion: A Compilation of the Official Records of the Union and Confederate Armies* (Washington, DC: Government Printing Office, 1880–1891), Series I, Vol. 19,

Part I, 218. Hereinafter cited as O.R.

84 J. B. Polly, *A Soldier's Letters to Charming Nellie*, Richard B. McCaslin, ed. (Knoxville, TN: University of Tennessee Press, 2007), 134.

85 Andrew M. Erskine, On the Winchester and Alexandria Turnpike, 20 miles from Washington City to Ann Johnson Erskine, September 2, 1862, Erskine Letters, 175–177; Alexander N. Erskine, Shepherdstown, Virginia, to Ann Johnson Erskine, September 18, 1862, Erskine Letters, 184.

86 Discussion of the Gillen brothers at Antietam from Susannah J. Ural, *The Harp and the Eagle: Irish-American Volunteers and the Union Army, 1861–1865* (New York: New York University Press, 2006), 115–116. See also Don Ersnberger, *Paddy Owen's Regulars: A History of the 69th Pennsylvania Irish Volunteers* (Bloomington, IN: Xlibris, 2004).

87 Sandburg op. cit., 310–311.

88 Guelzo op. cit., "Emancipation/Bill of Lading." Original quote from *Times* of London.

89 Cooper op. cit., 408.

90 McPherson, *Ordeal*, 320.

CHAPTER 3

91 Everson and Simpson op. cit., 178–183.

92 Everson and Simpson op. cit., 180–182. See also D. Augustus Dickert, *History of Kershaw's Brigade* (Project Gutenberg eBook, 2004), 207, http://www.gutenberg.org/files/13124/13124-h/13124-h.htm#CHAPTER_XVI. Last accessed December 29, 2012.

93 Everson and Simpson op. cit., 168–169.

94 Everson and Simpson, op. cit., xix.

95 Everson and Simpson op. cit., 195–196.

96 Stephen W. Sears, *Chancellorsville* (New York: Houghton Mifflin, 1996), 5.

97 For details on the Irish Brigade at the battle of Fredericksburg, see Ural op. cit., 122–135. See also St. Clair A. Mulholland Pension File, National Archives, Washington, DC.

98 *Southern Watchman* (Athens, Georgia), February 25, 1863. See an excellent discussion of the Confederate Irish at Fredericksburg in Kelly J. O'Grady, *Clear the Confederate Way! The Irish in the Army of Northern Virginia* (Mason City, IA: Savas Publishing, 2000).

99 William Corby, *Memoirs of Chaplain Life: Three Years with the Irish Brigade in the Army of the Potomac*, Lawrence Frederick Kohl, ed. (New York: Fordham University Press, 1992), 132; David P. Conyngham, *The Irish Brigade and Its Campaigns*, Lawrence Frederick Kohl, ed. (New York: Fordham University Press, 1994), 343; Joseph G. Bilby, *The Irish Brigade in the Civil War: The 69th New York and Other Irish Regiments of the Army of the Potomac* (Boston: Da Capo Press, 2001), 67.

100 *The Irish-American*, December 27, 1862.

101 Conyngham op. cit., 350.

102 Ruth and Emil Rosenblatt, eds., *Hard Marching Every Day: The Civil War Letters of Private Wilbur Fisk* (Lawrence, KS: University Press of Kansas, 1992), xii–xvi, 1–2.

103 Rosenblatt and Rosenblatt op. cit., xii–xvi, 1–2.

104 Francis Augustín O'Reilly, *The Fredericksburg Campaign: Winter War on the Rappahannock* (Baton Rouge, LA: Louisiana State University Press, 2006), 348.

105 Rosenblatt and Rosenblatt op. cit., 357. Thanks to Wilbur Fisk's great-grandnephew, Peter Fisk, for sharing his thoughts on the bonds between Wilbur and Edgar Dinsmore and how this may have played a role in Wilbur's actions that winter.

106 See Rosenblatt and Rosenblatt op. cit., eds., xii–xvi, as well as Foreword by Reid Mitchel, vii–xi.

107 Rosenblatt and Rosenblatt op. cit., 79–80.

108 McPherson, *Battle Cry of Freedom*, 584.

109 Sears, *Chancellorsville*, 5.

110 Gary W. Gallagher, ed., *Chancellorsville: The Battle and Its Aftermath* (Chapel Hill, NC: University of North Carolina Press, 2008), 3.

111 "The Battle of Chancellorsville," Civil War Series, The National Park Service, History eLibrary, http://www.nps.gov/history/history/online_books/civil_war_series/8/sec1.htm. Last accessed December 29, 2012.

112 McPherson, *Battle Cry of Freedom*, 584–585.

113 Sears op. cit., 70–80.

114 Rosenblatt and Rosenblatt op. cit., 69–70.

115 Ray Allen Billington, ed., *The Journal of Charlotte L. Forten* (New York: W. W. Norton & Company, 1981), 7–42, 172–175.

116 John Q. Anderson, ed. Brokenburn: *The Journal of Kate Stone, 1861–1868* (Baton Rouge, LA: Louisiana State University Press, 1972), 18, 184.

117 "The Navy Runs the Guns at Vicksburg: April 16–17, 1863," *Naval History Blog: U.S. Naval Institute—Naval History & Heritage Command*, http://www.navalhistory.org/2010/04/18/1045/. Last accessed December 29, 2012.

118 Rosenblatt and Rosenblatt op. cit., 81.

119 Watson Dugat Williams, Camp on Rapidan River Near Sommerville's Ford to Laura Bryan, May 30, 1863, and Williams to Bryan, June 23, 1863. Watson Dugat Williams Letters, Hill College, Hillsboro, Texas.

120 Stephen W. Sears, *Gettysburg* (New York: Houghton Mifflin Company, 2004), 107.

NOTES

121 John Marquis Smither, Camp Near Chambersburg, Pennsylvania, to Mother, New Waverly, Texas, June 28, 1863. John Marquis Smither Family Papers, Thomason Room Special Collections, Sam Houston State University, Huntsville, Texas.

122 Valerius Cincinnatus Giles, *Rags and Hope: The Recollections of Val C. Giles, Four Years with Hood's Brigade, Fourth Texas Infantry, 1861–1865,* compiled and edited by Mary Lasswell (New York: Coward–McCann, 1961), 174, 176.

123 James H. Hendrick, June 28, 1863. James H. Henrick Letters, Hill College, Hillsboro, Texas.

124 Edwin B. Coddington, *The Gettysburg Campaign: A Study in Command* (Dayton, OH: Morningside Books, 1983), 369–370. See also Garry E. Adelman and Timothy H. Smith, *Devil's Den: A History and Guide* (Gettysburg, PA: Thomas Publications, 1997), 17.

125 Albert Cuthburt "Cubb" Sims, Company F, 1st Texas, in Jasper (TX) *News-Boy,* May 17, 1911. Copy in A. C. Sims Diary, "Texas First Infantry Regiment" Folder, Box 9 of 21: North Carolina—Texas, Confederate Units/Confederate Officers, "The Gettysburg Campaign," Robert L. Brake Collection, U.S. Army Heritage and Education Center, Carlisle, Pennsylvania. Hereinafter the "Brake Collection."

126 Adelman and Smith op. cit., 29.

127 Zach Landrum, July 15, 1863, Zach Landrum Letters, Texas Confederate Museum Collection, United Daughters of the Confederacy, Haley Library and History Center, Midland, Texas.

128 Giles op. cit., 181, 183.

129 Mark H. Dunkleman, *Gettysburg's Unknown Soldier: The Life, Death, and Celebrity of Amos Humiston* (New York: Praeger, 1999); see also Dunkleman, "Amos Humiston: Union Soldier Who Died at the Battle of Gettysburg," *America's Civil War* (August 1997), http://www.historynet.com/amos-humiston-union-soldier-who-died-at-the-battle-of -gettysburg.htm. Last accessed December 29, 2012.

130 J. R. Loughridge, Camp 4th Texas to Mary Felicia Loughridge, July 26, 1863. James Rodgers Loughridge Papers, Pre 1838–1972, Pearce Civil War Collection, Navarro College, Corsicana, Texas.

131 Nugent op. cit., 115–118.

132 For more on Davis Bend and the enslaved on Jefferson Davis's plantations see Neil R. McMillen, "Isaiah T. Montgomery, 1847–1924 (Part I)," *Mississippi History Now*: An Online Publication of the Mississippi Historical Society at http://mshistorynow.mdah.state.ms.us/articles/55/isaiah-t-montgomery-1847-1924- part-I. Last accessed February 8, 2013.

133 Carol Lynn Mead, *The Land Between Two Rivers: Madison County, Mississippi* (Madison, MS: Friends of the Madison County–Canton Public Library, 1987), 243–247; see also Hugh Miller Thompson II, *The Johnstones of Annandale,* (privately published), 64; see also Henry Presley Posey, *The Flora Book: A History of the Town of Flora and Southwest Madison County, Mississippi* (Flora,

MS: First Street Publishing, 2002). Special thanks to Dr. and Mrs. William and Gay Yerger of Madison, Mississippi for sharing some of this information.

134 Everson and Simpson op. cit., 283–285

CHAPTER 4

135 For background on the Grants, see Joan Waugh, *Ulysses S. Grant: American Hero, American Myth* (Chapel Hill, NC: University of North Carolina Press, 2009) and Jean Edward Smith, Grant (New York: Simon & Schuster, 2002). Sharra Vostral, "The Moveable Home Front: Julia Dent Grant and the Maintenance of a General's Family," *Gateway Heritage*, 25(4), 2005: 22–33.

136 Vostral op. cit., 32.

137 Julia Dent Grant, *The Personal Memoirs of Julia Dent Grant*, John Y. Simon, ed. (Carbondale, IL: Southern Illinois University Press, 1988), 89. See also Vostral, op. cit.

138 Vostral op. cit., 28.

139 Frederick Dent Grant, "At the Front with Dad," ed. Peter Cozzens, *Civil War Times Illustrated*, December 1996, 35(6): 16–40. See also Waugh and Smith, op. cit.

140 Cashin op. cit., 147–151; Cooper op. cit., 516.

141 Cashin op. cit., 149.

142 Bowler op. cit., 27–28.

143 Bowler op. cit., 247.

144 Bowler op. cit., 253–254

145 Bowler op. cit., 256.

146 Bowler op. cit., 4.

147 Drew Gilpen Faust, *Mothers of Invention: Women of the Slaveholding South in the American Civil War* (Chapel Hill, NC: The University of North Carolina Press, 1996), 242.

148 Faust op. cit., 240.

149 The Bread Riots discussion is from Stephanie McCurry, "Bread or Blood!" *Civil War Times*, 50 (June 2011): 36–41. See also Stephanie McCurry, *Confederate Reckoning: Power and Politics in the Civil War South* (Chapel Hill, NC: The University of North Carolina Press), 2011.

150 John B. Jones, *A Rebel War Clerk's Diary at the Confederate States Capital*, Volume II (Philadelphia: J. B. Lippincott & Co., 1866), 100–101.

151 McCurry, *Confederate Reckoning*, 198.

152 Faust op. cit., 241.

153 McCurry, *Confederate Reckoning*, 202.

154 Shepherd op. cit., 258.

155 Shepherd op. cit., 295.

156 Shepherd op. cit., 296–297.

157 Shepherd op. cit., 308.

158 Shepherd op. cit., 310.

159 James I. Robertson, Jr., *Soldiers Blue and Gray* (Columbia, SC: University of South Carolina Press, 1988), 142.

160 Samuel S. Watson, Camp, 1st Texas to "dear Friend Harriet," location unknown, October 21, 1864. Samuel S. Watson Letters, 1st Texas File, History Research Center, Hill College, Hillsboro, Texas.

161 G. H. Freeman, Petersburg, Virginia, to Madam, August 19, 1864, in *Freedom's Soldiers: The Black Military Experience in the Civil War*, eds. Ira Berlin, Joseph Reidy, and Leslie S. Rowland (New York: Cambridge University Press, 1998), 128–129, also available online at http://www.history.umd.edu/Freedmen/Freeman.html. Last accessed December 29, 2012.

162 Martha Glover to Dear Husband, December 30, 1863, *Freedom's Soldiers*, 117–188. Also available online at http://www.history.umd.edu/Freedmen/Glover.html. Last accessed December 29, 2012.

163 Spotswood Rice, Benton Barracks Hospital, St. Louis, Missouri, to My Children, September 3, 1864, *Freedom's Soldiers*, 131–132, also available online at http://www.history.umd.edu/Freedmen/rice.htm. Last accessed December 29, 2012.

164 Spotswood Rice, Benton Barracks Hospital, St. Louis, Missouri, to owner of one of Rice's children, September 3, 1864, *Freedom's Soldiers*, 132–133, also available online at http://www.history.umd.edu/Freedmen/rice.htm. Last accessed December 29, 2012. For some background on Rice, see http://www.oxfordaasc.com/public/features/archive/0208/essay.jsp. Last accessed December 29, 2012.

165 Joseph Miller affidavit, Camp Nelson, Kentucky, sworn before E. B. W. Restieaux, November 26, 1864, *Freedom's Soldiers*, 138–139, also available online at http://www.history.umd.edu/Freedmen/JMiller.html. Last accessed December 29, 2012. For background on Miller and this incident, see Amy Murrell Taylor, "How a Cold Snap in Kentucky Led to Freedom for Thousands," *Weirding the War: Stories from the Civil War's Ragged Edges*, Stephen Berry, ed. (Athens, GA: The University of Georgia Press, 2011), 191–214; see also Jim Downs, *Sick from Freedom: African-American Illness and Suffering During the Civil War and Reconstruction* (New York: Oxford University Press, 2012).

166 Jason Phillips, *Diehard Rebels: The Confederate Culture of Invincibility* (Athens, GA: The University of Georgia Press, 2007), 159–163. For an example of the Resolutions of Hood's Texas Brigade, see *The Daily Dispatch*, Richmond, Virginia, January 28, 1865, http://www.perseus.tufts.edu/hopper/text?doc=Perseus%3Atext%3A2006.05.12 84%3Aar ticle%3D4. Last accessed December 29, 2012.

167 Sara Frear, "Augusta Jane Evans Wilson," *Encyclopedia of Alabama*, March 14, 2007, http://encyclopediaofalabama.org/face/Article.jsp?id=h-1072. Last accessed December 29, 2012.

168 Faust op. cit., 244–245. Phebe Ann Hanafard, *Daughters of America* (Augusta, GA: True and Company, 1882), 129.

169 Faust op. cit., 244–245.

170 Stone op. cit., 224.

171 Stone op. cit., 292.

172 Stone op. cit., 277.

173 Stone op. cit., 323.

174 Stone op. cit., 339–340.

175 Houston Tri-Weekly Telegraph, May 19, 1865.

176 William A. Fletcher, *Rebel Private: Front and Rear, Memoirs of a Confederate Soldier* (New York: Plume, 1997), xiv, 103–109, and 195. See also http://www.tshaonline.org/handbook/online/articles/ffldd. Last accessed January 15, 2013.

CHAPTER 5

177 Frances "Fanny" Seward Diary, April 12 and April 13, 1865, entries discuss Seward's medication and nightmares; April 15, 1865, explains events of the attack on the evening of April 14, 1865; April 5, 1865, describes the carriage accident. See website "Lincoln and His Circle," hosted by the University of Rochester's division of Rare Books and Special Collections, http://www.lib.rochester.edu/rbk/lincoln. Last accessed December 20, 2012. Hereinafter cited as "Fanny Seward Diary."

178 Deirdre C. Stam, "Growing Up with Books: Fanny Seward's Book Collecting, Reading, and Writing in Mid-Nineteenth-Century New York State," *Library & Culture*, 41(2006): 194.

179 Fanny Seward Diary, April 5, 1865.

180 *Ibid*.

181 Franny Seward Diary, April 11, 1865.

182 George F. Robinson, "An Account of the Attempted Assassination of Secy. Seward, Apr. 14, 1865," George F. Robinson Papers, 1879, Pearce Civil War Collection, Navarro College, Corsicana, Texas. See http://www.pearcecollections.us/fa_ind.php?fid=646. Last accessed December 20, 2012. See also Fanny Seward Diary, April 14, 1865.

183 For material about Powell's attempted assassination on Seward, see Fanny Seward Diary, April 14, 1865; Michael W. Kauffman, *American Brutus: John Wilkes Booth and the Lincoln Conspiracies* (New York: Random House, 2004), 22–27; Doris Kearns Goodwin, *Team of Rivals: The Political Genius of Abraham Lincoln* (New York: Simon & Schuster, 2005), 736–737; and George H. Robinson, "An Account of the Attempted Assassination of Secy. Seward, Apr. 14, 1865," George F. Robinson Papers, 1879, Pearce Civil War Collection,

NOTES

Navarro College, Corsicana, Texas, http://www.pearcecollections.us/fa_ind. php?fid=646. Last accessed December 20, 2012.

184 Robinson Account.

185 Shakespeare, *Macbeth*, Act V, Scene 5.

186 "Risest thou thus, dim dawn, again ...." Alfred, Lord Tennyson, *In Memoriam.*

187 Fanny Seward Diary, April 15, 1865. http://www.lib.rochester.edu/index.cfm?page=1420&Print=436. Last accessed December 20, 2012.

188 Patricia C. Johnson, "I Could Not Be Well or Happy at Home: Politics and the Seward Family," *University of Rochester Library Bulletin*, 31 (1978), http://www.lib.rochester.edu/index.cfm?page=1018. Last accessed December 20, 2012.

189 For detailed information about Mary Surratt's role in the events surrounding the Lincoln assassination, see Kauffman, *American Brutus*, and especially Larson, *The Assassin's Accomplice.*

190 For background on the Harris family and specifics on Henry Rathbone and Clara Harris, Stephen Berry, "Casualties of War: Clara Harris Rathbone," *Civil War Monitor*, 1 (2011): 18–19, 75; see also Michael E. Ruane, "A Tragedy's Second Act," *The Washington Post*, April 5, 2009.

191 Berry, *House of Abraham*, 154–155; Paul F. Boller, *Presidential Wives: An Anecdotal History* (New York: Oxford University Press, 1998), 123.

192 For details about the Lincoln Assassination, see James L. Lawson, *Manhunt: The Twelve-Day Chase for Lincoln's Killer* (New York: William Morrow, 2006); Kauffman, *American Brutus*; Kate Clifford Larson, *The Assassin's Accomplice: Mary Surratt and the Plot to Kill Abraham Lincoln* (New York: Basic Books, 2008); and Dorothy Meserve Kunhardt and Philip B. Kunhardt, Jr., *Twenty Days: A Narrative in Texas and Pictures of the Assassination of Abraham Lincoln and the Twenty Days and Nights That Followed ...* (New York: Castle Books, 1993).

193 Berry, "Casualties of War: Clara Harris Rathbone," 18–19.

194 Edward P. Crapol, *James G. Blaine: Architect of Empire* (New York: Rowan & Littlefield, 2000), 27.

CONCLUSION

195 Stone op. cit., 7–12.

196 J. David Hacker, "A Census-Based Count of the Civil War Dead," *Civil War History*, 54:4 (December 2011), 306–347.

197 W. Fitzhugh Brundage, "Redeeming a Failed Revolution: Confederate Memory," in William J. Cooper, Jr., and John M. McCardell, Jr., eds. *In the Cause of Liberty: How the Civil War Refined American Ideals* (Baton Rouge, LA: Louisiana State University Press, 2009), 127.

198 Brundage op. cit., 127.

199 Drew Gilpen Faust, *This Republic of Suffering: Death and the American Civil War* (New York: Alfred A. Knopf, 2008), 215–222, 250.

200 Homer, *The Iliad*, trans. by Robert Fagles (New York: Penguin Books, 1990), 208–212. See also Homer, *The Iliad*, trans. by Samuel Butler (New York: Jonathan Cape, 1925), 55.

201 "Varina Howell Davis, (1826–1906)," *Encyclopedia of the American Civil War: A Political, Social, and Military History* (Santa Barbara, CA: ABC-CLIO, 2000). *Credo Reference,* http://www.credoreference.com.logon.lynx.lib.usm.edu/entry/abcacw/davis_varina_howell_1826_1906. Last accessed February 6, 2013; see also "Jefferson Davis, (1808–1809)," *Encyclopedia of the American Civil War: A Political, Social, and Military History* (Santa Barbara, CA: ABC-CLIO, 2000). *Credo Reference,* http://www.credoreference.com.logon.lynx.lib.usm.edu/entry/abcacw/davis_jefferson_1808_1889. Last accessed February 6, 2013.

202 Nugent op. cit., 237.

203 Dorothy S. Shawhan and Martha H. Swain, *Lucy Somerville Howorth: New Deal Lawyer, Politician, and Feminist from the South* (Baton Rouge, LA: Louisiana State University Press, 2006), 1–5.

204 Everson and Simpson op cit., 295–298.

205 Berry op. cit., 185–186.

206 "Gordon at Khartoum" in James Rodgers Loughridge Papers, Pre 1838–1972, Pearce Civil War Collection, Navarro College, Corsicana, Texas. Some of the postwar history, including the authorship of Felicia's poem, was provided to the author by the Loughridges' great-grandson, David L. Loughridge, of Plano, Texas.

207 Shepherd op. cit., 315–316.

208 U.S. Federal Census, 1870, Non-Population Schedule, Guadalupe, Texas, Precinct 1. See also United States Federal Census, 1870, Guadalupe, Texas, Precinct 1. Some of this information was also shared by Erskine descendents Melissa Laird Lingwall and Melinda Laird Kilian, great-granddaughters of Blucher Haynes Erskine.

209 Bowler op. cit., 6–7.

210 Forten op. cit., 216–217, 219.

211 Forten op. cit., 37–39.

212 Fisk op. cit., xv–xvi, 346–369.

213 Homer, *The Iliad*, trans. by Robert Fagles (New York: Penguin Books, 1990), 588–616. For the story of Andromache's fate, see "The Trojan Women" in Euripides, *Ten Plays* (New York: Bantam Classic Edition, 1960), 173–204.

214 Homer, *The Iliad*, trans. by Robert Fagles (New York: Penguin Books, 1990), 208–212. See also Homer, *The Iliad*, trans. by Samuel Butler (New York: Jonathan Cape, 1925), 55.

⇒ BIBLIOGRAPHY ⇐

MANUSCRIPTS

Andrew M. Erskine Letters. Private collection of Erskine decedents Melissa Laird Lingwall and Melinda Laird Kilian.

James H. Henrick Letters, Historical Research Center, Hill College, Hillsboro, Texas.

St. Clair A. Mulholland Pension File, National Archives, Washington, DC.

Zach Landrum Letters, Texas Confederate Museum Collection, United Daughters of the Confederacy, Haley Library and History Center, Midland, Texas.

James Rodgers Loughridge Papers, Pre 1838–1972, Pearce Civil War Collection, Navarro College, Corsicana, Texas.

James Rodgers Loughridge Military Service Record. National Archives, Washington, DC.

William T. Shepherd Civil War Pension File C2485-519, National Archives, Washington, DC.

A. C. Sims Diary, "Texas First Infantry Regiment" Folder, Box 9 of 21: North Carolina—Texas, Confederate Units/Confederate Officers, "The Gettysburg Campaign," Robert L. Brake Collection, U.S. Army Heritage and Education Center, Carlisle, Pennsylvania.

John Marquis Smither Family Papers, Thomason Room Special Collections, Sam Houston State University, Huntsville, Texas.

United States War Department, *The War of the Rebellion: A Compilation of the Officials Records of the Union and Confederate Armies*. 128 vols. Washington: Government Printing Office, 1880-1901.

Samuel S. Watson Letters, 1st Texas File, Historical Research Center, Hill College, Hillsboro, Texas.

Watson Dugat Williams Letters, Hill College, Hillsboro, Texas.

NEWSPAPERS

Albany Evening Journal

Arkansas State Gazette

The Daily Dispatch

Houston Tri-Weekly Telegraph

The Irish-American

Nashville *Republican Banner*

New Bern *Weekly Progress*

New York Times

Southern Watchman (Athens, Georgia)

The Washington Post

PUBLISHED PRIMARY AND SECONDARY SOURCES

Adams, Charles Francis. *An Autobiography*. Boston: Houghton Mifflin, 1916.

Adelman, Garry E. and Timothy H. Smith. *Devil's Den: A History and Guide*. Gettysburg, PA: Thomas Publications, 1997.

Anderson, John Q., ed. *Brokenburn: The Journal of Kate Stone, 1861–1868*. Baton Rouge, LA: Louisiana State University Press, 1972.

Baker, Jean H. *Mary Todd Lincoln: A Biography*. New York: W. W. Norton & Company, 1987.

Basler, Roy P., ed. *The Collected Works of Lincoln*, IV. New Brunswick, NJ: Rutgers University Press, 1953.

Berry, Stephen. "Casualties of War: Clara Harris Rathbone." *Civil War Monitor* 1 (2011): 18–19, 75.

_____. *The House of Abraham: Lincoln and the Todds, A Family Divided by War*. New York: Houghton Mifflin, 2007.

Bilby, Joseph G. *The Irish Brigade in the Civil War: The 69th New York and Other Irish Regiments of the Army of the Potomac*. Boston: Da Capo Press, 2001.

Billington, Ray Allen ed., *The Journal of Charlotte L. Forten*. New York: W. W. Norton & Company, 1981.

Bleser, Carol K. and Lesley J. Gordon, eds. *Intimate Strategies of the Civil War: Military Commanders and Their Wives*. New York: Oxford University Press, 2001.

Boller, Paul F. *Presidential Wives: An Anecdotal History*. New York: Oxford University Press, 1998.

Brundage, W. Fitzhugh. "Redeeming a Failed Revolution: Confederate Memory." In

In the Cause of Liberty: How the Civil War Refined American Ideals. Edited by William J. Cooper and John M. McCardell. (Baton Rouge, LA: Louisiana State University Press, 2009), 126–135.

Cash, William M. and Lucy Somerville Howorth, eds. *My Dear Nellie: The Civil War Letters of William L. Nugent to Eleanor Smith Nugent. Jackson*, MS: University Press of Mississippi, 1977.

Cashin, Joan E. *First Lady of the Confederacy: Varina Davis's Civil War*. Cambridge, MA: Belknap Press of Harvard University Press, 2006.

Coddington, Edwin B. *The Gettysburg Campaign: A Study in Command*. Dayton, OH: Morningside Books, 1983.

Conyngham, David P. *The Irish Brigade and Its Campaigns*. Edited by Lawrence Frederick Kohl. New York: Fordham University Press, 1994.

Cooper, Jr., William J. *Jefferson Davis, American*. New York: Knopf, 2000.

Corby, William. *Memoirs of Chaplain Life: Three Years with the Irish Brigade in the Army of the Potomac*. Edited by Lawrence Frederick Kohl. New York: Fordham University Press, 1992.

Crapol, Edward P. *James G. Blaine: Architect of Empire*. New York: Rowan & Littlefield, 2000.

Davis, William C. *Jefferson Davis: The Man and His Hour*. Baton Rouge, LA: Louisiana State University Press, 1991.

Downs, Jim. *Sick from Freedom: African-American Illness and Suffering During the Civil War and Reconstruction*. New York: Oxford University Press, 2012.

Dunkleman, Mark H. *Gettysburg's Unknown Soldier: The Life, Death, and Celebrity of Amos Humiston*. New York: Praeger, 1999.

Emerson, Jason. *The Madness of Mary Lincoln*. Carbondale, IL: Southern Illinois University Press, 2007.

Ersnberger, Don. *Paddy Owen's Regulars: A History of the 69th Pennsylvania Irish Volunteers*. Bloomington, IN: Xlibris, 2004.

Euripides. *Ten Plays*. New York: Bantam Classic Edition, 1960.

Everson, Guy R. and Edward W. Simpson, eds. *"Far, Far from Home:" The Wartime Letters of Dick and Tally Simpson, Third South Carolina Volunteers*, 2nd ed. New York: Oxford University Press, 1994.

Faust, Drew Gilpin. *Mothers of Invention: Women of the Slaveholding South in the American Civil War*. Chapel Hill, NC: The University of North Carolina Press, 1996.

_____. *This Republic of Suffering: Death and the American Civil War*. New York: Alfred A. Knopf, 2008.

Fellman, Michael, Daniel E. Sutherland, and Leslie J. Gordon. *This Terrible War: The Civil War and Its Aftermath*. New York: Longman, 2002.

Fletcher, William A. *Rebel Private: Front and Rear, Memoirs of a Confederate Soldier*. New York: Plume, 1997.

Gallagher, Gary W. ed., *Chancellorsville: The Battle and Its Aftermath*. Chapel Hill, NC: University of North Carolina Press, 2008.

Giles, Valerius Cincinnatus. *Rags and Hope: The Recollections of Val C. Giles, Four Years with Hood's Brigade, Fourth Texas Infantry, 1861–1865*. Compiled and edited by Mary Lasswell. New York: Coward–McCann, 1961.

Goodwin, Doris Kearns. *Team of Rivals: The Political Genius of Abraham Lincoln*. New York: Simon & Schuster, 2005.

Grant, Frederick Dent. "At the Front with Dad." Edited by Peter Cozzens. *Civil War Times Illustrated* 35, no. 6 (December 1996): 16–40.

Grant, Julia Dent. *The Personal Memoirs of Julia Dent Grant*. Edited by John Y. Simon. Carbondale, IL: Southern Illinois University Press, 1988.

Grant, Ulysses S. *Personal Memoirs of Ulysses S. Grant*. New York: William S. Konecky Associates, 1999.

Hacker, J. David. "A Census-Based Count of the Civil War Dead." *Civil War History*, 54, no. 4 (December 2011): 306–347.

Hanafard, Phebe Ann. *Daughters of America*. Augusta, GA: True and Company, 1882.

Holzer, Harold. "Give Peace a Chance." *America's Civil War*, 23 (January 2011): 45.

Homer. *The Iliad*. Translated by Robert Fagles. New York: Penguin Books, 1990.

Jaffa, Harry V. *Crisis of the House Divided: An Interpretation of the Issues in the Lincoln Douglas Debates*. Chicago: University of Chicago Press, 1999.

Jones, John B. *A Rebel War Clerk's Diary at the Confederate States Capital*, Volume II. Philadelphia: J. B. Lippincott & Co., 1866.

Kauffman, Michael W. *American Brutus: John Wilkes Booth and the Lincoln Conspiracies*. New York: Random House, 2004.

Kunhardt, Dorothy Meserve and Philip B. Kunhardt, Jr., *Twenty Days: A Narrative in Texas and Pictures of the Assassination of Abraham Lincoln and the Twenty Days and Nights That Followed …* New York: Castle Books, 1993.

Larson, Kate Clifford. *The Assassin's Accomplice: Mary Surratt and the Plot to Kill Abraham Lincoln*. New York: Basic Books, 2008.

Lawson, James L. Manhunt: *The Twelve-Day Chase for Lincoln's Killer*. New York: William Morrow, 2006.

Lehrman, Lewis E. *Lincoln at Peoria: The Turning Point*. Mechanicsburg, PA: Stackpole Books, 2008.

McCurry, Stephanie. "Bread or Blood!" *Civil War Times* 50 (June 2011): 36–41.

McCurry, Stephanie. *Confederate Reckoning: Power and Politics in the Civil War South*. Chapel Hill, NC: The University of North Carolina Press, 2011.

BIBLIOGRAPHY

McPherson, James M. *Battle Cry of Freedom: The Civil War Era*. New York: Oxford University Press, 1988.

McPherson, James M. *Ordeal by Fire: The Civil War and Reconstruction*. New York: Knopf, 1982.

Mead, Carol Lynn. *The Land Between Two Rivers: Madison County, Mississippi*. Madison, MS: Friends of the Madison County-Canton Public Library, 1987.

Morgan, III, James A. "Ball's Bluff: 'A Very Nice Little Military Chance.'" *America's Civil War* 18 (2005), 30–56.

Nelson, James L. *Reign of Iron: The Story of the First Battling Ironclads, the* Monitor *and the* Merrimack. New York: William Morrow, 2004.

O'Grady, Kelly J. *Clear the Confederate Way! The Irish in the Army of Northern Virginia*. Mason City, IA: Savas Publishing, 2000.

O'Reilly, Francis Augustín. *The Fredericksburg Campaign: Winter War on the Rappahannock*. Baton Rouge: Louisiana State University Press, 2006.

Pease, William H. and Jane H. Pease. *James Louis Petigru: Southern Conservative, Southern Dissenter*. Columbia, SC: University of South Carolina Press, 2002.

Phillips, Jason. *Diehard Rebels: The Confederate Culture of Invincibility*. Athens, GA: The University of Georgia Press, 2007.

Polly, J. B. *A Soldier's Letters to Charming Nellie*. Edited by Richard B. McCaslin. Knoxville, TN: University of Tennessee Press, 2007.

Posey, Henry Presley. *The Flora Book: A History of the Town of Flora and Southwest Madison County, Mississippi*. Flora, Mississippi: First Street Publishing, 2002.

Reynolds, Donald E. *Editors Make War: Newspaper Editors in the Secession Crisis*. Carbondale, IL: Southern Illinois University Press.

Robertson, Jr., James I. *Soldiers Blue and Gray*. Columbia, SC: University of South Carolina Press, 1988.

Rosenblatt, Ruth and Emil Rosenblatt, eds. *Hard Marching Every Day: The Civil War Letters of Private Wilbur Fisk*. Lawrence, KS: University Press of Kansas, 1992.

Rubin, Anne Sarah. *A Shattered Nation: The Rise and Fall of the Confederacy, 1861-1868*. Chapel Hill: The University of North Carolina Press, 2005.

Sandburg, Carl. *Abraham Lincoln: The Prairie Years and the War Years*, Library of the Presidents Series. New York: Galahad, 2005.

Scarborough, William K. "Not Quite Southern." *Prologue* 36 (2004): 20–29.

_____. *Masters of the Big House: Elite Slaveholders of the Mid-Nineteenth Century South*. Baton Rouge, LA: Louisiana State University Press, 2006.

Sears, Stephen W. *Chancellorsville*. New York: Houghton Mifflin, 1996.

_____. *Gettysburg*. New York: Houghton Mifflin Company, 2004.

Shawhan, Dorothy S. and Martha H. Swain, *Lucy Somerville Howorth: New Deal Lawyer, Politician, and Feminist from the South*. Baton Rouge, LA: Louisiana State University Press, 2006.

Shepherd, William T. *To Rescue My Native Land: The Civil War Letters of William T. Shepherd*. Edited by Kurt H. Hackemer. Knoxville, TN: University of Tennessee Press, 2006.

Skaptason, Bjorn. "What I Saw of Shiloh: In the Footsteps of Ambrose Bierce." *The Ambrose Bierce Project Journal 3* (2007): 32.

Smith, Jean Edward. *Grant*. New York: Simon & Schuster, 2002.

Stam, Deirdre C. "Growing Up with Books: Fanny Seward's Book Collecting, Reading, and Writing in Mid Nineteenth-Century New York State." *Library & Culture* 41(2006): 194.

Strode, Hudson ed., *Jefferson Davis: Private Letters 1823–1889*. New York: Harcourt Brace Jovanovich, 1966.

Symonds, Craig L. *The Civil War at Sea*. New York: Praeger, 2009.

Tap, Bruce. "Inevitability, Masculinity, and the American Military Tradition." *American Nineteenth Century History 5* (2004): 19–46.

_____. *Over Lincoln's Shoulder: The Committee on the Conduct of the War*. Lawrence, KS: University Press of Kansas, 1998.

Taylor, Amy Murrell. "How a Cold Snap in Kentucky Led to Freedom for Thousands." *Weirding the War: Stories from the Civil War's Ragged Edges*. Edited by Stephen Berry. Athens, GA: The University of Georgia Press, 2011.

Thompson II, Hugh Miller. *The Johnstones of Annandale*. privately published.

Ural, Susannah J. *The Harp and the Eagle: Irish-American Volunteers and the Union Army, 1861–1865*. New York: New York University Press, 2006.

Vostral, Sharra. "The Moveable Home Front: Julia Dent Grant and the Maintenance of a General's Family." *Gateway Heritage* 25, no. 4 (2005): 22–33.

Waugh, Joan. *Ulysses S. Grant: American Hero, American Myth*. Chapel Hill, NC: University of North Carolina Press, 2009.

≋INDEX≋

251

INDEX

ꜗ ABOUT THE AUTHOR ꜗ

Susannah Ural is Professor of History and Co-Director of the Dale Center for the Study of War & Society at the University of Southern Mississippi. She teaches a variety of courses relating to nineteenth-century America, the field of war and society, and the U.S. Civil War era. Her first book, *The Harp and the Eagle: Irish-American Volunteers and the Union Army 1861–1865* (NYU Press, 2006) examined the motivations and experiences of Irish Catholic soldiers and their families. Her second work, the edited collection *Civil War Citizens: Race, Ethnicity, and Identity in America's Bloodiest Conflict* (NYU Press, 2010), chronicled larger ethnic experiences in the 1860s. She is currently finishing her narrative history of John Bell Hood's Texas Brigade, entitled *Hood's Boys*, which highlights the military experiences of the men and the families of this unit, the communities from which they came, and how they represent the larger Confederate experience. She is a frequent contributor to a variety of magazines and journals, including *America's Civil War*, *Civil War Times*, and *The Journal of Military History*. Ural also is a frequent lecturer at industry events and conferences for such organizations as Society of Civil War Historians, Society of Military Historians, and U.S. Army War College. Susannah Ural and her family live in Petal, Mississippi.